Jerusalem's Jewish Quarter
HERITAGE AND POSTWAR RESTORATION

Bracha Slae and Ruth Kark

Jerusalem's Jewish Quarter
HERITAGE AND POSTWAR RESTORATION

Bracha Slae and Ruth Kark

Published by ISRAEL ACADEMIC PRESS, New York
(A subsidiary of MultiEducator, Inc.)
180 E. Prospect Avenue • Mamaroneck, NY 10543
Email: nhkobrin@Israelacademicpress.com

ISBN # 978-1-885881-64-9
© 2018 Israel Academic Press

© 2018 All rights reserved by the authors Bracha Slae and Ruth Kark

Cover Photo: An old alley in the Jewish Quarter, by Mwinner, 2004, from Wikimedia Commons, the free media repository, https://commons.wikimedia.org/wiki/File:Jewish_Quarter_of_the_Old_City_of_Jerusalem.JPG

The right of Bracha Slae and Ruth Kark to be identified as authors of this work has been asserted (with exceptions in the case of the reading excerpts that are reprinted here with permission) in accordance with the US 1976 Copyright 2007 Act and Israel's ח"תשס ,יוצרים זכויות חוק. No part of this book may be reproduced or utilized in any form or by any means, electronic or mechanical, or by any information storage and retrieval system without the prior permission of the publisher. The only exception to this prohibition is "fair use" as defined by U.S. copyright law.

We dedicate this book
to our husbands
Menachem Slae
and
Jeremy D. Kark,
with whom we share our love of Jerusalem

Table of Contents

Preface 9

Introduction: Heritage, Conservation, and Tourism 11
    Heritage and Heritage Tourism
    Approaches to Heritage Presentation
    Israeli Conservation of Heritage Sites
    Continuing Concerns over Heritage Destruction

Chapter I: The History of Modern Jerusalem 18
    Ottoman and Mandate Periods
    Tourism in the Divided City, 1948–1967
    Postwar Jerusalem, 1967

Chapter II: Jerusalem's Jewish Quarter 35
    The Pre-1967 Jewish Quarter
    Jewish Quarter Renewal, 1967–1969
    First Steps in Planning, Policy Making, and Rebuilding

Chapter III: The Company for the Reconstruction and Development of the Jewish Quarter in the Old City of Jerusalem 46
    Centralized Planning of the Quarter
    Postwar Preservation and Reconstruction
    The New Jewish Community
    The Community and the Company
    The Jewish Quarter in Context

Chapter IV: Heritage Policy and Practice 67
    Residence, Tourism, and Commerce
    New and Unexpected Heritage
    Postwar Renovation of Jewish Holy Sites
    The Development of New Institutions

Chapter V: Preservation and Development of Historic Cities in Israel 100
    Jaffa
    Acre
    Safed

Chapter VI: Middle Eastern and European Cities 130
    Cairo
    Beirut
    Warsaw
    York

Chapter VII: Discussion and Conclusions 152
    The Jewish Quarter: Continuity or Opportunity for Change?
    The Influence of Unforeseen Factors, Conflicts, Disparities,
        and Private Initiatives
    Current Trends and Instruments
    The Place of Heritage

Bibliography 169

Notes 178

List of Maps and Plans

MAPS
Map 1: Divided Jerusalem and its Holy Places, 1949–1967 23
Map 2: Schematic map of Jerusalem, 1949–1967 28
Map 3: Jordanian map of the Old City—
Jordan the Holy Land. Al-Muadleen Jewish Quarter 1949–1967 37
Map 4: Netzer's proposed borders for the Jewish Quarter 42
Map 5: Avraham Halperin, Batei Mahse neighborhood in the Jewish Quarter
on the Eve of the War of Independence 53
Map 6: Map of population density and ruins in the Jewish Quarter, based on Sharon 1973 60
Map 7: The Jewish Quarter showing overlap of former sites of religious institutions,
ruins, and excavations 69
Map 8: Cairo map by regions 133
Map 9: The Jewish Quarter today 152

PLANS
Plan 1: The first Jerusalem town plan (British architect William McLean, 1918) 20
Plan 2: Old City Outline Plan AM/9, 1971 31
Plan 3: Jewish Quarter Master Plan, 1968 33
Plan 4: Mandel's proposal for renewal of Batei Mahse Plaza, 1970 54
Plan 5: Frankel and Ya'ar, Pilgrims' Route proposal, ca. 1968 58
Plan 6: Frankel and Ya'ar, Jewish Quarter commercial and tourist routes and terminal, ca. 1968 68
Plan 7: Shem Or's proposal 81
Plan 8: Old Town Acre Report, Monuments and Population Density, 1944 111

LIST OF FIGURES
Figure 1: View of Jerusalem's Old City from the King David Hotel, 1938 20
Figure 2: Barricaded Suq Street and British soldiers during Palestine disturbances, 1936 21
Figure 3: No man's land as seen from Mount Scopus, from the Tower of David to Mount Zion, 1964 ... 26
Figure 4: Imaginative rendering of a proposed national park, 1969 27
Figure 5: Elyada Merioz in his art gallery, 1973 40
Figure 6: The new Yehuda Halevy Staircase and Teutonic Knights complex, 1970 44
Figure 7: Funeral service for a Jewish rabbi at Batei Mahse Square, 1903 52
Figure 8: State Ceremony on the Tenth Anniversary of the Restoration of Batei Mahse, 1977 52
Figure 9: Aerial photo of Batei Mahse Plaza before reconstruction, ca. 1970 54
Figure 10: Batei Mahse rebuilt, 1972 55
Figure 11: HaKotel Yeshiva students moving into Batei Mahse, October 1967 61
Figure 12: Nachal Moriah soldiers with Torah scroll, 1968 62
Figure 13: Pierotti's plate of the entrance to the ruins of the Church of St. Mary, 1864 71
Figure 14: Inside the Teutonic Knights complex today 71
Figure 15: Etz Hayyim Yeshiva students renew studies, ca. 1968 74
Figure 16: Middle Synagogue desecrated, 1967 79
Figure 17: Middle Synagogue renovated, 2007 79
Figure 18: New Year's greeting card depicting the Hurva and Tiferet Israel Synagogues 82
Figure 19: Ruins of the Hurva Synagogue, 1967 83
Figure 20: Kahn's sketch for a new Hurva Synagogue 84

Figure 21: Hurva Synagogue complex as depicted on a 1935 Etz Hayyim calendar 84
Figure 22: Tiferet Yisrael Synagogue, ca. 1940 86
Figure 23: Destroyed façade of the Tiferet Yisrael Synagogue, ca. 1968 87
Figure 24: Porat Yosef Yeshiva before 1948 89
Figure 25: Ruins of Porat Yosef Yeshiva at the top of the new staircase
leading to the Western Wall Plaza, ca. 1970 89
Figure 26: Campus of Porat Yosef Yeshiva today 90
Figure 27: Destroyed façade of the Karaite Synagogue, ca. 1970 91
Figure 28: Restored interior of Karaite Synagogue, 2006 91
Figure 29: The Byzantine Cardo in front of the Habad Synagogue. Seen in the background:
the Hurva Synagogue arch and the Sidna Omar Mosque, 1984 92
Figure 30: Rivka Weingarten, founder of Old Yishuv Court Museum in family home, 1967 95
Rivka Weingarten, Prime Minister Levi Eshkol, Central Command General Uzi Narkiss,
and entourage tour the Jewish Quarter, 8 June, 1967 95
Figure 31: Preparations for a party in the Cardo, 2013 98
Figure 32: Aerial photo of Jaffa destruction, June 1936 105
Figure 33: Cutting new road through Old Jaffa, 1936 105
Figure 34: British Mandate photos of Old Acre 110
Figure 35: Cannons on the city wall, 2006 115
Figure 36: Crusader dining hall in restored Hospitaller complex, 2005 115
Figure 37: Old postcard of Safed, general view 118
Figure 38: Aerial view of the Safed Citadel and Old City, ca. 1930 118
Figure 39: Artistic rendering of the Kahal site 124
Figure 40: Street scene in Cairo, 1934 132
Figure 41: Ayyubid Wall, Al-Azhar Park, Cairo, 2006 136
Figure 42: "Good Morning from Beirut" 1958 139
Figure 43: Beirut downtown seafront, 2011 140
Figure 44: Destroyed Warsaw, capital of Poland, January 1945 142
Figure 45: Castle Square in Old Town Warsaw, 2005 144
Figure 46: Etching of Micklegate Bar, York, showing the ruined barbican still in place, 1814 147
Figure 47: York City Center, 2005 148
Figure 48: Aerial View of the Old City and Temple Mount, 1979 157

Preface

The Old City of Jerusalem is approximately a square kilometer in size, and of that, its Jewish Quarter consists of less than 15 percent. However, its geopolitical, religious, historic, economic, tourist, and heritage-related influence cannot be overestimated. Since the 1967 War, the Jewish Quarter has undergone major restoration, creating an entity far different from that of previous periods. Our case study of urban heritage and postwar rehabilitation in the Jewish Quarter in Jerusalem will examine the following parameters:

- Postwar reconstruction of one section of Jerusalem's Old City—the Jewish Quarter—after the unification of East and West Jerusalem in 1967.
- The Jewish Quarter as an example of both centralized planning and grassroots initiatives.
- The Jewish Quarter as a case study of changing heritage values in reconstruction of the historic city and in collective identity formation.
- The Jewish Quarter as an example of the use of inner-directed and outer-directed heritage narratives, and of changes in heritage narratives from place to place and time to time.
- The role of tourism-based heritage development in reconstruction of the historic Jewish Quarter.

The literature on Jerusalem has paid great attention to the architectural, archaeological, religious, and political aspects of the rebuilding of the Jewish Quarter. Tourist guides and histories of earlier periods abound. However, very little has been written about the process of regeneration that began in 1967, certainly not in the framework of historical geography or of heritage studies. We have attempted here to discuss this process in the context of the renewal of historic cities in the second half of the 20th century, and to compare these to current approaches to the same topic.

We have limited our research to the years 1967–1975. During this formative period the organizational framework for the restoration was established, the outline plan was completed, and precedents for procedures set. Towards the end of this period, there were several crises, including the Yom Kippur War in 1973, and confrontations between the Jewish Quarter Development Company and the Municipality, the local residents, and the State Comptroller, culminating in an overall revision of the Company—the end of an era.

Limiting our research to such a short time period and limited area allows us to examine the influence of governmental and municipal decisions on actual development, and the impact of individuals and NGOs on the centralized plans and policies—all of which constitute the dynamics of renewal.

We shall examine conservation theory and practice in a broad context, and how these have changed over the decades and from place to place. We shall also compare the renovation of heritage in Jerusalem to that in other historic cities in Israel and to Beirut, Cairo, Warsaw, and York.

In this study we made use of archival contemporary primary sources, including maps, plans, photographs, documents, and protocols of the various government and municipal offices, of NGOs and of the Company for the Reconstruction and Development of the Jewish Quarter. Newspaper articles and interviews with key players have filled out the picture.

The authors also drew on their experience and first-hand knowledge of the Jewish Quarter and of Jerusalem. Bracha Slae is a veteran resident and Ruth Kark a prolific researcher and writer of numerous studies of Jerusalem, its neighborhoods, and history. Both have witnessed the development of the Quarter since 1967. As a new resident, the uniqueness of the neighborhood architecture and design, the fascinating stories of its past, and the elusive heritage broadcast from every stone fascinated Bracha Slae and raised questions such as: What is old or new, what is changed, and why? What was life here like in earlier periods? What do we know about the Jewish Quarter's history? The search for answers to these questions, and acquaintance with defenders and former residents of the Quarter, as well as with architects and neighborhood activists, provided the basis for much of this book.

The authors would like to express their thanks to the following persons whose assistance was essential to our study: Prof. Noam Shoval of the Department of Geography at the Hebrew University of Jerusalem; Tamar Soffer and Michal Kidron, cartographers of the Department of Geography at the Hebrew University of Jerusalem; Alifa Saadya for assisting in the manuscript preparation; and the interviewees. Last but not least, we appreciate the support and encouragement from our families.

Bracha Slae
Ruth Kark
Jerusalem, January 2018

Introduction
Heritage, Conservation, and Tourism

Heritage and Heritage Tourism
Much attention has been paid to heritage—history passed over to us as knowledge or as a physical entity considered worthy of preservation, as negotiated and interpreted within specific cultural and intellectual parameters. The value of heritage is dependent upon the opinion of the bystander who endows it with a subjective, current value that is dependent upon a particular time and place. History becomes heritage, and heritage becomes a commodity, defining and defined by collective memory, and determining social, ethnic and national identity (Graham et al. 2000, 11). Heritage, by definition, must have cultural significance—an aggregate of aesthetic, religious, national, ethnic, political, and other values. Without this, there is no reason to preserve it.

"Selling" heritage to others for cultural consumption may be seen as an expansion of the pilgrimage tradition. In turning outward, care must be taken that commercialization and tourism not overwhelm and destroy heritage sites. Along with providing a basis for "heritage tourism," preservation and presentation strengthens collective identity of the local population, enriching and strengthening the collective self-image of users of the space (Fenster 2004, 109–10, 307–10; Orbasli 2000, 29; Sheeran 2003). According to Meethan, this may be problematic in an era of globalization in which the particular heritage of a place may have several different narratives, or in which the local residents at present do not share the historical heritage of the past. In addition, enhancing heritage values often entails gentrification of residential and commercial neighborhoods and changes in their population. "The creation of heritage can therefore be seen as an attempt to establish historical identity in the face of global change." A shift of emphasis from the elite to the vernacular has led to heritage becoming "a form of mass consumption" (Meethan 1996, 322–25).

A sense of the past provides us with stability and expresses our values. Heritage is extremely valuable as a didactic instrument. The historical value of monuments and heritage sites derives directly from their ability to provide an authentic testimony of the past, of both ordinary life and how people lived, and of extraordinary events. Heritage utilizes the past to produce and promote desired presents and futures (Ashworth and Tunbridge 1990, 125–30).

David Lowenthal elaborates on the dangers and misuses of heritage as well as on its central role in modern society. He sees neither heritage nor history as objective. "History explores and explains pasts grown ever more opaque over time; heritage clarifies pasts so as to infuse them with present purposes" (Lowenthal 1998, xv).

Furthermore, "polarized knowledge" spawns "wildly divergent accounts of the past.... I have my past, and you have yours, and never the twain shall meet" (Lowenthal 2015, 585). We attempt to safeguard the past by preserving its relics. However, "every mode of honouring the past to some extent transforms, even destroys it" (Lowenthal 2015, 413). Just as recall modifies memory and subjectivity slants history, handling relics refashions their appearance and meaning. Interaction with the past's residues ceaselessly alters their nature and context, unwittingly if not intentionally (Lowenthal 2015, 516).

Although value was attached to heritage preservation in different parts of the world, including the Middle East, China, and Europe, from the middle ages onward, the preservation movements of the 19th and 20th century developed in response to the technological revolution and to growing exposure to different civilizations. Since the nineteenth century, "Grand Tours," religious pilgrimage, and tourism to faraway heritage destinations became popular, particularly among the Western upper class. In addition, pilgrimage changed: it had formerly been mostly Catholic and Orthodox Christians traveling to holy shrines, but Protestants and Evangelicals became an increasingly important segment in pilgrimage to the Holy Land. With increased mobility and a rise in the standard of living and leisure time in Western culture, the range and extent of tourism increased greatly. Thomas Cook's "Eastern tours" revolutionized pilgrimage to Palestine as early as 1869, making it a must in British and American travel itineraries and affordable even for ordinary people. Tens of thousands of tourists and pilgrims used his services. This led to the building of new hostels and hotels, development of travel and guide services, restaurants and cafés, and even to philanthropic tourism—visits to mission schools, support of medical facilities, and so on. Cook's "heritage tours" in Palestine brought economic gains and modernization to the local society even before World War I. At the same time, they enriched Western society by making the Holy Land accessible to thousands (Kark 2001, 154–74). These tours may be seen as the connecting link between pilgrimage by homogenous groups seeking a religious experience and tourism by heterogeneous groups united only in their interest in visiting specific sites.

Approaches to Heritage Presentation

Ashworth lists three processes that developed consecutively: preservation (from the beginning of the 19th century), conservation (from the 1960s), and heritage (from the 1980s). In the first, the past was to be preserved for its own sake. "The main unquestioned assumption is that the past is real...and it can be preserved through its sites...and bequeathed to the future" (Ashworth 2011, 6–8). According to this, prevention of future physical damage to a monument or site is the sole purpose of preservation. Its present or future use is irrelevant. This is the basis of the Athens Charter of 1931, the Venice Charter of UNESCO of 1964, and of the National Historic Preservation Act of the United States of 1966. The Venice Charter led to the foundation of ICOMOS in 1965, among whose responsibilities it is to advise UNESCO on World Heritage Sites, and to safeguard monuments for the sake of future generations.[1] Preservation is considered an end in itself, didactic in purpose, and independent of economic or tourism interests.

Over the decades, the focus of preservation efforts has gradually shifted to include whole areas, not merely individual sites. Conservation means keeping the "spirit of the city," and thus comes under the jurisdiction of city planners and developers, expanding the vocabulary to terms such as "renovation," "revitalization," "renewal" and "regeneration," where considerations of present and future usage become integral parts of the process.

This connection between past, present, and future is developed further in the heritage paradigm, in which structures and sites become the means to achieve social, political, religious, and economic goals. In heritage-oriented development, present use of the past becomes the focal point, involving a broad spectrum of actors—academic, governmental, entrepreneurial, etc., and including a constantly changing and adapting repertoire of narratives. This approach is undoubtedly the most versatile, and the one most effective for social, economic, and political gains. However, it is also the approach raising the most conflicts and dilemmas. These three paradigms illustrate a gradual change from preservation for its own sake to a more open-ended approach of negotiation and private initiative (Ashworth and Tunbridge 1990, 23–25; Meethan 1996, 326).

A quick review of the vast amount of literature on preservation, conservation, and heritage over the last century shows an overwhelming preponderance of references to the Western World. However, in recent decades developing nations in Asia and Africa have come to realize the economic value of heritage tourism and the significant role heritage conservation can play in raising national pride. UNESCO, ICCROM, and ICOMOS[2] have been key players in renewal of sites in Africa, Asia, and the Near East and in developing national identity along with heritage tourism (Stubbs 2009, Appendix B). The integration of the different aspects of recognition of cultural heritage, whether physical, intangible, or living, and the motivation and involvement of society in safeguarding it, is one of the challenges of the 21st century (Jokilehto 2011, 3).

One of the most problematic aspects of heritage presentation is that of conflicting narratives. There may be multiple dissonant heritages relating to a particular time or place, particularly in sites contested by opposing groups, in areas of conflict, and in areas whose population is unstable. Each side in the conflict will embrace a particular set of heritage values in order to achieve its goals, and this heritage will serve to fortify the collective identity of the site or group it represents. These narratives may be used to promote political or other goals (Ashworth and Tunbridge 1990, 28–31; Graham et al 2000, 101–20; Tunbridge and Ashworth 1996, 273). Conflicting narratives may themselves become a tourist attraction (McDowell 2008, 405–21).

Heritage reinforces social identity and fosters feelings of belonging to a community, thereby enhancing its social fabric and resilience. Conversely, lack of social cohesion and community fragmentation can adversely affect heritage conservation and preservation. Lowenthal writes,

> Enthralled by the past, we deploy it for present benefits of every kind. A goodly heritage persuades us we belong to a community of like-minded folk and act within a tradition sanctified by age-old experience. Heritage is all the more valued in a world where turbulent change and global fears make the present seem frightful and the future fearsome. Yet the very zeal with which heritage is pursued leads to countless abuses of the treasured past. Roots and relics become weapons to foment hatred of others, to warp historical truth, to deform our own legacy, to further some class or cause. Despite new recognition that the world's diverse legacies belong to and require the care of all mankind, heritage passions remain animated largely by self-regarding chauvinism (Lowenthal 1998, 156).

When heritage becomes a tourism goal, its development is further complicated. The focus of heritage tourism is the city core, with its historic, ethnic, spiritual, national, and cultural values; however, visits to these sites will not necessarily entail any expenditure. The economic value of a heritage site depends rather on opportunities for entertainment, hotels and restaurants, shopping, and transportation in the vicinity. Tourism usage of a heritage site may be of minimal significance to the site itself, or to the historic city in general, but a particular site may be of supreme value for the tourist. Thus, the tourist-heritage site relationship may be beneficial or damaging to the heritage site.

Another issue involves the mechanisms for heritage preservation. The European approach, cemented by ICOMOS charters, has been one of definition, preservation, supervision, and development of heritage sites by local or national authorities. In America, on the other hand, preservation developed as a didactic, free market voluntary movement whose goal was to protect and restore sites deemed representative of American values and history, and to use them to inculcate American heritage to the great wave of emigrants who flooded the country at the beginning of the 20th century. This approach advanced the American idea of becoming a "melting pot," for the great multicultural waves of immigrants in the 19th and 20th centuries. Although the American preservation movement has joined ICOMOS, preservation is still primarily the concern of local NGOs and not of the Federal government.[3] As Margaret Mead declared, "Never doubt that a small group of thoughtful, committed citizens can change the world. Indeed, it is the only thing that ever has."[4]

If America was a "melting pot," then Israel is "a pressure cooker." It is incredibly rich in heritage sites, and rich in heritage issues mentioned above: sites in danger, numerous conflicting and complementing narratives, sites integral to national and religious identity, and sites whose chief characteristics are their tourism potential. The number of such sites in Jerusalem is extraordinary.

Israeli Conservation of Heritage Sites

In his study on conservation of the architectural heritage of abandoned urban neighborhoods following the 1948 War, Yair Paz described the conflict between two opposing tendencies in the early years of the State of Israel—development on the one hand, and conservation of the architectural heritage on the other. In his study based on archival primary sources, he demonstrated the form this conflict took in Tiberias, Jaffa, and Acre. Paz traced the formation and development of a school of thought that supported conservation while allowing for controlled development, a tendency that gained wide public support only two decades later. Paz pointed out that these two elements acting together were responsible for a high degree of awareness and sensitivity during a period in which this issue was not very popular. A unique group of leading professionals, educated in Europe or in British Palestine, held responsible positions in the Planning Division, the Department of Antiquities, and in several departments in the Ministries of Religious Affairs and of Tourism. The second element which added impetus to the influence of these individuals was the legislative (and perhaps the educational) heritage of the British Mandate administration in Palestine which provided a relevant body of administrative and statutory guidelines. Practical results of the conservationist attitude were the successful checking—at least partially—of plans to destroy ancient sections of Jaffa, Acre, and elsewhere. In addition, there was the establishment of a high-ranking government committee, which shaped a uniform, nationwide policy and conducted and publicized surveys and studies.

Through these processes, the Israeli public gained awareness of the importance of conservation. Paz concluded that if one takes into account the variegated conservation issues with which the high-ranking government committee dealt, and especially the attitude they adopted in relation to the preservation of entire "historic" neighborhoods, one may definitely conclude that most of the seeds of the contemporary movement for conservation in Israel were planted in the hectic early years of the State of Israel (Paz 1998, 95–135).

Continuing Concerns over Heritage Destruction

A city's heritage sites embody its identity and values. Therefore, destruction and reconstruction of heritage sites often accompany changes in identity and values. For example, it has been suggested that during Gamal Abdel Nasser's rule in Egypt, many historic and religious monuments in the old city of Cairo were destroyed because of Nasser's socialist nationalist ideology. To Nasser, the Mamluk and Ottoman dynasties were "invaders," not authentic Egyptians, and thus their heritage presence in Old Cairo was unworthy of preservation. As a result, his regime demolished historic buildings and whole quarters in historic Cairo to create new squares and free standing housing projects (Nour 2012, 117–18).

Modernization often led to erasure of heritage while attempting to address modern life and needs, such as improving infrastructure, providing for parking, expanding the road network, and increasing building dimensions to accommodate an increased population. For example, the Swiss-French architect Le Corbusier, one of the leaders of modern architecture at the turn of the 20th century, proposed bulldozing most of central Paris and replacing it with his sixty-story cruciform towers, but his proposal was rejected. This approach reflects a lack of appreciation of all preceding urban heritage in the area, but it is not a tool of warfare. Rejection or exchange of one heritage and collective identity for another can occur peaceably, as noted above, or through internal (civil war) or external conflict. In times of external conflict, the resulting destruction may be radical.

It is accepted military strategy to eradicate an enemy's cultural heritage in order to destroy his morale. Within the more general history of the loss or conservation of cultural heritage, the First and Second World Wars undoubtedly represent a watershed, raising heritage awareness definitively to international concern. Together with the loss of millions of lives and the immense destruction of property all over the world, there was also vast destruction of works of art, ancient monuments, and large parts of historic cities such as Warsaw, Gdansk, Munich, London, Coventry, Louvain, Cologne, Hamburg, and Dresden. As a result, people became painfully aware of the values and cultural and social identity associated with destroyed places and objects.

Today, ISIS fighters regularly take control of world heritage sites and destroy them systematically as part of their fight against non-Muslim society. This includes archaeology museums and outdoor sites, churches, and sacred graves. It conveys a hostile attitude to the areas under its control; a desire to harm the West and its values; a way of making headlines, and the development of a profitable commerce in antiquities, supposedly in order to "save" them. Through the UN and its relevant organizations, worldwide protest has been expressed. However, the international community has not yet succeeded in preventing the deliberate destruction of cultural heritage in this or in other parts of the world.[5]

The natural reaction to this hostile strategy is an immediate resolve to restore the collective heritage, even if before the war it had been obsolescent (Stanley-Price 2005, Introduction). Wholesale demolition and modern rebuilding, as done in Frankfurt and West Berlin, were almost universally rejected. Functional structures were usually rebuilt according to paradigms of modern architecture; but symbolic structures were replicated in traditional form. In many countries, a major objective in the aftermath of war was to pay particular attention to damaged works of art and architecture. This resulted in new norms and legislation at the national and local levels, as well as renewed international efforts to respond to emerging needs, to share acquired knowledge through conferences and training programs, to agree on universally valid principles for safeguarding, and to designate special funds for restoration and reconstruction of monuments and heritage sites (Jokilehto 2011, 5–6). Historicist reconstruction sends a message of continuity, a return to normal after exceptional events, together with the assertion of national cultural identity and an encouragement of those dispersed by war to return home. "Awareness of a shared past allows for the creation of a present and future common identity...." (Skaf 2013, 125–32).

We now turn to a short summary of the past shared by Jewish residents of the 19th and 20th centuries in Jerusalem.

Chapter I
The History of Modern Jerusalem

Ottoman and Mandate Periods

The growth of Jerusalem during the British Mandate period (1920–1948) is well known; less known is the unprecedented growth of Jewish neighborhoods under Ottoman rule. Many factors contributed to this growth, including a disastrous earthquake in Safed in 1837 that led to a sizable Jewish emigration to Jerusalem, coinciding with the rise to power of Muhammad Ali and Ibrahim Pasha; the subsequent reforms upon resumption of Ottoman rule; the entrance of European powers into the Ottoman Empire; and the granting of privileges to Christians and Jews.

The Jewish population of the Old City increased from about 2,000 in 1806 to 20,000 at the turn of the 20th century. The first Jewish hospitals, banks, printing presses, workshops, and educational institutions were founded in the Old City and only later moved to the New City. By the 1880s, Jews constituted the majority of Jerusalem's population in both Old Jerusalem and in the new city (Kark and Oren-Nordheim 2001, 26–30; Ben-Arieh 1984, 353–61). From the 1860s until World War I, more than a hundred Jewish, Arab, Christian, and mixed neighborhoods were built outside of the old city walls; 78 of these were Jewish (Kark and Nordheim 1996, 67). By 1910, the total population of Jerusalem had increased to more than 75,000, with a Jewish population of at least 45,000 (Ben-Arieh 1984, 358). Tourism and pilgrimage to holy sites flourished. The increasing numbers of Christian pilgrims and tourists who came not only to visit specific holy sites on a religious pilgrimage but also to tour the Holy Land was both a consequence and a causal factor in the development of improved, faster, and more comfortable transportation to and within the Holy Land. The rise of organized tour companies such as Thomas Cook from the 1840s on accelerated the establishment of new hotels and hostels, both religious and commercial. The flourishing trade in guidebooks, souvenirs, and religious artwork also stemmed from the growing demand by visiting pilgrims and tourists (Kark 2001, 155–74; Cohen-Hattab and Shoval 2014, 1–2; Cohen-Hattab and Bar 2011, 126–48).

This phenomenon was not limited to Christians. Jews visiting Palestine did not confine themselves solely to the traditional holy sites, but also took interest in its geography, history and archaeology, and in the newly-established villages, agricultural development, and so on. The first modern Hebrew guidebook to the Holy Land was published in 1876 by Avraham Moshe Luncz, who called it his "Baedeker" (Luncz 1876, reprint 1979; Witztum and Kalian 2013, 49–51). There was also small scale Muslim tourism from neighboring countries. Other modern inventions which made the Near East more attractive for tourists were photography, the presence of European and American consulates, the newly-paved Jaffa-Jerusalem road, the introduction of electricity, and improved mail and bank services. Hotels, hostels, travel agencies, museums, and shops opened both within and without the Jerusalem city walls. It is estimated that about 5,000 pilgrims and tourists debarked at Jaffa port per season at the turn of the century. These numbers doubled and tripled in the decades before World War I (Cohen-Hattab 2010, 197–210; Cohen-Hattab and Shoval 2014, Ch. 2).

In the course of the First World War, the total population of Jerusalem fell to about 55,000, and the Jewish population to about 30,000, due not only to the war and the deportation of non-Ottoman citizens, but also to disease, starvation, and difficult living conditions (Kark and Oren-Nordheim 2001, 28). Palestine was cut off from the West during the war, bringing a complete halt to tourism and pilgrimage from Europe and America.

One of the first things Britain introduced into Mandatory Palestine after the war was town planning. William McLean's Jerusalem plan of 1918 established Jerusalem as the functional capital of British Palestine. Modern technology was introduced in various spheres, such as electricity, improved water supplies, sewage systems, telephones, roads and public transportation, and construction using reinforced concrete. The High Commissioner's residence, the Central Post Office, and other important economic, cultural, and governmental buildings were constructed in Jerusalem. The "New City," influenced by British and European culture, soon offered modern tourism facilities, public parks, attractions such as the Rockefeller Archaeological Museum, the archaeological exhibit in the Tower of David, theatres, concerts and other cultural activities, and the newly established Hebrew University of Jerusalem (Cohen-Hattab 2006, Chapter IV).

British planners William McLean, Charles Robert Ashbee, and Patrick Geddes took a completely different approach to the Holy Basin, including the walled Old City and the Mount of Olives. It was carefully excluded from modernization in order to preserve its historic and religious character. Regulations prohibited new construction or demolition without special permission. A green belt was demarcated around the walls, separating old from new and preserving the "medieval aspect" of the Ottoman city. In fact, Sir Ronald Storrs, the first military governor of Jerusalem, wrote that the primary goal for which McLean had been invited was "to advise upon the best method of preserving intact the appearance and atmosphere of Jerusalem...." (Hyman 1994, 50). With its inspiring landscape, bustling *suq*, and religious and historical landmarks of the three monotheistic religions, it was to remain a magnet for pilgrimage tourism. "In an attempt to preserve the architectural quality of the Old City, laws were enacted and imposed safeguarding antiquities and sites...the city walls were repaired, as too was the Dome of the Rock...." The British, in keeping with their definition of "historic," removed the Clock Tower, built by the Ottomans in 1907 above Jaffa Gate. These plans reflected the attempt to enhance the sacred nature of the city, and preserve it as a living museum, distancing the city enclosed in a wall from new industrial and commercial developments" (Kark and Nordheim 1996, 58–86).

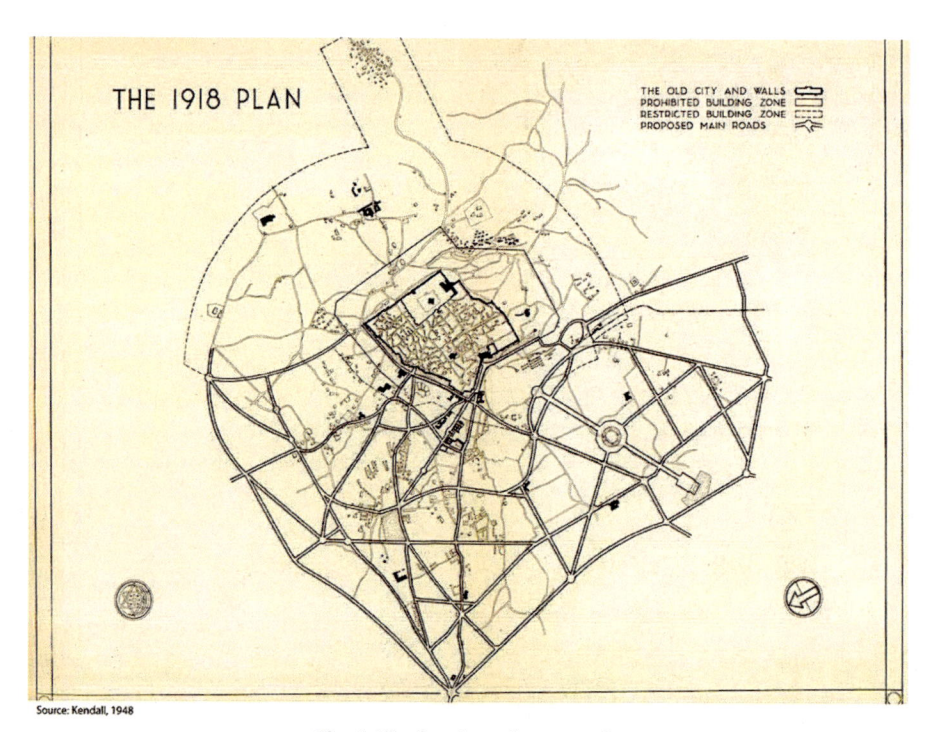

*Plan 1: The first Jerusalem town plan
(British architect William McLean, 1918). Source: Kendall, 1948.*

*Figure 1: View of Jerusalem's Old City from the King David Hotel, 1938.
Source: Matson Collection, Library of Congress, Washington, D.C.*

The Pro-Jerusalem Society was founded in 1918 to protect Jerusalem's natural resources, to establish cultural and educational institutions, to encourage and preserve local arts and handicrafts, and to protect and preserve antiquities in and around Jerusalem. Charles R. Ashbee was secretary of the Society as well as Jerusalem's Civic Advisor. For the first time in Jerusalem's history, an Antiquities Department with legal authority worked to renovate and to preserve the Tower of David, the city walls, and Christian holy sites. Recommendations were made for renovation and preservation of Muslim holy sites, including the Dome of the Rock. On the other hand, development of Jewish holy sites in the Old City, including the Western Wall, was sharply restricted. Porat Yosef Yeshiva (rabbinical seminary for religious studies; pl. *yeshivot*), was the only new building built in the Jewish Quarter during the Mandate Period, and that was a continuation of construction begun before the outbreak of war. Most of the veteran institutions moved to the New City. The green belt around the Old City walls and limitations on building preserved the view but further isolated the walled city (Kark and Oren-Nordheim 2001, 143–46; Efrat 1993, 377). While this approach encouraged religious pilgrimage to ancient Jerusalem, it led to its decline as a desirable residential and commercial center. Nevertheless, these plans formed the basis for all future planning, including that of the State of Israel after 1967.

A second factor in the decline of the Old City was the deteriorating security situation. Effectively, the Old City was divided into violently conflicting Jewish and non-Jewish Quarters as early as 1929, when serious riots broke out around claims to the Western Wall. Jews were isolated inside a shrunken Jewish "Quarter" constituting only about 15% of the walled city, and the Jewish population gradually decreased from about 20,000 throughout the Old City to less than 2,000 concentrated in the Jewish Quarter (Kark and Oren-Nordheim 2001, 143–44; Izrael 1987, 222–41).[6]

Figure.2: Barricaded Suq street and British soldiers during Palestine disturbances, 1936. Source: Matson Collection, Library of Congress, Washington, D.C.

Understandably, following the 1929 "disturbances" the number of tourists also plummeted (Cohen-Hattab 2006, 245). Nevertheless, the opening of the King David Hotel in 1931 marked the prosperous modernization and westernization of Jerusalem. More and more lucrative tourism facilities opened—all located outside of the walls (Cohen-Hattab 2004, 279–302). The Arab Rebellion of 1936–1939 with World War II on its heels again led to a tourism crisis. However, "military tourism"—visits by Allied forces on leave to Palestine—more than made up for this (Cohen-Hattab 2006, 43).

At the same time, Jews from Palestine toured Lebanon, particularly the resort city of Beirut, and skied on Mount Hermon. They also visited Egypt and Syria, looking for the "authentic" and the exotic, in the spirit of the times (Pan 2014).

According to the 1945 Mandatory Government estimate, 97,000 residents—an overwhelming majority of Jerusalem's total population of 157,000—were Jewish (Kark and Oren-Nordheim 2001, 28). However, less than 2,000 Jews were living in the Jewish Quarter when war broke out in 1948, and only a few hundred were fit to defend it. In less than two weeks, they surrendered to the Jordanian Arab Legion, and were evacuated on May 29, 1948. Israel managed to retain an army outpost on Mount Zion, but all the rest of East Jerusalem came under Jordanian control.

Tourism in the Divided City: 1948–1967

Jerusalem had been intended by the United Nations to be an international city, but was divided between Jordan and Israel into East and West Jerusalem under the armistice agreement of 1949. For nineteen years, from 1948 to 1967, West Jerusalem was the capital of Israel, while East Jerusalem, including the Old City and environs, was part of the Hashemite Kingdom of Jordan. Both parts of the divided city suffered greatly during the war in 1948, but after a few years, both began to recover.

Israel made West Jerusalem its capital, but its legal status as capital or even as part of the State of Israel was not recognized by the world at large. Israel built its parliament—the Knesset, along with other new national institutions, the Israel Museum, and a second campus of the Hebrew University of Jerusalem in Givat Ram, forming the new national center in West Jerusalem. Theodor Herzl, the political prophet of Zionism, was reinterred on Mount Herzl in a new national cemetery for Israeli leaders near the national military cemetery. Nearby, Yad Vashem memorialized the Holocaust. In addition, hospitals, educational and scientific institutions, and light industry contributed to the socio-economic growth of the city.

Jerusalem was divided, not only politically, but also in terms of heritage. Most tourism infrastructure and subsidiary services were in West Jerusalem, but it was blatantly lacking in heritage sites. The most important holy sites, such as Haram al-Sharif—the Temple Mount; the Holy Sepulchre, Via Dolorosa; and the churches on the Mount of Olives were in East Jerusalem under Jordanian rule.[7] Throughout this period, the Western (Wailing) Wall—although inaccessible to Jews—continued to serve as Israel's most significant heritage symbol. Tourists in Israeli Jerusalem, whose major holy sites were the Room of the Last Supper and the Tomb of King David on Mount Zion, generally spent no more than a day in the city. Over the years, Jordan was able to establish the necessary tourism services for visitors to the East Jerusalem holy sites, making this the most important branch of Jordanian Jerusalem's economy. Most visitors were Christian or Muslim pilgrims. Jewish sites in the Old City were destroyed and the Kingdom of Jordan did not grant visas to Jews.

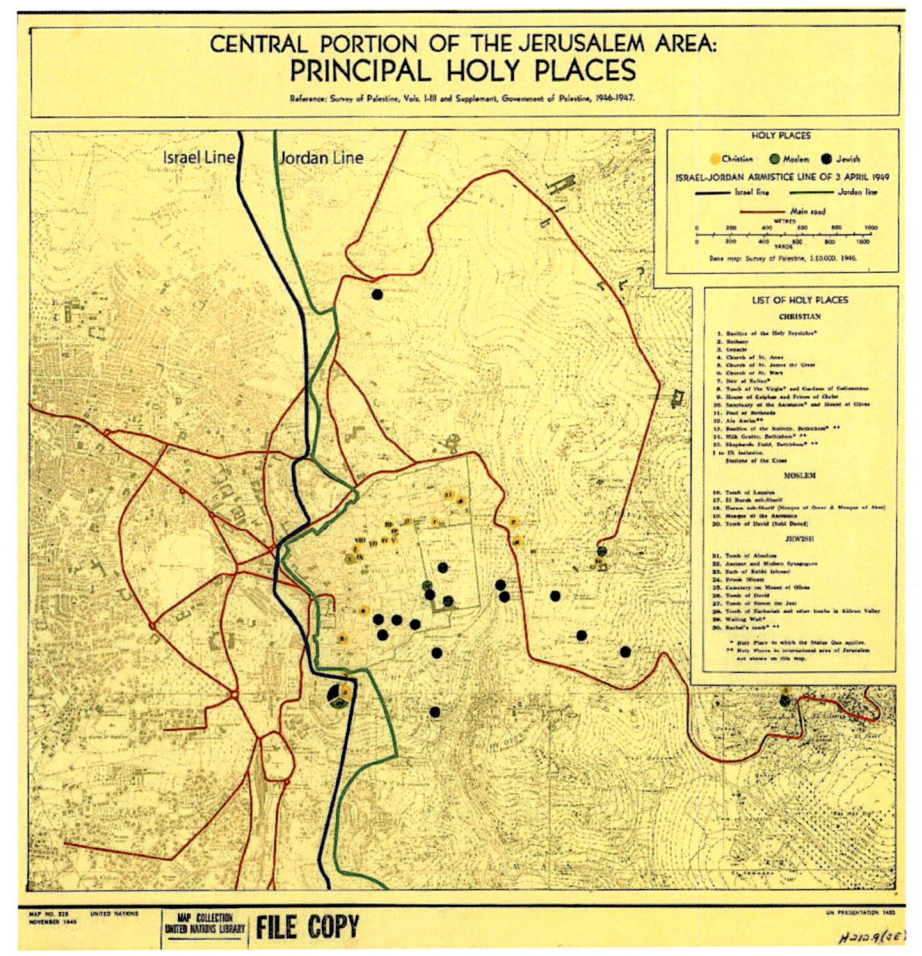

Map 1: Divided Jerusalem and its Holy Places, 1949–1967.
Source: Cartography Department, Hebrew University of Jerusalem, 2016, based on UN map 299, 1949.

The mayor of Jordanian Jerusalem, Ruhi al-Khatib, described its development from 1948 until 1966:

> Perhaps the most conspicuous achievement in the city during this period was in the field of tourism. In the second half of 1948 not a single hotel was operating in the city, while now we have 70 hotels and 3 pensions.... The establishment and development of the Jerusalem airport [in Atarot of today (B.S. and R.K.)], encouraged local, Eastern and foreign airline companies to open branches in Jerusalem.... many of our young men specialize as tourist guides...thus helping to raise their number from about 20 in 1948 to 215 at present.... The souvenir industry also witnessed a revival.... The number of taxis working in the field of tourism alone is more than 600 today....[8]

Other indirect effects of heritage tourism in East Jerusalem were an increase in population from 33,000 to 70,000, publication of two English and three Arabic daily newspapers, repair of the Golden Dome, and a planned repair of the Holy Sepulchre. It should be noted that most tourism was religiously oriented, and there was no entrance fee to holy sites. Thus, tourism profits were secondary, stemming from hotels and restaurants, transportation, guides, souvenirs, and so on. Since tourism is always in flux, this economic base was undependable. Nevertheless, religious tourism remained East Jerusalem's primary economic growth factor (Hopkins 1969; Al-Khatib 1966 [note 8 above]).

The Old City in general, including its mosques and madrasas, was in poor condition. The historian Aref al-Aref, former Mayor of Jerusalem and Director of the Rockefeller Institute in East Jerusalem, charted the fate of Jerusalem's historic mosques under British and Jordanian rule. Sixty Mamluk Madrasas lay abandoned by the end of the Mandate Period, and were being used as living quarters for the poor, schools, jails, and so on. Seven out of twenty-seven mosques were also abandoned or used for some other purpose. Under King Hussein, the "King Solomon's Throne Mosque" adjacent to Al-Aqsa was used as a weapons arsenal for the Jordanian Legion. When Aref al-Aref's summary was written in 1968, only ten mosques were active in the Old City, including those on Haram al-Sharif. The only mosque to be renovated and renewed by Jordan was on Haram al-Sharif to which purpose the Gulf States and other Muslim countries contributed generously (Al-Aref, 1961, 491–504).[9]

A UNESCO expert in the preservation of archaeological and historic sites wrote of the Old City in 1960:

> Picturesque and romantic though this aspect may be, there should be no deception about the necessity of large scale future improvements

to prevent part of the Old City becoming ever increasing slums.... [E]lements of architecture...have decayed, disappeared or been replaced by ugly modern additions....[10]

In 1962, Jordan ordered a survey of Jerusalem from Brown Engineers International Corporation of New York, titled "Jerusalem General Plan." The survey described the Old City thus: "The Old City, on the other hand, has resisted modernization.... [I]t is still in large measure a town of pedestrians, and most of its streets and houses are still medieval in character." It recommended "the reconstruction and rehabilitation of destroyed or deteriorating areas in the Old City... similar to the original... after a rehousing program has provided alternate living space for the inhabitants...."[11]

From 1961–1967, British archaeologist Dame Kathleen M. Kenyon excavated in the City of David–Silwan and outside the southern wall of the Temple Mount. During the latter excavation, she found Byzantine remains, but failed to identify structures and relics from other periods. Later, from the early 1970s on, Prof. Binyamin Mazar and others excavated the same area and more, discovering major finds from First and Second Temple, Byzantine, early Muslim, Crusader, and other periods. As will be noted later, this greatly enriched the heritage value of the Old City from 1967 on. Kenyon's failure to uncover Muslim and Christian heritage during the Jordanian occupation was a real missed opportunity.

Another unexploited resource during the Jordanian period was the PAM (Palestine Archaeological Museum, popularly known as the Rockefeller Museum). The museum was built in 1930 to house the large antiquities collection left by Ottoman authorities along with extensive finds from excavations carried out during the Mandate. Just before termination of the British Mandate late in 1947, a board of international trustees was assigned management of the museum. This board of trustees remained until 1966, when Jordan suddenly took over the museum, claiming that the trustees had done little more than "keep the place clean." For 18 years, Jordan missed an opportunity to develop the museum and to enhance Jerusalem's attraction as a heritage tourism site. Instead, it sent new archaeological finds to Amman, Jerash, or Petra after 1948.

Then, in 1967, Israel gained sovereignty over the East Jerusalem museum.

Ironically,... the dissolution of the international board of trustees served Israel's interests; Israel now took over the management of the PAM.... The atmosphere of peace and scholarship was replaced by the industrious activity of the Israel Antiquities Authority Management, which now occupies most of the building (Kletter 2006, 174–91).

Figure 3. No man's land as seen from Mount Scopus, from the Tower of David to Mount Zion. Elan Tal, 1964. Source: Wiki Commons.

Postwar Jerusalem, 1967

In the assessment of Teddy Kollek, Jerusalem's mayor, "With the reunification of the city after the Six-Day War, and its restoration to its rightful place at the center of the country, a new future opened before Jerusalem" (Teddy Kollek, 1975, quoted in Gilbert 1977, 123). Israel took steps to ensure that its newly declared sovereignty over united Jerusalem would endure despite opposition by the Arab countries and the United Nations. Militarily, politically, legally and demographically, the government took whatever steps it could to strengthen this sovereignty (Dumper 1997, 39–43). There is no doubt that the heavy losses Israel incurred in the wars of 1948 and 1967, and the very visible physical scars of these wars in the built environment, reinforced Israeli determination to make both East and West Jerusalem integral and inseparable sections of the capital of Israel. Even without these losses and scars, as the religious and political capital of an independent Jewish State in the First and Second Temple periods, Jerusalem has never ceased to be the symbol par excellence of Jewish sovereignty and independence. First, Israel urgently needed to alter its demography by re-introducing a Jewish population into East Jerusalem, and particularly into the Old City and environs, where no Jews had resided for nineteen years, in order to prevent any possibility of these areas becoming part of a Jordanian or Palestinian state (Dumper 1997, 53).

As Rabbi Shear Yashuv Cohen, Deputy Mayor of the Jerusalem Municipal Council, stated on August 13, 1967:

We must do everything within our power to make Greater Jerusalem the largest Jewish city in the world, a real Jewish city, both in terms of the population numbers and in giving a permanent Jewish character to the whole city (cited in Dumper 1997, 53).

Upon the annexation of East Jerusalem in 1967, Israel attempted to merge the two municipalities and their services into one. The challenges were great. A huge gap existed in salaries, services, and taxes between the two municipalities. East Jerusalem residents and the Muslim *Waqf* (religious endowment) Council refused to recognize Israeli sovereignty or even to receive compensation for damages from the government, as this might be understood as a form of recognition. The physical state of the Old City was very poor, with infrastructure dating back to the Ottoman Period or earlier. Almost 24,000 Muslims and Christians lived in the Old City in 1967 (including some 5,000 in the ruined Jewish Quarter.) About 40% of these households lived in one room, almost 60% had no running water, almost 40% had no indoor plumbing, and 30% had no electricity (Shalem 1968).[12] On June 11, 1967, the government established a Ministerial Committee for Jerusalem, which included the Ministers of Justice, Security, Religious Affairs, Foreign Affairs, Interior, Housing, and Minister without Portfolio Menachem Begin. Later, the Ministers of Justice, the Treasury, Labor, Tourism, and Housing also sat on the committee. The Mayor of Jerusalem would be invited to participate as needed.[13]

For the first three weeks after the ceasefire in June 1967, Jerusalem remained under military rule. During that period, the Municipality worked together with the military authorities, the Department of Housing, and the National Parks Authority (then part of the Prime Minister's office) to remove roadblocks and repair war damage and dangerous structures. Jerusalem Mayor Teddy Kollek immediately began fundraising and planning the renovation of the Old City, including restoring Jewish life to the Jewish Quarter, renovating historic monuments such as Jaffa Gate and the Tower of David, and creating a new national park encircling the walls of the Old City.[14]

Figure 4: Imaginative rendering of a proposed national park. R. Dvir, 1968. Source: Israel State Archives.

Planning began simultaneously in three concentric circles: erecting new Jewish and non-Jewish neighborhoods in greater "United Jerusalem"; regeneration of the Old City and Environs; and rebuilding the destroyed Jewish Quarter. In the negotiations between the various national and municipal bodies involved, it is difficult to separate one aspect from another.

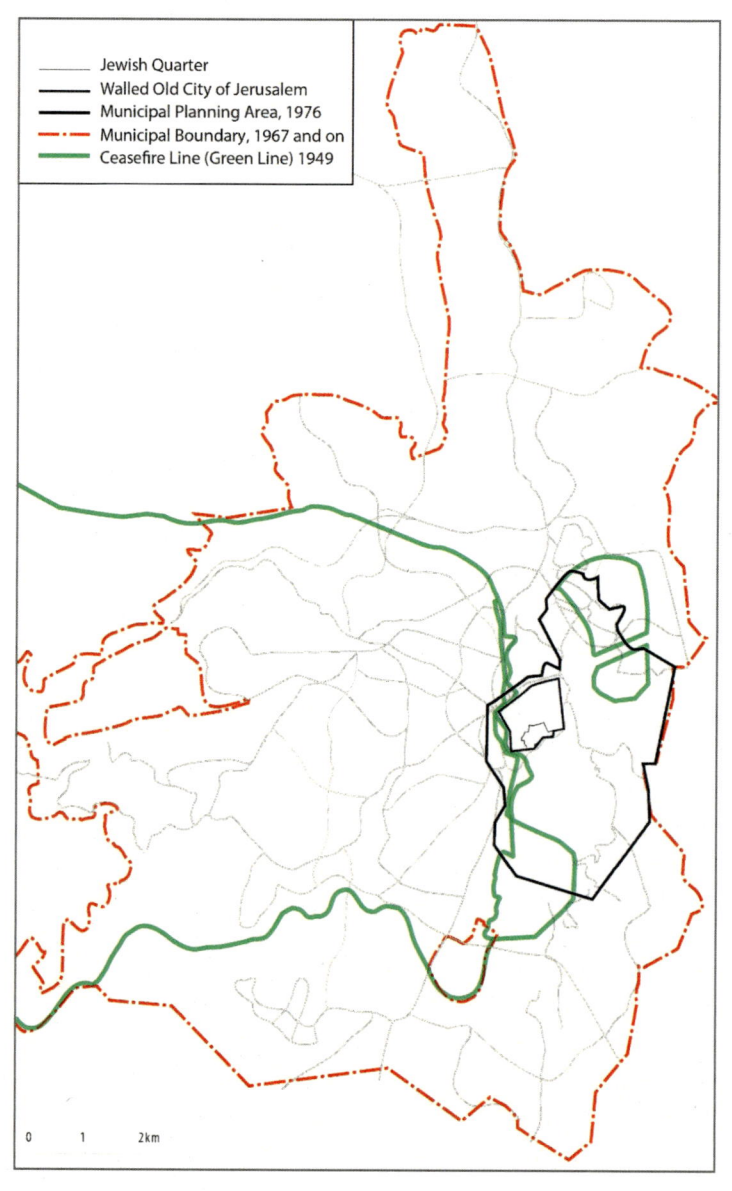

Map 2: Schematic map of Jerusalem, 1949–1967.
Source: Cartography Department, Hebrew University of Jerusalem, 2016.

The Housing Ministry began to create a plan for the regeneration of the Old City, beginning with the Jewish Quarter, continuing on to the Muslim Quarter, and then to special projects in the Armenian and Christian Quarters.[15] According to two early censuses taken in the Old City in the summer of 1967, its population was almost 24,000, most under the age of 30. Almost 5,000 Muslim Arabs lived in the Jewish Quarter, many in appalling conditions. About 13,500 lived in the Muslim Quarter, and about 5,000 Christians and 1,000 Muslims in the Christian and Armenian Quarters. There were no Jewish residents. The plan was to compensate and relocate the non-Jewish occupants of the Jewish Quarter and replace them with Jewish residents. Later, as renewal of the rest of the Old City progressed, plans were to "thin out" the Muslim Quarter to no more than 8,000. It was estimated that the first stage of planning would take only eight months.[16]

On June 27, 1967, the Knesset enacted the Protection of Holy Places Law 5727 (1967), signed by Prime Minister Levi Eshkol, Minister of Religious Affairs Zerach Warhaftig, and President Shneur Zalman Shazar, providing that:

> The Holy Places shall be protected from desecration and any other violation and from anything likely to violate the freedom of access of the members of the different religions to the places sacred to them or their feelings with regard to those places.

Infringement of this law would be punishable by imprisonment for a term of five to seven years. The Minister of Religious Affairs was charged with the law's implementation.[17] By this law, Israel proclaimed its intention to protect all Christian, Muslim, and Jewish Holy Sites and to prevent the kind of purposeful desecration of holy places discussed above and so common in times of war. Israel took upon itself to conserve and rehabilitate both Jewish and non-Jewish religious heritage, with emphasis on the destroyed Jewish heritage of the Jewish Quarter. Although Israel promised freedom of religion to all, there is no mention of the "status quo" in the earliest statements made by Prime Minister Eshkol and by Minister of Religion Warhaftig, "apparently due to Israel's concern that mention of the status quo might invoke the restrictive, humiliating regulations existing during the Mandate concerning the Jewish holy sites, particularly as regards the Western Wall" (Guinn 2006, 42).

On June 29, 1967, the cement walls and legal barriers separating East Jerusalem from West came toppling down. Teddy Kollek was now the Mayor of United Jerusalem. There was a euphoric atmosphere in Jerusalem, as Jews and Arabs freely crossed over the borders and visited old friends. Despite all the concern beforehand, thousands of Jews and Arabs reunited over cups of coffee on both sides of the town. There was hope that peace would speedily be achieved, and that a wonderful future lay ahead.

What would the Old City and the Jewish Quarter be like? There were many different visions—stemming from different ideologies and cultural, religious, ethnic, and social orientations. All these visions were based on different understandings of Jerusalem's heritage and how to best realize it.

Planning Jerusalem

One of the questions raised was whether renovation of the Old City and its environs came under the jurisdiction of the State or of the Municipality. By law, city planning is done by the city. However, Interior Minister Haim Moshe Shapira was not willing to allow Mayor Kollek sole authority in planning and rebuilding the Old City. Jerusalem was a "universal" city and the Old City a "special area," warranting concern on the national and international levels. In an urgent letter on July 7, 1967, the Jerusalem Municipality was warned not to initiate any building projects in East Jerusalem. Although it was inside the Municipality boundaries, "[t]he Minister of Interior has not yet declared it a part of the Local Planning Authority of the Jerusalem Municipality."[18]

Mayor Kollek and the City Council Members objected strongly and garnered support from leading public officials, municipalities, and architects all over the country. This step was seen as dividing Jerusalem anew, as creating a dangerous precedent for other cities, and as necessitating a complicated and artificial planning framework that simply would not work. "The government has many worries and responsibilities; the Jerusalem Municipality has only one—Jerusalem," declared Kollek.[19]

While this issue was still being debated, Prime Minister Levi Eshkol decided to intervene by appointing a special advisor in the Prime Minister's office, Yehuda Tamir, as head of the new Unit for the Population of Jerusalem, directly responsible to Eshkol alone.[20] Tamir was given authority over planning, renovation and population of East Jerusalem, including full responsibility for the renewal of the Jewish Quarter.[21] His staff included representatives of the Israel Lands Authority, the Housing and Religious Affairs Ministries, the Jerusalem Municipality, and the Interior Ministry. Tamir immediately set to work, and on September 3, 1967 presented a plan for building new Jewish neighborhoods in East Jerusalem (later known as Ramat Eshkol, Ramot, Armon HaNeziv, and Gilo), as well as renovation of the Old City. These proposals were to form the basis for future planning and construction policies.

On September 6, 1967, Israel's Minister of Interior Haim Moshe Shapira officially expanded the municipal limits of Jerusalem, at the same time declaring the Old City and its environs "a special area" which would remain under the Jerusalem Regional Planning Authority, belonging to the Ministry of Interior. The Regional Planning Authority then established a secondary committee responsible for the Old City, composed of representatives of the Municipality, the Ministry of Interior, and professionals in planning and construction, which began work that same month.[22]

The Municipality's reaction to loss of authority over the Old City was to erect yet another committee—a special advisory committee made up of the best town planners in the country—to direct and advise the secondary committee to the regional planning committee. The outline plan devised by this committee, headed by renowned planner Aryeh Sharon, came to be known as AM/9. It attempted to embody "the religious, historical, and national values of Israel, and take into consideration the special values of other religions as well."[23]

This outline plan for the Old City and Environs was completed in 1971. The outline plan for all of Jerusalem, completed only in 1975, defined the relationship between the New and Old Cities, reiterated the commitment to establish a national park all around the Old City Walls, and called for an effective public transportation system providing easy access to the Old City (Schweid 1975). Control over planning and construction in the Old City and Environs was returned to the Jerusalem Municipality in 1971, following completion of outline plan AM/9. Every stage of planning and construction was to be examined by a panel of architects, and approved by the various committees.[24] The situation was further complicated by the fact that neither the Greater Jerusalem Outline plan nor the Jerusalem Master Plan had been completed and approved by then. The planners demanded more time in order to plan correctly. Meanwhile, construction took place without planning permits and without following plans and orders.[25]

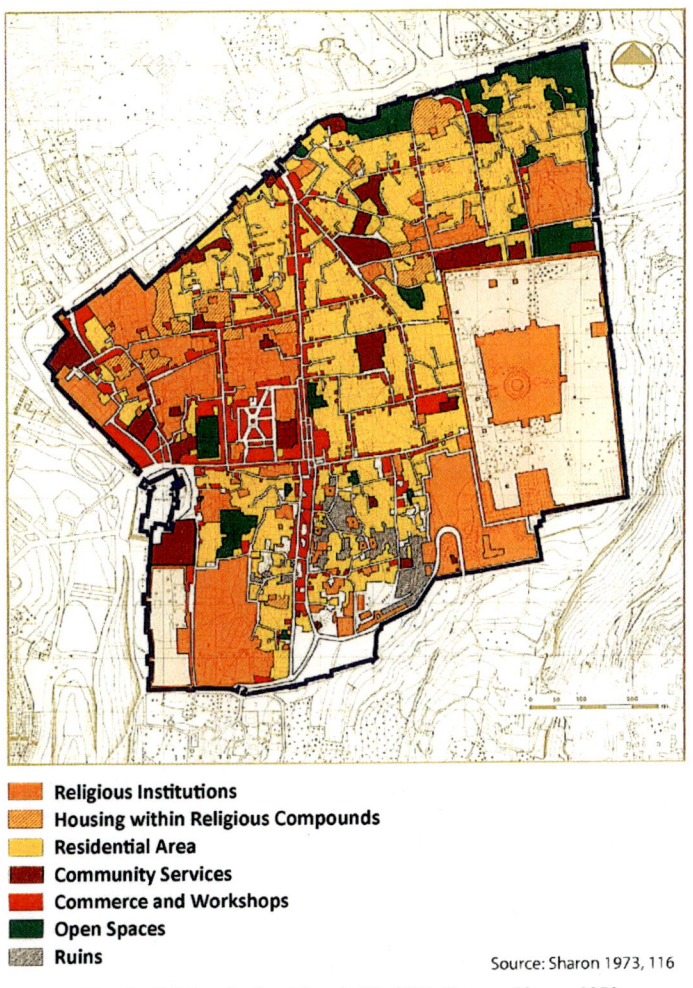

■ Religious Institutions
▨ Housing within Religious Compounds
■ Residential Area
■ Community Services
■ Commerce and Workshops
■ Open Spaces
▨ Ruins

Source: Sharon 1973, 116

Plan 2: Old City Outline Plan AM/9, 1971. Source: Sharon 1973.

The Jerusalem Master Plan

In 1964, about two years before the Six Day War, the Planning Division of the West Jerusalem Municipality began to devise a new Master Plan for the divided city. This plan was based on the prediction that in the long range there would be a gradual normalization of relations between Jordan and Israel, allowing free access from one side of the city to the other. No state of war between the two states was expected. Therefore, it was recommended to plan to connect the two cities with roads capable of carrying a heavy load of traffic. All that was needed after the unification in 1967 was to further expand this plan, but not to drastically revise it.[26]

The 1967 plan's three objectives in renovating the Old City and environs were preservation of landscape and religious, historic, and archaeological sites; commercial, cultural, and tourism development; and gentrification of residential neighborhoods, including thinning out overcrowded areas.[27] The special architectural qualities of the Old City were to be preserved by continuing building with limestone, retention of scale, and upgrading infrastructure and physical conditions. Motor traffic would not enter the Old City, which would be surrounded by a national park. The landscape would further be protected by prohibiting construction in the surrounding areas: Mount Zion, the City of David (Silwan), the Kidron Valley, and the Mount of Olives. Construction inside the city walls would remain low and at a distance from the walls. Wide boulevards would lead from the city gates to the commercial center and government buildings in West Jerusalem, and to Mount Scopus. Ring roads carrying heavy traffic would encircle the Old City at a distance.[28] (In 1967, one of every ten Israeli households owned a car. It was estimated that by 2010, the number of motor vehicles would be identical to the number of households (Benziman 1973, 271; *Hazofeh*, 12 June 1967, 4).

We have noted that the authors of the master and outline plans followed the British approach to preservation of the Holy Basin, including separation of the old from the new by a green strip all around the Old City walls and restricted motor access into the Old City. One of the results of this isolation would be the limited demographic, political, and economic relevance of the Old City to Greater Jerusalem and to Israel in general, despite its religious significance and symbolic title as the heart of the united city.

In October 1967, the Jerusalem master plan staff began to prepare an index of sites for preservation upon which future plans would be based. Planners were advised to put economic considerations on the side and emphasize the value of creating cultural continuity by integrating modern elements with foundations from the past. However, since the Antiquities Authority did not yet exist, there was no legal basis for enforcing preservation. It remained no more than a recommendation, dependent on the good will of the relevant body in each particular case—archaeologists, the National Parks Authority, the Ministry of Religion, the Municipality, private enterprise, and so on.[29]

In both the Master Plan and the statutory Outline Plan, the total number of residents in the Old City would gradually be reduced to between 14,000 to 20,000. The Christian population of about 6,000 would remain static, but the Muslim population would be lowered from 16,000 to 4,000–8,000. The Jewish population would grow from 0 to 3,500 within the Jewish Quarter, with an additional 1,000–2,000 dormitory students in educational institutions. Thus the total number of Old City residents would decrease gradually from over 23,000 in 1968 to about 14,000 by 1990.[30]

This Master Plan aroused much controversy, on the municipal, national, and international levels. It was never approved and a consensus never reached on issues such as roads and transportation, despite the fact that the Outline Plan drawn shortly after was based on this Master Plan.[31]

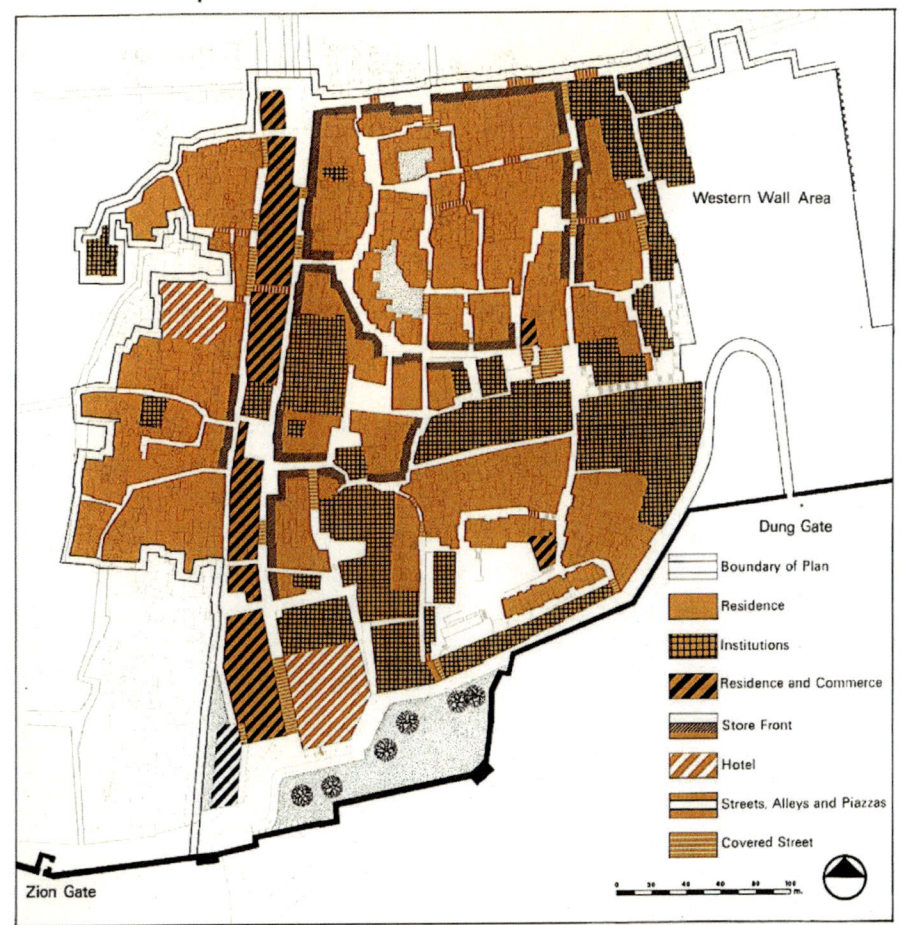

Map 5: Jewish Quarter Master Plan, 1968

Plan 3: Jewish Quarter Master Plan, 1968. Source: Sharon 1973.

The Jerusalem Committee

In 1968, in reaction to the internal political and ideological struggles over the Master and Outline Plans for Jerusalem, and to the importance of Jerusalem to the world at large, Mayor Kollek established the "Jerusalem Committee"—an international, non-affiliated advisory council for planning United Jerusalem, consisting of some seventy renowned architects, urban planners, historians, and philosophers from many countries. The first convention of the World Advisory Council of the Jerusalem Committee was held in July 1969. Among the speakers were Mayor Kollek, Prof. Bruno Zevi of Italy, American sculptor and landscape designer Isamo Noguchi, Oxford historian Sir Isaiah Berlin, former President of the Philippines Carlos Garcia, Dr. Willem Sandburg of Amsterdam's Municipal Museum; architects Dan Tanai, Louis Kahan, Ehud Netzer (then Menczel), David Anatol Bruzkus, and Buckminster Fuller. Archaeologist Prof. Binyamin Mazar, City Counsellor Meiron Benvenisti, Hebrew University of Jerusalem President Prof. Avraham Harman, and City Engineer Amikam Yaffe also spoke.

The committee recommended restoration of the Old City walls, clearance of Jewish and Muslim slums adjacent to them, and renovation of important ancient sites. Its support for the proposal to erect a national park surrounding the Old City walls was undoubtedly one of the factors that influenced its implementation. At the same time that the UN seconded Jordan's protest against Israel's annexation of East Jerusalem, the Jerusalem Committee affirmed its confidence in the Municipality and in Mayor Kollek's ability to rebuild the unified city.[32] Although no Muslim countries agreed to participate in the conference, Jerusalem's significance as a city holy to all three monotheistic religions was emphasized, and the conference organizers expressed the wish that "our Muslim brothers" would attend future conferences.

A second conference took place in December 1970, and its program was similar to the first. Criticism was expressed of the road plans that would lead to heavy traffic on the roads around the Old City, to the conservative architecture of the new buildings, and to the preference accorded the residential character over the archaeological character of the Jewish Quarter (Benziman 1973, 270–72). As a result of the controversy and criticism, the Jerusalem Municipality established the Planning Policy Department in the City Planning Division, headed by City Engineer Amikam Yaffe and the renowned British planner Prof. Nathaniel Lichfield. One of the most successful projects of this department was the international competition for renovation of the Cardo, held in 1971.[33] In an effort to involve the local population in planning, the committee held an exhibition in the Tower of David on municipal plans for restoration of sites in the Jewish, Muslim, and Christian Quarters.[34]

Chapter II
Jerusalem's Jewish Quarter

The Pre-1967 Jewish Quarter

One of the reasons for the overcrowding of the Jewish Quarter during the Ottoman Period was the ban on acquisition of land by non-Ottoman Jewish subjects. The Jewish and Christian populations increased enormously during the 19th century due to immigration from Russia and Europe. However, in the first half of the 19th century foreign citizens could not purchase and register land in their names, with the rare exception of an individual who obtained a special *firman* from the Sultan. In spite of the authorization given in the Hatt (1856) for foreigners to buy land, and the publication of the Ottoman Land Laws of 1858, final legal permission was withheld for another decade. Only in 1867 were subjects of foreign powers officially allowed to acquire land and to build on it (Kark 1984, 357–84).

As Ricca notes, "Since the destruction of the Temple in 70 C.E. until the construction of the imposing dome of the Hurva in 1864, no Jewish building, apart from the striking mass of the Wailing Wall, characterized the city's skyline" (Ricca 2007, 17). Until then, dozens of synagogues and other institutions kept a low profile, concentrating their talents and resources on interior decoration. From the second half of the 19th century onwards, the number of synagogues and *yeshivot* within the ancient city grew from about eight to almost eighty.

Along with the population growth, the area in which Jews were concentrated expanded, and the "Jewish Quarter" spread to areas north of the Street of the Chains, which had served as the dividing line. An estimated 5,000 Jews and a dozen or more institutions were located outside of the nuclear Jewish Quarter. In many cases, Jews and Arabs lived in close proximity, sometimes even in the same courtyard. Relations were generally good, and sometimes very good. However, Jews were always *dhimmi*, second class citizens under Muslim rule, despite their newfound right to acquire property and to erect new structures. As noted in Chapter I, this population largely moved to the New City during the 20th century, particularly after the Arab riots under the British Mandate in 1920, 1921, 1929, and 1936–39. Many of the wealthier Arab families, especially Christians, also left the Old City before and during the 1948 war.[35]

By the time war broke out in 1948, no Jews lived in the Old City outside of the shrunken Jewish Quarter—a tiny isolated enclave surrounded by thousands of hostile neighbors. The quarter's defenders fought for two weeks, and then surrendered to the Arab Legion. As in many violent ethnic and religious conflicts, Jewish institutions and holy places were targeted for destruction both during and after the war, and a concerted attempt was made to erase all evidence of a Jewish presence within the walls (Ben Eliezer 1975; Desecration 1967). One-third of the Jewish Quarter's buildings were totally destroyed and another third partially destroyed. Most of the remaining historic Jewish Quarter of the Old City was in advanced stages of deterioration, its infrastructure outdated or non-existent, exasperated by weather damage and years of neglect. Nevertheless, during the nineteen years of Jordanian rule that followed its surrender in May 1948, the Arab population of the (former) Jewish Quarter increased to 5,000—many of whom were poverty-stricken families from Hebron who lived in absentee property, ruins, and makeshift hovels. Many of the wealthier families, especially Christians, left the Old City before and during the 1948 war. Under Jordanian rule, the Jewish Quarter was renamed Al-Munadileen, but was also known as Haret ash-Sharah or Haret ash-Sharaf (the neighborhood of honor), and al-Mu'asker (Military Camp [Kailani 2007, 71–75]). Although most of the Jewish Quarter was in ruins, the northern section, from which Jews had been evacuated during the last two decades of the British Mandate, remained relatively undamaged, and population density there reached 90–100 people per dunam (1 dunam = 1,000 square meters) by 1967.

In 1963, Brown Engineers International Corporation of New York submitted their Jerusalem town plan to King Hussein. He then issued orders to evict all inhabitants from the destroyed Jewish Quarter, to clear away the damaged synagogues and homes, and to turn the area into a national park or a joint Jordanian-American amusement park. In 1966, he signed an additional royal order for evacuation of the area. Alternative housing for the evacuees was to be found in northeastern Jerusalem (today French Hill and Shuafat). Thus, the Six Day War found the Jewish Quarter in the process of being cleared out. In the 1960s, much of its Arab population was evicted. Many of these inhabitants returned in 1967, only to be compensated and relocated outside of the Jewish Quarter again (Israel Information Centre 1973 (Kailani 2007, xv, 73–75).

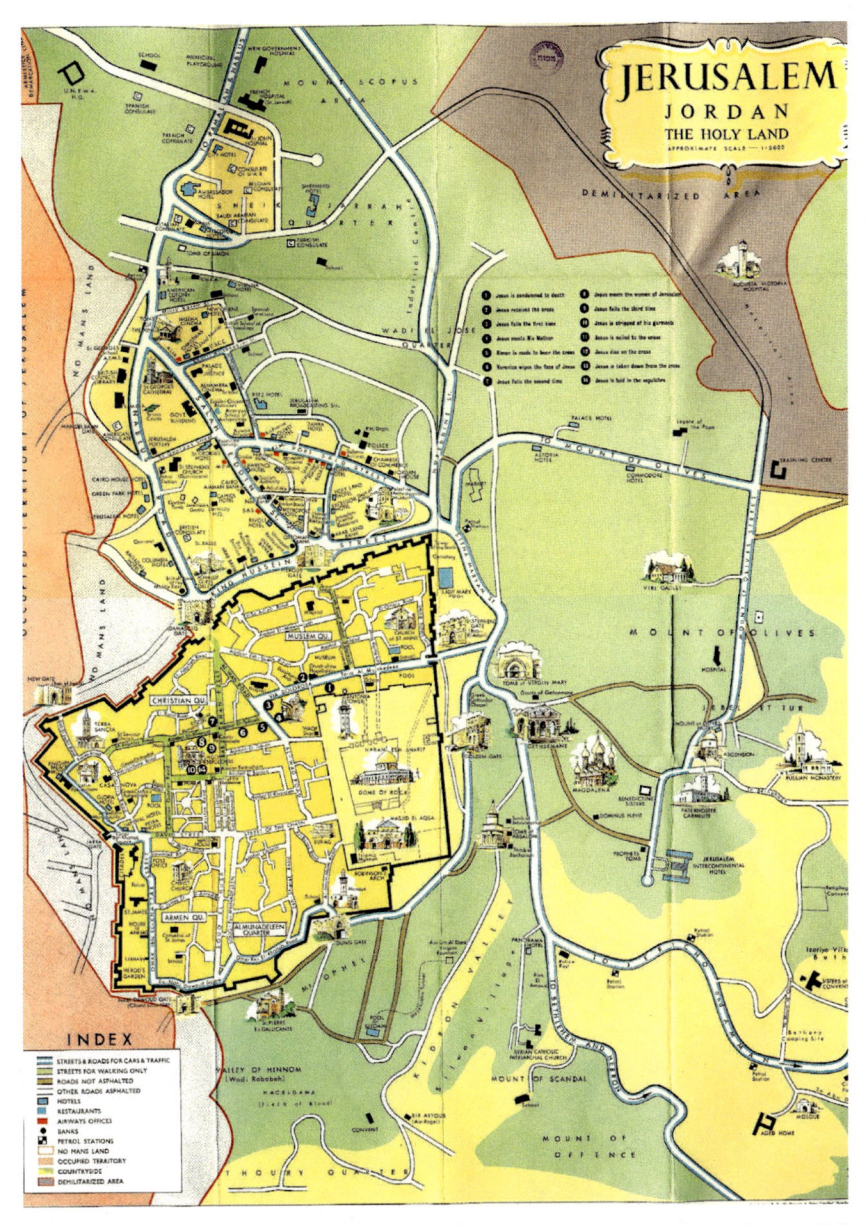

Map 3: Jordanian map of the Old City—Jordan the Holy Land. Al-Munadeleen Jewish Quarter 1949–1967. Source: Hebrew University of Jerusalem, Mount Scopus, Map Library.

Jewish Quarter Renewal, 1967–1969

After 1967, rebuilding the Jewish Quarter and the Western Wall Plaza were Israel's top priority. This would restore the beloved Jewish holy sites and put them on par with those of the Muslims and Christians. It would signify Israeli sovereignty over the heart of Jerusalem, not merely military or political hegemony. It would also enhance the self-image and satisfy the desires of the Israeli man in the street. Despite its small size, the heroic and traumatic battle over the Jewish Quarter in 1948 and its ensuing destruction and desecration had made it the symbol of Israel's return to its historic and religious capital. As with destroyed Warsaw after World War II, physical renewal embodied the spirit of the nation, reflecting both past and present collective memory and identity. This intangible cultural heritage played an important role in the formation of collective identity, but different representations of national identity reflected the cultural and ideological diversity that led to conflicting choices of past intangible heritage. In the rebuilding of the Jewish Quarter after 1967, the choice of tangible and intangible heritage to be presented aroused lively debate. These differing interpretations led to several approaches to development of heritage-based tourism (or pilgrimage).

Israel was still new at planning. Its regulatory system, in the framework of the Planning and Construction Law of 1965, was the first comprehensive attempt to create an obligatory legal framework for physical development in Israel, making planning approval obligatory before construction. One of the principles of local outline schemes was listed as "preservation of every building or site of architectural, historic, or archaeological importance," allocating the authority to decide on criteria for preservation to the local authorities. This law had no "teeth" to enforce preservation. In addition, the Planning and Construction framework was highly centralized and required approval of plans on three levels: national, regional, and municipal. This was typical of the centralized socialist approach of Israeli governance at the time.

Between the years 1948–1953 Israel underwent major changes as the country's population doubled. Concomitant to establishing and organizing the new state, architect Arieh Sharon led a series of new planning paradigms in order to cope with the massive waves of immigration and the increased state land holdings. Guided by European models, Israel adopted proactive planning to create a new settlement map for the new state, with successes and failures along the way (Kark 1995, 461–94). Needless to say, a planning framework tailored to large-scale urban development was not the most appropriate for rehabilitating historic cities. This problem was not unique to Israel, as Stefana Bianca has noted (Bianca 2014, 97).

In addition, the lack of coordination between the Master and Outline Plans for the Old City and the slow pace of planning led the regulatory committee to approve building without a clear contextual framework. With such a complicated, unwieldy regulatory system, it is easy to see how construction could take place de facto without planning permits, with little or no relation to the larger context, and without following plans and orders.[36]

The revitalized city was intended to attract large numbers of tourists and pilgrims, providing them with tourism services such as shops, hotels, and restaurants, as well as cultural and religious opportunities. The gap between the vision of a gentrified Jewish Quarter, conserving and presenting religious and historic values in an aesthetic and tourist-friendly built environment, and the difficult social and physical conditions existing then with the potential continuation of Arab-Israel violence, proved almost impossible to bridge. To cope with this challenge, another centralized government agency was established—a high-level Ministerial Committee on Jerusalem, headed by Yehuda Tamir, Prime Minister Eshkol's trusted and experienced advisor, and including Minister without Portfolio Menachem Begin and the Justice, Security, Interior, Religious Affairs, Foreign Affairs, and Housing Ministers.[37] These competing bureaucracies and the unwieldy regulatory system complicated and delayed planning the Jewish Quarter. In part, it was a result of the system itself, but it also reflected the extremely sensitive religious, ethnic, and political issues involved.

In the case of Jerusalem, the struggle for control between national and municipal authorities reflected not only personal and political friction, but basic questions about presentation of Jerusalem's heritage: Should Jewish values or universal values take priority? Which Jewish values should be emphasized: modern or traditional, secular or ultra-Orthodox, Zionist or post-Zionist? Another issue was the approach to be taken—modernization or conservation? Should speed or meticulous planning take priority? The public debate at all levels of Israeli society was intense. It was not only personal ambition that drove every minister or public figure to strive to be included in the decision-making. These were vital ideological decisions.

The first Jewish efforts to live in the Jewish Quarter were grassroots undertakings. About two months after the 1967 war, when official planning was just beginning, the first new residents of the Jewish Quarter moved in: One rabbi, two artists, and a handful of *yeshiva* students. The rabbi had received permission to reside in and renew the Habad Synagogue —one of the few important synagogues still standing in the Jewish Quarter. The artists simply purchased property from local residents and opened studios. The *yeshiva* students lived and studied in abandoned, partially destroyed buildings, establishing a Jewish presence in the Quarter and at the Western Wall. These private initiatives are barely mentioned in official documentation, although they occurred concurrently with the centralized planning and development described here.[38]

Figure 5: Elyada Merioz in his art gallery, 1973. Source: Government Press Office.

The Batei Mahse Team

Prime Minister Eshkol's advisor Yehuda Tamir was charged with directing the rehabilitation. He began by appointing two teams. Architect Ehud Netzer (then Menczel) was chosen to survey the area and prepare a master plan.[39] Architects Ora and Ya'akov Ya'ar, Sa'adia Mandel, and Ya'akov Frankel, the award-winning team which had developed Old Jaffa, were chosen to be the first to work on a specific site in the Jewish Quarter—the Batei Mahse neighborhood.

A few of the hundred-year-old structures in the Batei Mahse Plaza had survived the 1948 War, and were known to be owned by the charitable endowment of the Organization of P'kidim and Amarcalim. The large open plaza had been heavily bombed during the war. Here the residents and fighters of the Jewish Quarter surrendered to the Arab Legion on May 29, 1948, and were then driven out of their homes. Sa'adia Mandel recalled:

> The war [of 1967] was barely over when I was invited to come to Jerusalem and quickly get to work. In the center of the Batei Mahse Plaza was a public toilet [from the Jordanian period] constructed of Jewish gravestones from the Mount of Olives Cemetery. The government decision to begin renovations immediately was a direct reaction to this—a clear political statement about Jerusalem and who would inhabit the new houses we were to build (Mandel interview 2006).

The speedy renovation of Batei Mahse with Jewish residents was seen as a national priority with high symbolic, historic, and political value, one that would bring the typical townscape of the Jewish Quarter of a century ago back to life. Only two months after the ceasefire following the Six Day War, Ya'ar, Mandel, and Frankel presented a plan and timetable for the restoration of the Jewish Quarter:

1. Survey of the Jewish Quarter, preparation of a master plan, and measurements in preparation for restoration work.
2. Establishment of a restoration framework—evacuation of squatters, clearance of ruins, supervision of conservation activities.
3. Preparation of infrastructure plans (water, sewage, electricity, gas, telephone, television, and so on).

Proposed order:
4. Planning the street scheme and the infrastructure
5. Paving streets, designing public spaces
6. Restoration and preservation of existing structures
7. New construction

Moving Jewish tenants into temporary housing in the quarter was scheduled to begin immediately after laying the infrastructure. There was a strong desire to restore the Jewish population of the quarter, but it was clear that this would not happen until the ruins were cleared, the squatters removed, and the plans and infrastructure for the new neighborhood completed.[40] This could not be done overnight.

First Steps in Planning, Policy Making, and Rebuilding

In July 1967, only one month after the Six Day War, Ehud Netzer was appointed to conduct a survey of the physical state of the Jewish Quarter and to create a master plan for it. To this purpose, the Treasury Ministry took possession of all property in the Jewish Quarter for one year, beginning September 1967.[41] It was not easy to set boundaries to the Jewish Quarter. At its height, the Jewish population of the Old City had reached some 20,000, and Jewish neighborhoods, such as "Hebron Street" (north of the Street of the Chains) reached as far as the Damascus and Lions Gates. But by the time the 1948 war broke out, the Jewish Quarter had shrunk from 150 metric dunams to 70 (1 metric dunam equals 1,000 square meters) (Ben-Arieh, 1984).[42]

As mentioned above, there was no running water, the sewage system was inadequate, and modern infrastructure non-existent. Netzer completed the difficult physical survey of the quarter in 1968 and prepared a first draft of a master plan for a Jewish Quarter of 120 dunams, a close approximation to the extent of the Jewish Quarter at the turn of the century. Differentiation between the Jewish and the Armenian Quarters was based on land ownership, rather than location.[43] A political decision was taken to disregard Jewish-owned property and institutions in former Jewish neighborhoods north of the Street of the Chains, and to concentrate on the area that the British had designated the "Jewish Quarter."[44]

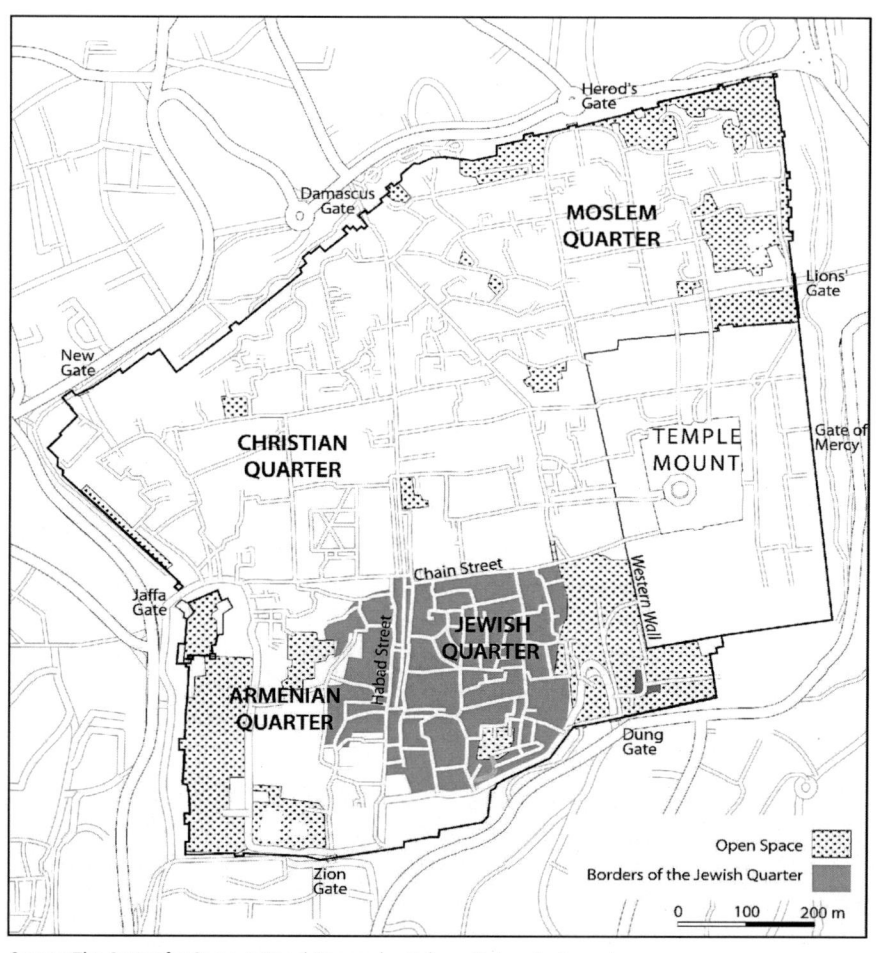

Source: The Center for Computational Geography, Hebrew University Jerusalem

Map 4: Netzer's proposed borders for the Jewish Quarter.
Source: Cartography Department, Hebrew University of Jerusalem, 2009.

In April 1968, the 120 dunams that would become the Jewish Quarter were expropriated by the Israeli Government, including both Jewish and non-Jewish owned properties. This was only part of a much larger scale expropriation in all of East Jerusalem, in order to enable construction of new housing and services for both Jews and non-Jews. Had the government not completed this blanket expropriation, it would have been extremely difficult to resolve issues regarding the legal status of properties whose ownership was registered and held in Ottoman, British, Jordanian, and Israeli archives. Charitable foundations of the Muslim *Waqf*, the various churches, and Jewish institutions were dealt with individually. After establishment of the Company for the Reconstruction and Development of the Jewish Quarter, it leased the Jewish Quarter from the Israel Lands Authority (Gardi interview 2007).[45]

Netzer's master plan, accepted on December 12, 1967, prescribed preservation of the scale and urban fabric of the quarter, including the traditional narrow winding lanes. As for the buildings themselves, only about one hundred (a third) of the old structures were deemed suitable for restoration. The last paragraph of his master plan related to land usage and the character of the rebuilt quarter. However, its socio-economic status, the way in which it would (or would not) preserve and express national, religious, historic, and cultural values, and its relationship to the rest of the Old City, were not addressed at all. This plan apparently served as precedent for both the Jerusalem Master Plan of 1968 and Outline Plan AM/9 (Rabinovich 1969).[46]

1. Exterior walls and rooftops are to be faced with natural hewed limestone. Tiled rooftops will only be allowed in special cases.
2. The heights of buildings will conform to the general topography and in no case exceed 4 stories.
3. Sites designated for preservation may not deviate from their original form nor include additions.
4. Sites that undergo general renovation shall conform to the general streetscape. Additions and changes for the benefit of residents or to fill in incidental spaces are permitted so long as they conform to the general pattern.
5. All domed rooftops and the skyline are to be preserved.
6. The Jewish Quarter is intended to be occupied by residents and by educational, cultural and religious institutions that fit its character, including services necessary for such residents, institutions, and for visitors. Nightclubs, wedding halls, large hotels and commercial centres will not be built in the Jewish Quarter.[47]

Netzer's proposal contained two new ideas: Creation of a new tourist route from the Western Wall Plaza to the Jewish Quarter via the remains of the destroyed Hurva, Karaite, and Tiferet Yisrael synagogues. This meant clearing a wide path in the center of the quarter and construction of a new staircase at the eastern edge. The large-scale destruction in the center of the quarter made such a project feasible.

Second: Construction of an underground parking lot and terminal in the southwestern corner of the quarter, and pedestrianization of the Jewish Quarter, particularly of the road inside the city wall from Zion to Dung Gate, as it had been during the British Mandate (Netzer [Menczel] interview 2005).

In those parts of the quarter that had not been destroyed, Netzer attempted to preserve the layout of the streets and old buildings as much as possible. Only about 200 old buildings were still standing, most in very poor condition. It was estimated that 100–140 could be preserved. There was much controversy regarding the materials and style of new construction. It would conform in scale and in use of stone facing, but how new and modern should it look? (Rabinovich 1969).

The government approved Netzer's plan, established a ministerial committee for development of the Jewish Quarter, and passed emergency measures that would allow the planners and architects exemption from the bureaucracy requiring approval of construction plans, building permits, and so on, in order to speed up the process. All work was to be carried out by the Housing Ministry (Benziman 1973, 265).[48]

The first ten months of work were spent clearing away ruins and debris and planning the layout of streets and infrastructure. Several partially destroyed synagogues a century or more old were cleaned and initial repairs begun, along with the Zion Gate plaza and sections of the city wall. On the eastern edge of the Jewish Quarter, the remains of a large Crusader complex were unearthed, and construction of the new staircase to the Western Wall Plaza alongside it was begun. (Within two years, the remains of a Turkish Bazaar and a Second Temple period structure would be discovered in the same area.)

Figure 6: The new Yehuda Halevy Staircase and Teutonic Knights complex. Source: Eisenstark Photographic Collection, 1970. Israel State Archives.

The Housing Ministry held negotiations with about 800 squatters and resettled them outside of the quarter. It also began to lay the underground infrastructure of water, sewage, electricity, telephone, and television, to keep the skyline clean. Several old buildings were partially renovated to serve as dormitories for a few rabbinical seminaries (*yeshivot*) already opened in the quarter. Plans were completed for a residential neighborhood of about 600 households (2,400 persons) and another 1,000 dormitory residents. About half of the new construction was designated for housing, 40% for institutions, and 10% for commerce. Services such as schools, clinics, parking, and so on were planned to serve the estimated population, but no specific locations were chosen. It was decided that archaeological discoveries in the future would be preserved in open parks or in underground cellars. Seventeen of the most famous synagogues of the Jewish Quarter were designated for restoration.[49]

Still, there were numerous and varied visions of what the renewed Jewish Quarter in the rehabilitated Old City of Jerusalem should or could look like: There was a desire to turn the Jewish Quarter into a national and international cultural, educational, and tourism center. There seems to have been an implicit assumption that if it were properly rebuilt, that is what it would become. City planner Eliezer Brutzkus recommended "settling for a limited number of traditional institutions and residents willing to live in refurbished homes and unmodern conditions."[50] Architect Aviyah Hashimshony preferred a limited number of institutions rather than families (Hashimshony et al 1973). Planner Yosef Schweid preferred a community that would bring the quarter back to life 24 hours a day, but limited in size. According to his calculations, if all four quarters of the Old City were to be properly renovated, its total population would have to be reduced to 8,000, with another 7,000 employees and about 2,000 students in educational institutions (Schweid [Shavid] 1976, 66–69). Architect David Cassuto preferred "a living community… whose residents also work in the quarter (Cassuto 1976, 71–73).

In the Jewish Quarter of Jerusalem, responsibility for planning, preservation, and renovation was given neither to the Municipality nor to the Ministry of Tourism, but rather to a central authority representing all sectors of the government, as the rebuilding of the Jewish Quarter was not only about heritage and tourism, but also a political and religious statement to the world. The Company for the Reconstruction and Development of the Jewish Quarter (hereafter the Company or JQDC) was a non-profit government organization with great legal and political power, as befits Jerusalem.

Chapter III
The Company for the Reconstruction and Development of the Jewish Quarter in the Old City of Jerusalem

Centralized Planning of the Quarter

A year after the unification of Jerusalem, in light of the slow pace of renovation, the controversies aroused, and increasing pressure from the international community, Prime Minister Levi Eshkol suggested setting up a centralized government agency which would concentrate in one body all the different functions and offices involved in renewing the Jewish Quarter. Establishment of the Company for the Reconstruction and Development of the Jewish Quarter in the Old City of Jerusalem (henceforth the Company, or JQDC), was approved in September 1968. Due to the illness and subsequent demise of the prime minister, it did not begin to function until April 1969. The directorate consisted of members of the Ministerial Committee for Jerusalem. However, each minister was entitled to appoint a professional staff member of his office as a "substitute," and these ran the committees on finance, population, construction, and so on. Interestingly, no committee was created to develop and organize heritage conservation, pilgrimage and tourism, one of the chief functions of the JQDC today. Until the end of 1969, Prime Minister Eshkol's advisor Yehuda Tamir had been involved in the creation of new Jewish neighborhoods such as Ramat Eshkol and Gilo in East Jerusalem. Now he resigned from the job of executive director of the Division for the Population of Jerusalem, and was appointed executive director of the Company.

The goals of the Company, as set forth in its statement of policy in April 1969, were to renovate and develop the Jewish Quarter

> in order to turn it into a national, religious, historical, and cultural center…, a tourist attraction and residential neighborhood…, to provide public services and maintenance…while preserving the special character of the area…. The Company will continue to initiate, plan and fund national institutions in the Jewish Quarter…. First, the Company will develop a pedestrian route through the quarter and to the Western Wall, lay infrastructure underground to preserve the Old City atmosphere, and negotiate alternative housing solutions for squatters….[51]

Israel planned to renovate and develop all quarters of the Old City, with renovation of the Jewish Quarter as the first stage. Priority was given to re-establishing the centuries-old Jewish community in the Jewish Quarter, not only to reverse the destruction incurred, but also to emphasize its Jewish character and the importance of the Old City to the State of Israel and to Jews worldwide.[52] The other goals specified above—making the quarter "a national, religious, historical and cultural center, a tourist attraction"—all use heritage to enhance Israeli sovereignty in Jerusalem.

The Company was responsible for all planning and physical construction in the Jewish Quarter, as well as for policy and decision-making regarding population, housing, commerce, institutions, tourism, and culture. That included negotiation, compensation, and relocation of pre-1967 Arab residents of the Jewish Quarter, co-ordination and supervision of archaeological excavations, preservation and reconstruction of old houses, laying infrastructure, planning and constructing new residences, institutions, commercial areas and open spaces, providing community services, population of the quarter, and more.

It soon became evident that the physical renovation alone was a Herculean task. Ottoman period structures had been built on the ruins of previous periods without proper support. In addition to wartime damage, snow and rain on roofless buildings in the following two decades had caused further serious deterioration. Often, while laying new infrastructure and beginning renovations, the foundations of buildings were shaken, causing them to collapse. In other cases, the structures were so far above bedrock that steel or cement reinforcements and pillars had to be inserted beneath their foundations in order to guarantee stability. Economic and technical demands exceeded initial expectations. The great number of unexpected archaeological discoveries and the difficulties encountered during preservation and renovation activities made surprises more frequent than not. Few contractors had the necessary expertise, and this made the government policy of accepting bids impractical (Naor 1987, 326–36).

The Commercial Network

During its first years, the Company dealt primarily with compensation—relocation, infrastructure, and excavations, and with populating the quarter anew. Besides heeding the preservation guidelines outlined above, it designed the layout of streets and public areas to accommodate the high volume of tourists and pilgrims expected in Jerusalem. City Planner Doron Klinghoffer and Jewish Quarter Chief Architect Shalom Gardi followed Eliezer Frankel and Ora and Ya'akov Ya'ar's 1970 plan to separate residential and commercial areas, protecting residential areas by narrow winding lanes and courtyards opening inward. These plans formed the basis for all plans of the Jewish Quarter.

In 1970, Klinghoffer surveyed the quarter's existing commercial network along Jewish Quarter Street. He found that most of the existing commercial activity dated no earlier than Jordanian rule:

The quarter, physically devastated...and cut off from the municipal and tourist hinterland, was used for the lowest level services of storage, stables, and workshops, typical of deteriorating commercial areas.... The poor physical condition of the shops at the northern edge of Jewish Quarter Street in particular, justifies reconstruction of the old city center (Klinghoffer 1970, 8–22).

He suggested creating some 200 tourist-oriented services and separating them from those catering to the local population. Along Jewish Quarter and Habad streets (a continuation of the Suq street from Damascus Gate later to become the Cardo) would be the commercial center. There would also be a new tourist route from Jaffa Gate to the Western Wall and to the Temple Mount/Haram al-Sharif, as Frankel and Ya'ar had proposed.

In order to reap maximum benefits from these tourist-oriented services, Klinghoffer recommended a very centralized structure:

- One authority (the Company) will plan and build the entire commercial network.
- It will thus be able to coordinate the main services and ensure a unique and uniform architectural style.
- The Company will ensure adequate infrastructure.
- Even the street furniture will be in harmony.
- Careful planning of function as well as style will ensure the optimal number of each type of shop and service.
- This will enable efficient development of a relatively small area.
- There will be no stairs, and it will be a pedestrian only walkway.
- Most of the area will be roofed over, to allow all weather activity.

Klinghoffer emphasized the importance of centralization in the hands of the Company as a way to achieve both high quality urban fabric and the coordination of commercial services. Everything would be included in this centralization—parking, service vehicles for delivery of merchandise, security and surveillance, maintenance, and so on. For the most part, his plan was very similar to the plan of Frankel and Ya'ar. However, Klinghoffer's plans for commercial development were never realized. In 1972, the Company reported the completion of only 30 shops, most of which did not open until several years later.[53] Thus, the financial profit accruing to the Jewish Quarter from tourism was minimal and underdeveloped. Nor was the planned commercial development of the quarter tied to its heritage. It was simply assumed that the heritage would attract tourism and that tourists would be attracted to the commercial services, often situated adjacent to historic areas.

The only commercial venture based upon heritage and historic values was the area of the Roman-Byzantine Cardo, a continuation of the colorful traditional market streets of the Muslim and Christian Quarters. Although plans for renovation of the Cardo were submitted in the early 1970s, actual renovation only began in 1976 and continued well into the 1980s. (See Chapter IV below)

Klinghoffer counted 500,000 tourists and pilgrims from abroad and 1,000,000 Israeli visits to Jerusalem in 1968. He predicted that the tourist load would hit 5 million in 1975. By 1985, he estimated that 13 million people would visit the Jewish Quarter annually, an average of 36,000 visits a day (Klinghoffer 1970, Table 41, 121). He estimated that about 20% of these would be Muslim tourists. Shalom Gardi, Chief Architect of the JQDC, projected his estimate one step further. Assuming that the average tourist spent about two hours in the Jewish Quarter, and that more visitors came on the Sabbath and holidays, 10,000–15,000 people might be walking in the Quarter's public lanes at any given time—and this would be its maximum carrying capacity (Gardi 1972, 62). However, between the years 2000–2012, total foreign tourism to Israel was less than 2 million a year.[54] It rose to a record high of 3.5 million foreign visitors in 2013, 68% of whom visited the Western Wall, 64% the Jewish Quarter, and about 50% Christian holy sites in and around the Old City.[55] It is difficult to estimate the numbers of Israeli visitors. A recent study by the municipality estimates that about 100,000 people enter and leave the eight gates of the Old City on a summer weekday. This includes about 10,000 Old City residents along with pilgrims, students, and tourists. Of these, only about 26,000 enter through Zion and Dung Gates, those closest to the Jewish Quarter and the Western Wall.[56] Despite the fact that these statistics are lower than the initial predictions, it often seems that Jewish Quarter tourism today has exceeded its carrying capacity, especially during holidays and festivals.

During the first years, the Company did little to develop a program for heritage tourism or to document and present the rich heritage of the Jewish Quarter. Perhaps it was felt that such planning was unnecessary, as tourism and public interest in the rebuilding were high from the beginning; people felt that history was being made before their eyes, and that the city would always be a magnet for visitors.

Postwar Preservation and Reconstruction

In 1971, Executive Director Moshe Avnieli of the Company participated in a summer course on renewal and preservation of historic cities in York, England. The preservation guidelines recommended historic and architectural documentation before beginning professional preservation, advice applicable to the Jewish Quarter but not always followed by its architects and planners. These guidelines held that it was the government's responsibility to preserve historic monuments for their intrinsic values and not for economic or societal benefits. The preservation agency was also responsible for maintenance, independent of profits accrued. The tendency was "to allow tourism" if it did not harm preservation projects.[57]

Architect Shalom Gardi visited Warsaw, whose historic old town had been reproduced after its deliberate destruction in World War II. Gardi considered the approach taken in Warsaw non-authentic. In many cases, modern buildings were constructed behind the old style façades, and much of the restoration carried out was not an accurate replication of the twentieth century Old Town, but rather an idealized representation of it. Warsaw architects had succeeded in secretly preserving architectural sketches of its historic buildings during the war, and thus could have more accurately reproduced the façades, but other factors were also taken into account. Nevertheless, the rebuilt Old City of Warsaw succeeds in conveying the character and heritage of the city over the centuries (see Chapter VI below). No such documentation was available to architects of the Jewish Quarter. In addition, the Company had no experienced preservation staff and was not familiar with the principles guiding preservation. Architects and administrators learned while on the job (Gardi 2007 and Mandel 2006 interviews).

The consensus was that there was very little outstanding architecture in the Jewish Quarter and few important monuments, but the general fabric of the historic city could be preserved by restoring the street layout and as many historic structures as feasible. The Company did not consider postwar reconstruction of synagogues and *yeshivot* its responsibility, but rather that of the ethnic groups or organizations to which they belonged. Only two synagogues, the Hurva and Tiferet Yisrael, were considered to have been imposing landmarks. Fitting the new building in with the old was the achievement of Chief Jewish Quarter Architect Shalom Gardi:

> There are almost no historical monuments, but it does excel in close stonework, narrow lanes, inner courtyards, arched spaces and domes—which are worth preserving. It is to this end that reconstruction is carried out in keeping with the existing style (Gardi 1986; Gardi interview 2007).

This was accomplished by limiting density, height and style of new building, keeping the lanes open for pedestrians only, keeping the skyline clear with views of the Temple Mount and Mount of Olives on the east, and preservation of the traditional courtyard pattern with its internal open patios, gradated apartments, and open rooftops for maximum privacy, light, and air. At first, the Company reasoned that restoring old buildings would cost less time and money than archaeological excavations, new planning and construction. This proved to be wrong.[58]

Batei Mahse: A Case Study

The Batei Mahse (Alms Houses) neighborhood has a rich history spanning almost a century from the end of the Ottoman period until the War of Independence. The neighborhood was built between the years 1859–1890 by a German-Dutch charitable organization, Kollel Hod (Holland and Deutschland). The organization purchased empty plots of land and built "modern" courtyards with two-room apartments around an open square, the first public park in Jerusalem. About 100 lucky families won the lottery entitling them to subsidized housing for 3 years. The impressive Rothschild Building, with its elegant arched porch, was reserved for honored rabbis and community leaders. There were three synagogues, a free soup kitchen, and a dozen water cisterns for the community. This was the first and largest new housing project built in the Old City; it parallels in time and concept the history-making first Jewish neighborhoods built outside of the Old City walls such as Mishkenot Sha'ananim, Nahalat Shiva and Meah Shearim.

During the 1948 War, the open square served as the main training area for the Jewish Quarter's defenders. Secret military headquarters were located on the top floor of Sha'ar Hashamayim Yeshiva on the west. The sunken apartments on the south served as hospital, headquarters, and shelters during the war. On May 28, 1948, less than 2,000 Jewish survivors of the battles and about 30 fighters gathered in the square to surrender to the Arab Legion and to be evacuated from the quarter. They left behind over 60 comrades and neighbors killed during the fighting, buried in a common grave at the edge of the square (Philips 1976).

Under Jordanian rule (1948–1967), the Jewish Quarter was out of bounds, but from tall buildings in West Jerusalem, one could catch a glimpse of the Batei Mahse rooftops. Many of the buildings were destroyed, and the square was piled with rubble, which remained there until 1967. In the center of the square, a new public toilet was constructed, using gravestones from the nearby Mount of Olives Jewish cemetery. This desecration triggered the immediate declaration in 1967 by the State of Israel that the Jewish Quarter would be rebuilt and populated with Jews, and the first area to be rebuilt would be the Batei Mahse Square. Thus, Batei Mahse symbolized the productivation process that characterized the Jewish community in Jerusalem from the mid-19th century, the fierce battle and loss of 1948, the Arab desecration of holy sites, and the renewal of the quarter in a unified Jerusalem.

*Figure 7: Funeral service for a Jewish rabbi at Batei Mahse Square, 1903.
Source: Library of Congress, Washington, D.C.*

*Figure 8: State Ceremony on the Tenth Anniversary of the Restoration of Batei Mahse.
Photographer: Moshe Milner, 1977. Source: Government Press Office.*

The architectural qualities of the neighborhood were unique to the Old City—a large open grassy space surrounded by 1- to 4-story buildings, with a view of the Mount of Olives and the Temple Mount on the east. In some places the neighborhood was enclosed by a low wall with gates, and in others, the houses themselves served as the wall.

This was the first neighborhood to be rebuilt. Planning and implementation were awarded to the architects who had renovated ancient Jaffa—Ya'akov and Ora Ya'ar, Eliezer Frankel, and Sa'adieh Mandel. Each took a different section of the square to renovate. The goal was to create a combination of public and private building, with two or three small shops in the square. Mandel realized that the Rothschild building dominated the square, and proceeded to design reconstruction of the square as an open-air theatre facing the Rothschild building. He also made it into a more intimate space by the addition of new buildings on the north and east, thereby narrowing the original size of the square and cutting off the view of the Mount of Olives and the Temple Mount on the east. (Mandel interview 2006).

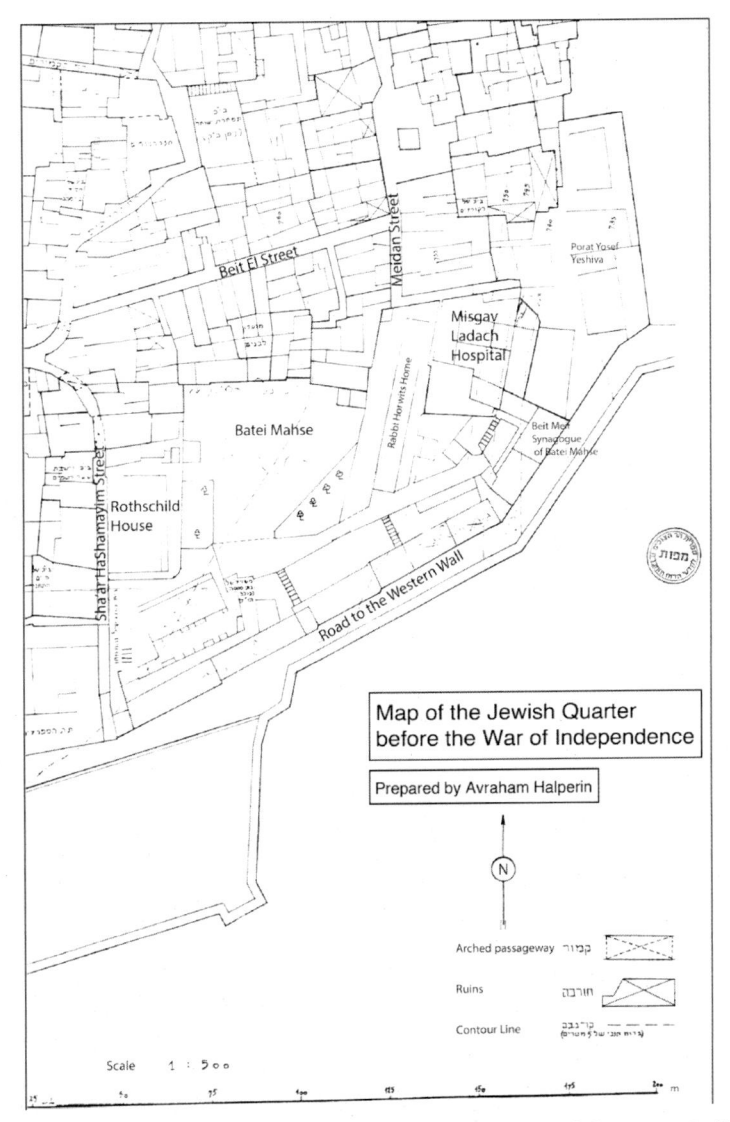

Map 5: Avraham Halperin, Batei Mahse neighborhood in Map of the Jewish Quarter on the Eve of the War of Independence. Source: Hebrew University of Jerusalem Mount Scopus Map Library.

54 | JERUSALEM'S JEWISH QUARTER

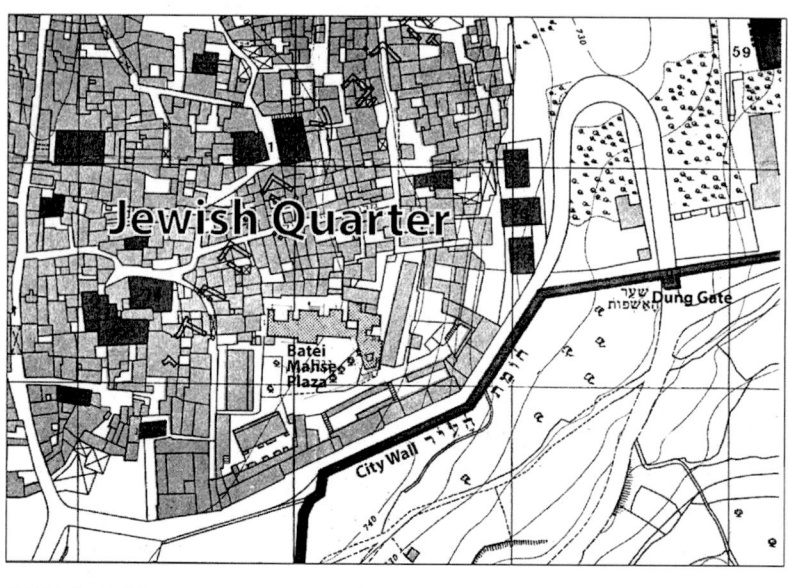

Plan 4: Mandel's proposal for renewal of Batei Mahse Plaza, 1970. Source: JCA.

Figure 9: Aerial photo of Batei Mahse Plaza before reconstruction, c. 1970. Source: Naor 1987. Courtesy of the Company for the Reconstruction and Development of the Jewish Quarter.

Figure 10: Batei Mahse rebuilt. Source: Gardi, 1972. Courtesy of the Company for the Reconstruction and Development of the Jewish Quarter.

The general architectural heritage of the Batei Mahse Square was conserved, but not much else. None of the historic, religious, social, or national values of this neighborhood are apparent at first sight. Historic structures still standing were preserved according to the principle of strengthening all original elements and completing the missing parts with new construction that blends in but is not a copy of the old.

The historic values of the neighborhood were not recognized; no attempt was made to document the past or to present it to the public by means of physical representation. There are almost no signs on the buildings, except for the Rothschild insignia hanging high up on the building (which apparently has no historical precedent). Only one of the four original gates to the neighborhood survived the war and was partially preserved. There are no markers to indicate the places where the other three once stood. The red roof rafters have disappeared, as they were a modern European innovation in the Old City in the early 20th century, and Mandel in 1967 considered them a foreign element. The public park with its greenery has been replaced by stone pavements with a few trees, making the neighborhood much more urban looking than it was originally. Street levels, the ratio of built to open spaces, and the open view to the east were also changed. Old buildings that were destroyed were not rebuilt, and the new buildings were arranged differently in the square, which itself became narrower and tilted west instead of east.

No consideration was given to wheelchair accessibility or to making the stone pavements user friendly. Public awareness of these issues was very limited in the 1960s and 1970s. The architect was more interested in creating a pleasant urban environment combining new and old architecture. There was no attempt to recreate or even to commemorate the synagogues, soup kitchen, or subsidized housing projects (Mandel interview 2006). Except for the preservation of the area where the war victims had been buried in 1948, there is no physical evidence of the fierce battle that took place. In front of Rothschild House, two enormous pillars from the Second Temple Period were placed. Impressive as these pillars are, they were found at another site and have no integral connection to the Batei Mahse Square. One heritage replaced another.

Heritage which could have served as an educational and tourist springboard was ignored. Had a museum been founded in the Rothschild House, telling the story of this historic neighborhood and its inhabitants, of the 1948 War and the fall of the Jewish Quarter, a visit to the square would have been a much more meaningful experience.

Infrastructure, Townscape, Street Levels, and Street Names

After the general outline scheme for Jerusalem was completed in 1971, authority over new construction reverted to the Jerusalem Municipality. That obligated the Company to present a detailed outline scheme for the Jewish Quarter to the Municipality planning authority. Gardi's plan attempted to separate residential quarters from tourist routes and commercial areas, taking advantage of courtyards turning inward to allow maximum privacy. Separation of residential land use from commercial and institutional (as in Bruges, Belgium) preserves the urban fabric of the historic areas and also improves the quality of residents' lives (Orbasli 2000, 267–71). However, it was only partially successful in the Jewish Quarter. Small electric vehicles able to navigate most of the lanes were intended to provide services such as deliveries and garbage collection. The main tourist and commercial routes were to run along the eastern edge of the quarter and from east to west via the destroyed synagogues. Educational and religious institutions for the local population and for visitors would also be located in these areas. Six to seven hundred households, up to 2,000 students in dormitory institutions, and about 250 visitor-focused commercial establishments would populate the Jewish Quarter. Prices were set on the same level as apartments built by the Housing Ministry in the new Ramat Eshkol neighborhood, despite the fact that construction costs were far higher in the Jewish Quarter (Avnieli 1976, 103; Naor 1987, 377).

Architect Shalom Gardi had planned the Jewish quarter as a residential neighborhood, dependent on metropolitan Jerusalem for most medical, cultural, educational, commercial, and vocational services. Only those necessary for daily life, such as grocery shopping, basic medical care, nursery, kindergarten and elementary school, small open spaces, and a community center would be provided inside the quarter. The location and size of the above institutions were not built into the outline scheme, but left open until such time as the population of the quarter would justify opening them. Since only one or two new structures were built specifically to serve communal needs, old buildings were remodeled ad hoc to serve as classrooms, medical clinics, and so on, as the population grew and the need increased. As a result, these communal institutions were often housed in inappropriate sites, contrary to Gardi's outline plan.[59]

In residential neighborhoods, lanes were renovated—some at a minimum width to allow passage of small electric service and emergency vehicles, and others—stepped and narrow—for pedestrian use only. This was done purposely, to prevent them from becoming tourist thoroughfares, and to safeguard the privacy of the residents (Gardi interview 2007). About a third of the Jewish Quarter was designated for public spaces, including the Western Wall Plaza. Only 80 dunams remained for new construction. Three archaeological sites were earmarked to become open sites: the area slated to become a terminal, the Crusader complex, and the Broad Wall.[60]

Once the outline scheme was completed, the Company's main function was to carry it out. That included compensation and resettlement of pre-1967 Arab residents, coordination and supervision of archaeological excavations, preservation and reconstruction of old houses, laying infrastructure, planning and constructing new residences, institutions, commercial areas, and open spaces, providing community services, population of the quarter, and more. This turned out to be extremely complicated and challenging, with few precedents to follow. David Zifroni, assistant executive director of the Company, explained:

> Any attempt to follow the rules was impossible in the quarter.... no matter how many plans there were, after they started to dig, they didn't know what to do next.... We worked by trial and error.... We should have gotten all the details and then built a framework around them: First, we should have surveyed every single corner. Second, we should have done all the calculations, and then prepared a master plan and outline scheme. Land function is the result of all the previous steps. Only later on were we asked to obtain documents and building permits.... I claimed that no outline scheme was possible before we had all the relevant information. Things were built according to circumstances, and this is the result. We couldn't plan it in advance (Zifroni interview 2005).

In the center of the quarter, an open plaza was created around the ruins of the Hurva Synagogue. From the plaza, a relatively wide path led west to Jaffa Gate and east to the new staircase leading down to the Western Wall Plaza. On the way, this new path passed many of the major synagogues of the quarter (at the time, most in ruins), and it connected to the Batei Mahse Plaza on the south.

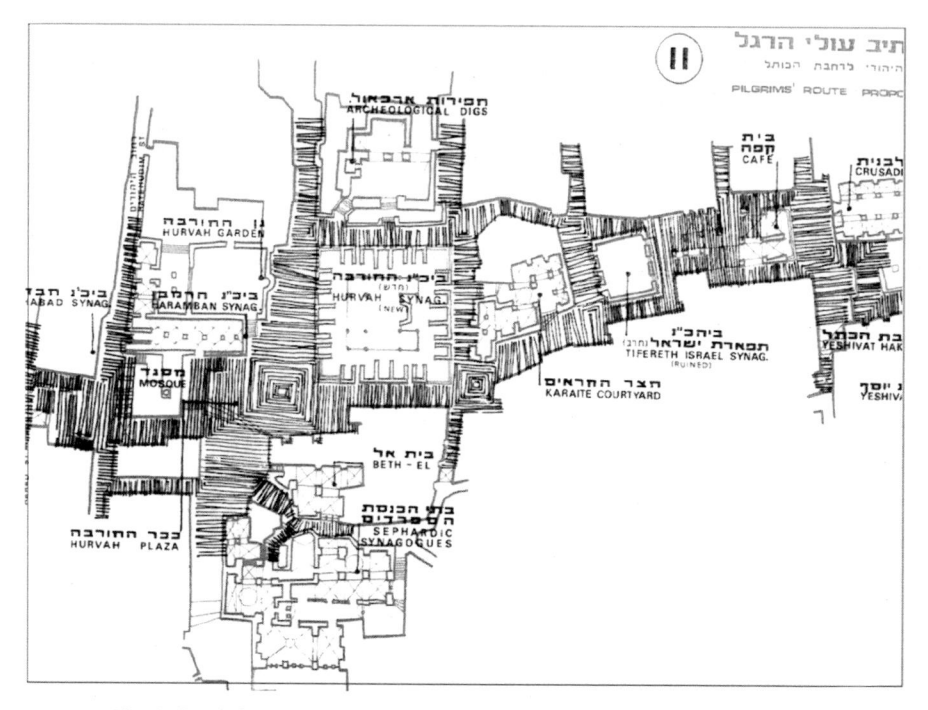

Plan 5: Frankel and Ya'ar, Pilgrims' Route proposal, ca. 1968. Source: Yaakov Ya'ar.

Street levels were adjusted according to the requirements of the new infrastructure, the need to allow drainage of rainwater, and the archaeological excavations. Because the Quarter was renovated piecemeal as building sites became available, sharp differences in street level between adjoining areas were created. For example, the infrastructure of Jewish Quarter Street, one of the main south-north avenues of the quarter, was laid at the beginning. About ten years later, when the Cardo was excavated, planners realized that the level of Jewish Quarter Street was a meter or two too high, but it was too late to make substantial changes (Zifroni interview 2005).

Another important decision pertained to street names. As a matter of principle, it was decided not to name the new lanes after individuals, but rather to give them names associated with the history of Jerusalem. New street names embody the heritage visible today in the Jewish Quarter: The First and Second Temple Periods, and the 19th and early 20th century Jewish community. Old streets such as Habad Street generally retained their traditional names as part of their preservation.[61] New street names were accorded over a period of about 20 years, as the quarter was rebuilt. Elchanan Reiner has suggested that these changes in street names reflect the desire to bequeath to the Jewish Quarter a different identity than it had before 1948. Indeed, the quarter itself was often designated the "Upper City" (as Josephus Flavius called it), instead of the Ottoman and British term "Jewish Quarter," or "Old City" (Reiner 1978).

The New Jewish Community

At the very beginning of Israeli military rule, and with the agreement of Jerusalem Mayor Teddy Kollek, the engineering corps demolished several dangerous structures in the Jewish Quarter that had been occupied by Arab refugees since the 1948 War (Narkis 1991, 335–36). Squatters were also removed from buildings identified as synagogues and *yeshivot*.[62] The Ministerial Committee on Jerusalem authorized Mayor Kollek to compensate Muslim inhabitants evacuated from the Jewish and the Mugrabi Quarters in 1967.[63] However, many of these inhabitants refused compensation in protest against the Israeli government. While still under military rule, it had been psychologically easier for them to accept compensation.[64]

Slum clearance through negotiations and with mutual consent had limited success. Not all tenants agreed to negotiate, resulting in several lawsuits and in about ten percent of the non-Jewish occupants remaining in the quarter. Negotiations took a long time and were quite expensive. Nevertheless, that may have been the best option under the circumstances. Between 1967 and 1971, the Housing Ministry and the Municipality compensated and relocated about 2,700 people (out of some 5,000), and 45 shopkeepers. However, during that same period, the remaining Arab population grew by almost the same number, whether by natural increase or by the return of those who had left. In 1973, an estimated 1,400 Arabs were still living in the Jewish Quarter, alongside less than a hundred Jewish households and a few hundred students.[65] In 1975, seven years after renewal of the quarter had begun, Arab residents still constituted a majority in the Jewish Quarter.[66]

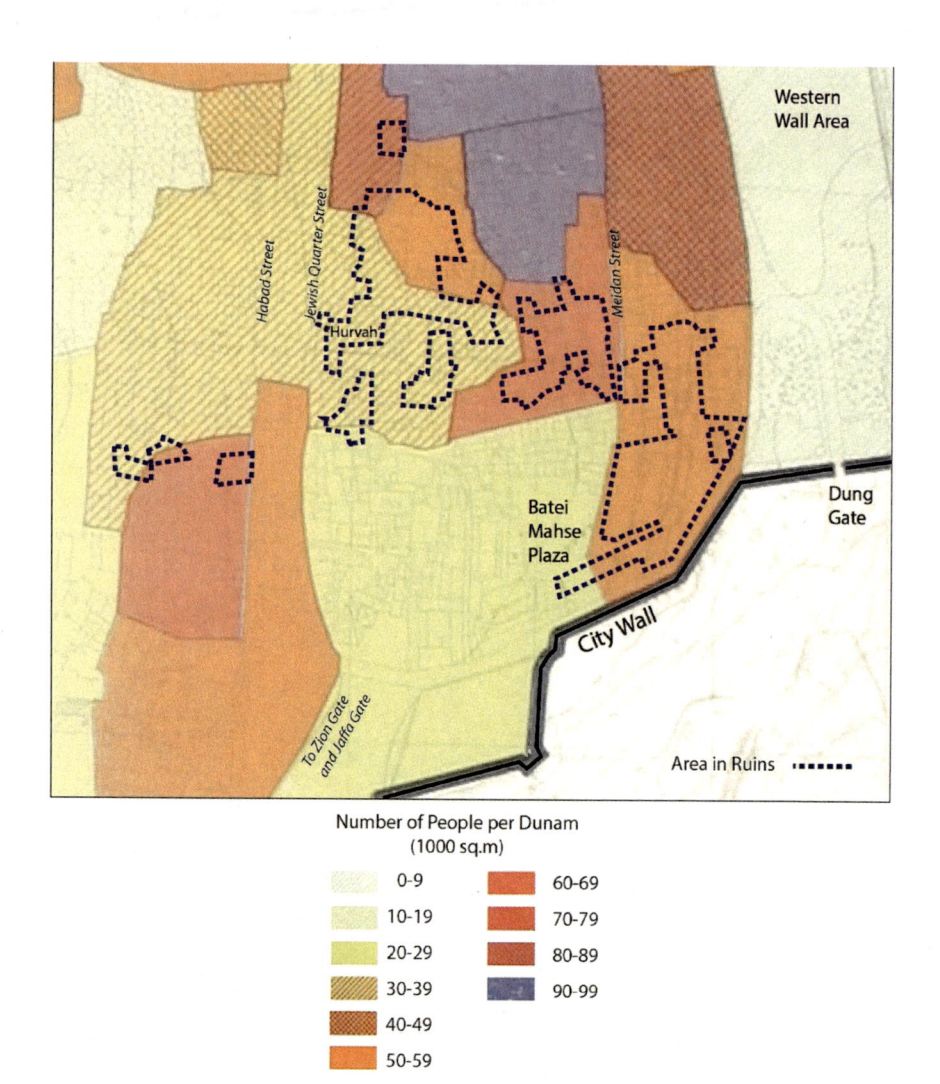

Map 6: *Map of population density and ruins in the Jewish Quarter, based on Sharon 1973. Source: Cartography Department, Hebrew University of Jerusalem, 2009.*

Creation of a "living city" in the Jewish Quarter was one of the top priorities of the Israeli government. Political and ideological goals converged with the strong popular consensus in favor of reviving the Jewish neighborhood so viciously destroyed during and after the war in 1948. Unable to provide adequate housing and services to establish a residential community during the first years of reconstruction, the Company encouraged the establishment of educational institutions with dormitories. This had many advantages: Such an institution has a permanent or semi-permanent social structure, but its residents are only temporary, and able to tolerate difficult living conditions for short periods. The population density of an institution is usually greater than that of private households, and therefore a preferred option for sparsely populated areas. An institution provides the social milieu and support that can compensate for tough physical conditions. In addition, institutions whose staff and student body live on the grounds are active around the clock, in contrast to commercial or cultural establishments that close at night and on holidays.

Only a few months after the war in 1967, two new *yeshivot* opened, HaKotel Yeshiva and HaHistadrut Yeshiva, with about fifty students of college age and up (N.a., "Yeshivat HaKotel Revitalizes Jewish Quarter," *Israel Digest* 13 [1969]: p. 5; Abramowitz 1980). In addition, Hayyei Olam Yeshiva, the Sephardic Metivta, Etz Hayyim Yeshiva, and Porat Yosef Yeshiva reopened their historic institutions in the quarter. Two more dormitories in historic buildings for new immigrant university students were quickly renovated, in part by the students themselves. Nachal Moriah, a division of the IDF whose members combined guard duty and security-related activities with apprenticeship in trades such as printing, metal working, and carpentry, set up a branch in the Jewish Quarter.

The Nachal corps of the IDF had been established to guarantee security in border areas by stationing semi-permanent staff there in a combined military and civilian capacity. Most Nachal groups settled agricultural settlements along the country's northern and eastern borders. About thirty members of the Moriah group settled in the Jewish Quarter, where a handful of Jews and tens of students coexisted with an Arab population of thousands. Both Nachal Moriah members and HaKotel Yeshiva students lived in Jewish-owned but as yet unrenovated buildings such as those in Batei Mahse (Shefer 2008 and Markovitz 1998 interviews). In 1973, when security had improved and there was the beginning of a Jewish community in the quarter, the Nachal was disbanded. Note that most of the above initiatives were taken by private or semi-private organizations (NGOs), not by the government.

Figure 11: HaKotel Yeshiva students moving into Batei Mahse, October 1967. Source: HaKotel Yeshiva Archive.

Figure 12: Nachal Moriah soldiers with Torah scroll, 1968. Eliezer Shefer archive.

In 1969, when the Company was established, there were about 160 Jews living in the Jewish Quarter, most of them affiliated with one of its educational institutions (Avnieli 1976, 103).[67] The Company planned to settle another 150–200 people in the quarter and to renovate several of the better-known religious institutions that year. Deputy Prime Minister Yigal Alon and his wife Ruth moved into their newly renovated state apartment in the quarter in 1969 (*Australian Jewish News*, 8 Aug. 1969), followed shortly after by State Comptroller Dr. Yitzhak Nebenzahl and his married children (Glatt interview

2008). About 2,000 Jews had applied for apartments in the Old City, most of them families of pre-1948 residents. However, the preliminary steps took much longer than planned. By 1972, the number of students in HaKotel Yeshiva had grown to 140 and it had renovated four dormitory apartments,[68] but only 88 other Jewish households (less than 200 adults) lived in the quarter. Almost half of these were connected to one of the dormitory institutions.[69] By 1973, this number had doubled, but Jews were still only one-quarter of the population.[70]

The Community and the Company

Motor access, even to the edges of the quarter, was difficult or impossible. The quarter, in its first years, was one big building site and archaeological dig in which donkeys did most of the work. New and recently renovated buildings were side by side with ruins. Nevertheless, the aesthetic, historic, cultural, and religious values evident everywhere, the new discoveries and ongoing construction, the famous persons who came to visit, the close community and the support that residents gave each other–made it an exciting and enriching place to live. Beginning in 1971, residents elected a committee that successfully lobbied the municipality to provide them with basic health, cultural, and educational services. However, attempts at community involvement in participatory planning with the Company did not bear fruit. This, despite the fact that many of the residents held important positions in public and governmental institutions in Jerusalem, and were responsible for many public and private sector initiatives in the rebuilding of the quarter.

Creation of a gentrified neighborhood was expensive, but the Company was determined to prevent the quarter from again becoming a densely occupied lower class neighborhood "rich in spiritual values and poor in material wealth" (Margalit, *HaModia*, 28 June 1976). Until the mid-1980s, apartments cost much more to build than their sale price, partly because the quarter was still a construction site and demand was limited. Attempts by the Company to control the socio-economic profile of homeowners, whether directly or by the interior design of apartments and the availability of community services for specific sectors, did not work. The population was largely religious from the start. Relatively few artists, artisans, or other tourism-related professionals settled in the quarter. Nor did more than a handful of pre-1948 residents return to their former homes. Above all, rebuilding and repopulating the quarter proceeded extremely slowly.

A public outcry arose, calling for investigation or even for disbanding the Company altogether.[71] Finally, in 1975, the Company was restructured. No longer would the directorate of the Company be identical to the Ministerial Committee on Jerusalem. Its board would be composed of government-appointed officials and headed by Housing Minister Avraham Ofer, in place of the Justice Minister who had replaced the Prime Minister after the demise of Levi Eshkol.[72]

Time was also a crucial factor. Despite the fact that rebuilding the Jewish Quarter took two or three times as long as had been initially planned, had the reconstruction been carried out "according to the books," it would have taken much longer. Public opinion, along with the political and security pressures, led to necessary but premature planning and decision-making. In 1975, the Outline Scheme of the Jewish Quarter and about forty detailed building plans (some for projects that had already been built) were completed and submitted. Explicit guidelines for future building were spelled out (Efroni and Sheinberg 1975; Gardi 2007 and Mandel 2006 interviews). The circle had closed. In 1967, the Jerusalem Municipality and the Housing Ministry vied for a mandate to rebuild the Jewish Quarter and the Old City, but national and international concerns led the government to consign planning and policy-making to a government-appointed body. In 1975, the Municipality and the Housing Ministry were recognized as the main actors.

The Jewish Quarter in Context

As noted above, the division of the Old City into four quarters according to religion is a geographical oversimplification that does not reflect the demography or legal status of the quarters. For the first years after 1967, attempts were made to functionally and architecturally blend the Jewish Quarter into the rest of the Old City. Restoration of the Jewish Quarter was intended to be the first step in the restoration of the whole Old City. The Cardo, with its many tourist shops, is the natural continuation of the Suq street leading to Damascus Gate. The food shops, post office, and medical services of the Jewish Quarter were intended to serve the whole Old City. In the late 1960s, Jewish mothers visited the mother-child clinics near Damascus Gate. HaGai (in Arabic Al-Wad) Street was widened and connected via a tunnel to the Western Wall so as to enable vehicular and pedestrian access from Lions' Gate to Dung Gate. Above the junction of the four quarters, a rooftop promenade was constructed as a meeting and lookout point for all Old City residents and visitors (Shtern 2017).[73]

From 1971 on, both the Company for the Reconstruction of the Jewish Quarter and the Company for the Development of East Jerusalem participated in renewal projects throughout the Old City.[74] The city engineer planned and oversaw, and the JQDC sent workers to lay new infrastructure, including preparation for a central underground television and telephone antenna, improvement of façades and street furnishings. The Company sought to take advantage of the technical expertise and experience of its engineers and construction workers to carry out renewal projects in the other quarters. The need to use traditional building methods and the unique limitations of working within the walls meant that workers were drawn from the Old City, as they were familiar with the requirements. This arrangement was approved by the Minister of Justice from 1971–1974.

However, this plan encountered tremendous political opposition. Despite the huge sums of money invested by the Jerusalem Fund in central antennas and underground infrastructure for electricity, telephone, television, and so on, residents and institutions outside of the Jewish Quarter refused to take advantage of it. To this day, the antenna and satellite free skyline of the Jewish Quarter clearly denotes its boundaries within the Old City.

The Jerusalem Foundation and the Treasury Ministry funded efforts to narrow the gap between living conditions in the Jewish and other quarters. However, attempts to "thin out" the population and renovate buildings in non-Jewish areas were viewed as attempts to expel residents. As a result, requirements for planning and building permits outside of the Jewish Quarter were not enforced; population density increased greatly, and sanitary conditions and social and educational services decreased. A survey of buildings in the Muslim Quarter had indeed been completed in 1973, but renovations and improvements based on the survey were limited to public spaces, and no attempt was made to relieve population density, which had increased by 30% since 1967.[75]

Israel did not foresee the strong, unyielding Muslim and Christian opposition to its sovereignty. Architect David Kroyanker summarized Israel's reaction in 1975:

> A political facet is added to the purely social dimension of the problem when plans are discussed to reduce the population congestion in the Muslim Quarter of the Old City...now 60 persons per dunam.... The outline scheme for the Old City and the environs recommended the dilution of the existing population in the quarter by about 10,000 persons, by means of resettling in the eastern part of the city.... The plan was regarded by the Arab community as intended dispossession, which led to a complete stoppage of all further action in the matter. That is a typical example of the confrontation experienced by the planners with the socio-political problem without any possible solution being offered in the foreseeable future (Kroyanker 1975, 77).

According to Kroyanker (2007), one of Teddy Kollek's most egregious errors as mayor was allowing for this vast discrepancy to arise between the impressive scope and level of renovation in the Jewish Quarter of the Old City and the state of disrepair in the Muslim Quarter. Gad Soen, a high-ranking official in the Commerce and Industry Ministry and one of the first residents of the Jewish Quarter, also petitioned the municipality:

> The greater the gap between the Jewish and the Muslim Quarters (insofar as population density, standard of living, ethnic differences, facilities and services), the worse the situation will become. The earlier [we correct the situation] the better.[76]

As Ruth Amir and Michael Dumper have aptly pointed out, despite the formal extension of Israeli jurisdiction, Israel has not fully asserted its sovereignty over all the areas annexed in 1967, and international interests in the city have placed considerable constraints on Israeli policy makers (Amir 1999, 172–74).

It is unnecessary to elaborate on the effect this has had on the gap in standard of living between the Jewish Quarter and the rest of the Old City. The level and extent of services is unequal despite the government decision of 1967. The more time passes, the greater the gap in living standards between the different quarters (Kroyanker 1975, 50).[77] The euphoria that engulfed Israelis immediately after the 1967 War has gradually evaporated. The "Jerusalem of Jews, Arabs, and Peace" described in the media has not yet happened. In 1982, a municipality publication put it this way:

> The municipality has helped to restore and renovate many of these structures, including a number of sebils, mosques, public buildings, and schools. However, while almost all of these buildings are in a quite deteriorated state and often falling apart, most are occupied by families who do not wish to move. Moreover, most of these inhabitants are unaware of the special qualities, remarkable artistic features and historical value of their legacy.... The situation is even more complicated by the fact that inevitably these medieval structures are Waqf.... Additional complications arise from age-old rivalries of many Muslim families....There is hope that slowly things may improve...and eventually a route for tourists could be established thus permitting the visitors to discover and better appreciate these structures... [as well as] the local population (Out of Jerusalem, Summer 1982).

International refusal to recognize Israeli sovereignty over Jerusalem also served to limit freedom of action of national and municipal bodies, particularly in East Jerusalem. The Jewish Quarter remained isolated both from the modern metropolis and from the other quarters of the Old City. Had the whole Old City been treated as one integral unit, the result would have been quite different. These conflicts over planning and developing East Jerusalem reflect both geo-political and ideological power struggles. Religious and cultural values, conceptions of Jerusalem as a national and international capital, and of the Jewish Quarter as an integral part of the Old City or as an independent unit—all find physical expression in the urban fabric.

Chapter IV
Heritage Policy and Practice

In the previous chapter, we described planners' visions of and decisions regarding the Jewish Quarter as a "living city"—both a residential neighborhood and a tourist attraction. What heritage did they choose to present in the Jewish Quarter? What connection did they make between development of heritage, tourism, and the other functions planned for the quarter? What crucial decisions were made in the first years? What changed as reconstruction progressed?

Residence, Tourism, and Commerce

In the early 1970s, architects Eliezer Frankel and Ya'akov and Ora Ya'ar presented the Company with a general plan for rehabilitation of the Jewish Quarter as a living city (Frankel and Ya'ar 1968). This plan attempted to rebuild the historic city to include three very different functions, each in its proper place. Reconstruction of the residential neighborhood and the physical presence of Jewish households was essential to establish Israeli sovereignty and to counter the Jordanian attempt to eradicate all signs of past Jewish life within the Old City. Restoration of the traditional city fabric and monuments, archaeological parks, museums, and so on were intended to attract tourism. Commercial projects were expected to support and grow out of tourism. Little concrete attempt was made to integrate these functions or use them to complement each other. Other national functions, such as establishment of government, religious or cultural centers in the Jewish Quarter were considered but never realized.

As presented in preceding chapters, planners proposed spatially separating the residential from the commercial and tourist areas, concentrating tourist activity along the routes passing holy, historical, and archaeological sites. A new main route (the Pilgrims' Route) would begin at Zion and/or Jaffa Gate and proceed east to a new staircase leading down to the Western Wall Plaza, passing the central synagogues (whether rebuilt or left in ruins) and other tourist attractions. Secondary services such as tourist-oriented shops, hotels, and restaurants would be located along this route.[78] Intersecting it would be the commercial route, beginning with Jewish Quarter Street in the south (from Zion Gate), and merging with the ancient Old City Suq street in the north (until Damascus Gate), bordering on all four quarters. In one of the historic buildings would be a hostel, and in another, a hotel. Adjacent to Zion Gate would be a terminal, including parking, an amphitheater, a cultural and commercial center, and an apartment hotel. This would also be the entrance point for emergency and service vehicles into the Old City (Gardi interview 2007; idem 1986, 177).[79]

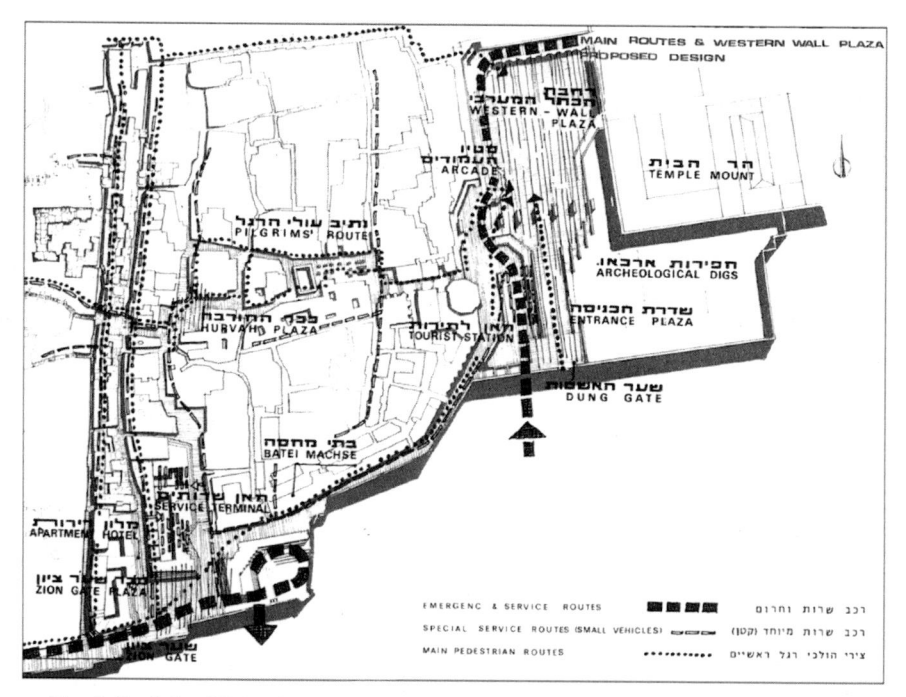

Plan 6: Frankel and Ya'ar, Jewish Quarter commercial and tourist routes and terminal, ca. 1968. Source: Ya'akov Ya'ar.

New and Unexpected Heritage

As early as 1967, the Old City and Environs was declared an archaeological site according to the Antiquities Law, thus prohibiting any new construction without preliminary excavations and official approval. Until 1969, Architect Ehud Menczel (later Netzer) was Chief Architect of the Jewish Quarter of Jerusalem. From the beginning, even before official excavations had begun, he contributed significantly to the identification, exposure, and preservation of archaeological findings in the quarter. At first, expectations were that findings would date back no earlier than the Crusader period, but these soon changed.

In 1969, Professor Nahman Avigad of the Hebrew University of Jerusalem began the first official digs. He excavated several sites simultaneously, passing from one to another according to construction plans. In principle, every building site was to be excavated prior to new building. However, every old building that could be saved would be, particularly in the narrow lanes that were designated to be part of the preserved urban fabric. Thus, most of the excavations took place in the ruined areas in the center of the quarter, the area planned as the Pilgrims' Route. In the first three seasons, from 1969–1971, nine sites were excavated. Over the years, over twenty metric dunams of land were dug, one of the largest archaeological sites in the State of Israel. Many sites were documented but not preserved, and have yet to be published (Geva 2007).

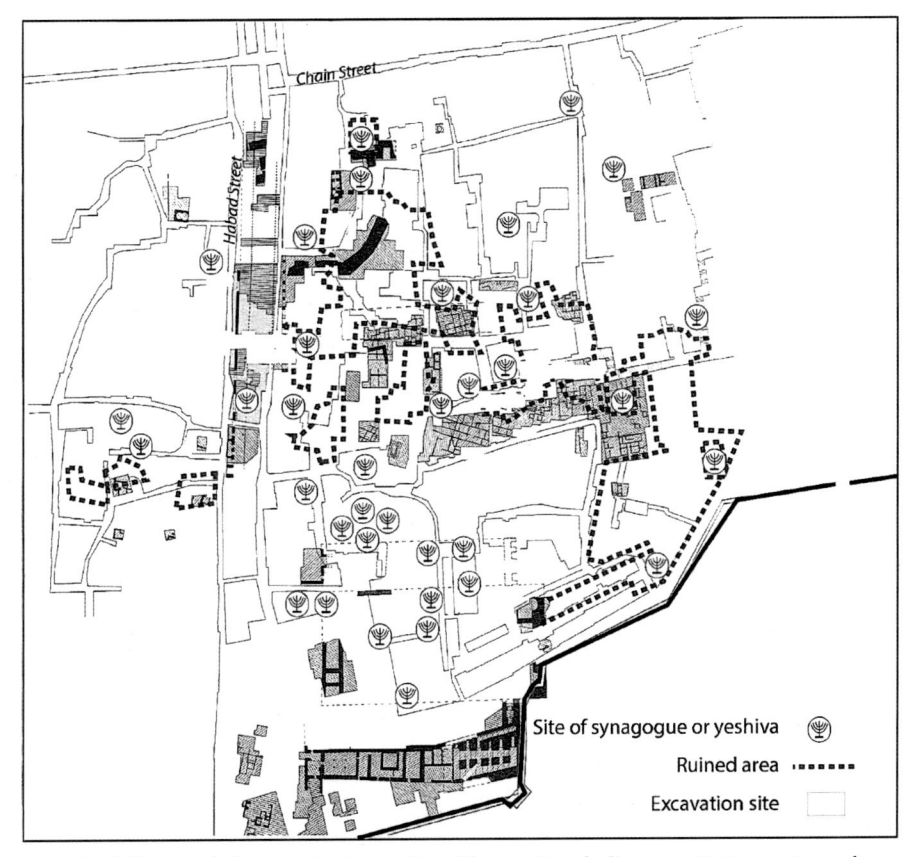

Map 7: The Jewish Quarter showing overlap of former sites of religious institutions, ruins, and excavations. Source: Cartography Department, Hebrew University of Jerusalem, 2016.

Avigad's first excavation uncovered a seven-meter wide wall from the middle of the First Temple Period (ca. 800 BCE). That settled the debate between the "maximalists" and the "minimalists" on the size of Biblical Jerusalem, extending it to include the Western Hill as well as the City of David. The quality and size of the wall show that Jerusalem of that period was an important and well-developed city. This impressive wall aroused international interest, and stimulated a debate on how to preserve and exhibit it. Originally, forty apartments had been planned for the site. As their foundations were being dug, Second Temple Period structures were uncovered. The Company revised its plans, deciding with Avigad that an open archaeological park would rise on the site, with apartments on stilts 5–9 meters high above the open park. However, after the

First Temple Period wall was discovered, professional and public opinion demanded no new building at all on the site. "Leaving this area open to the public will prove our historic connection to Jerusalem no less than an additional twenty housing units," wrote Teddy Kollek.[80] An open archaeological park now surrounds the wall, with apartment buildings to the north and south.

Other First Temple Period findings nearby include remains of an "Israelite Tower" and other segments of defensive wall. Near the tower, in a layer of ash from the sixth century BCE, three typical Israelite spearheads and one sophisticated Babylonian spearhead were discovered, reminders of the Babylonian destruction of Jerusalem in 586 BCE. Hundreds of typical Israelite ritual figurines were also found. In this case, a different form of preservation, first used in the Herodian Mansions under HaKotel Yeshiva, was chosen. Massive cement pillars were sunk into the dig, supporting the building on top of it, along with preservation and exhibition of the tower underground.

One of the earliest and most dramatic discoveries was that of the Second Temple Period Burnt House, a section of a residence and possibly of a workshop for incense, apparently belonging to the well-known priestly family of Katros, who were charged with preparation of the incense used in the Temple. The site was restored and later became a museum in a basement, while the apartment house planned for the site was built on top of it.[81]

Five magnificent Second Temple Period mansions were uncovered underneath the planned campuses of HaKotel and Porat Yosef Yeshivot, as well as artifacts and remains of the First Temple Period. Concrete pillars sunk into the area of the dig support the *yeshiva* buildings above (Gardi [2007] and Netzer [2005] interviews). This seemed like an original and exciting way to both preserve and present ancient Jerusalem and at the same time erect a residential neighborhood. Romantically, planners imagined tourists wandering through the narrow lanes and now and then "going underground" to see archaeological finds in the basements of the buildings (Bahat 1988, 183–92).

Discoveries from the Byzantine Period include the Cardo, the main street of Jerusalem in the 4th to 7th centuries, and the Nea Church complex. The finest piece of Crusader architecture uncovered was the German Teutonic Knights Church, Hospice, and Hospital of St. Mary, which had already been described by Italian engineer and archaeologist Ermete Pierotti, the city engineer of Jerusalem in the mid-nineteenth century. It had since been buried under debris and was exposed a second time in 1969.[82] The relicts were incorporated in an archaeological garden beside the new stairway down to the Western Wall Plaza. In addition, there are Crusader relicts in the Cardo and fortifications near the Nea Church and the Southern Wall. There are also relicts of Ayyubid fortifications on the southern border of the quarter, and an Ottoman "Turkish Bazaar" adjacent to the Burnt House and the Crusader Church of St. Mary.

Figure 13: Pierotti's plate of the entrance to the ruins of the Church of St. Mary, 1864. Source: Plate xxxviii, Pierotti: Project Gutenberg.

Figure 14: Inside the Teutonic Knights complex today. Source: Baruch Slae, 2017.

In the beginning, excavating and planning took place simultaneously, and if there were significant findings, the Company would revise its plans. From 1972 on, archaeologists began to demand that excavations precede all planning to avoid such problems. This of course caused great delay in construction and in populating the quarter.[83]

The excavations aroused public interest and enthusiasm, both nationally and internationally. Rami Izrael, an expert on the history and geography of Jerusalem, was one of the first guides for the Ben-Zvi Institute tours. He recalled the difficulties and the rewards of these tours:

> You never knew if you would be able to see again what you had seen yesterday. On the one hand, we were eyewitnesses to archaeological discoveries and to the process of restoration in the Jewish Quarter. On the other hand, doing a tour in a building site was very problematic. Future tourism sites were raw and unfinished, but people wanted to see for themselves what they had seen last night on TV, especially the discoveries from the First and Second Temple Periods (Izrael interview).

Planners found themselves in a unique situation. As in Warsaw and other war-damaged cities, reconstruction of Jewish holy sites in the Old City had great symbolic value. Israel was determined to rebuild what had been desecrated and destroyed, but the revelation that beneath these sites were two- to three-thousand-year-old archaeological sites of great consequence presented a difficult choice: preserve and present the findings from the First and Second Temple Periods, or restore 19th-century Jerusalem. Which heritage would be more meaningful to the late 20th-century Israeli public and to the international tourism industry?

Postwar Renovation of Jewish Holy Sites

There had been about eighty synagogues and *yeshivot* in the Old City in the Ottoman and Mandate periods, fifty of them in the Jewish Quarter. Until the end of the nineteenth century, non-Muslims were rarely allowed to erect new religious institutions, so most of these were located in already standing buildings transformed into study and prayer halls. As such, they kept a low profile and had no external architectural distinctiveness. However, each of the eighty institutions represented a unique Jewish ethnic group and prayer style. Almost every single one was damaged or destroyed in 1948, many after hostilities had ceased and all Jewish residents had been evacuated. Those holy sites that were not destroyed were densely inhabited by refugees or used for stables, workshops, and storerooms. The Protection of Holy Places Law, 1967, stipulated that the Israeli Ministry of Religious Affairs was responsible for the renewal of the desecrated religious institutions of the Old City of Jerusalem. Minister Zerach Warhaftig planned to renovate about 17 central institutions and to integrate them into the general renovation plans for the Old City, using them for religious and national ceremonies.

Despite public declarations that Jewish religious institutions would be renewed, it soon became clear that the government expected them to perform the restoration themselves. However, many religious institutions belonged to charitable organizations that no longer existed, many had no resources or competence to perform renovations, and most structures were damaged or destroyed. A year after the reunification of Jerusalem, a public committee was finally established to deal with property belonging to religious and charitable organizations.[84] An agreement was reached with Company Director Tamir that each institution would present its own plan for renewal. The Company, in turn, would assist in finding funding for renovations and would subsidize up to 25% of the cost, especially in the case of dormitory institutions. In return, the Company demanded that the charitable organizations prove ownership, provide a suitable professional building plan, fund 75% of the construction cost, and maintain the reconstructed holy site. This was a demand few could meet.

The renewal of the synagogues was connected to the larger question regarding the socio-economic and religious character of the newly-rebuilt Jewish Quarter, and of the heritage valued and considered worthy of presentation. These synagogues and *yeshivot* were not viewed by the Company (and the government) or by the public as relevant to anyone except the group that would be praying or studying there. The socio-economic status of the Old City's Jewish residents under the British Mandate—and of those for whom the synagogues embodied the character of the Old City—had been quite low. The Company was simply not interested in turning back the clock and "returning to the atmosphere in the Jewish Quarter before 1948."[85] However, the powerful symbolism of these holy sites and their rehabilitation was decisive in attracting tourism and pilgrimage, as well as in influencing the type of population who would be attracted to residence in the Jewish Quarter. The Western Wall itself is a powerful symbol of highly different values to different groups. (Guinn 2006, 68-70).

Figure 15: Etz Hayyim Yeshiva students renew studies, ca. 1968. Source: JCA.

As early as 1967, individual activists and veteran religious endowments initiated the renewal of the Habad and Or HaHayyim synagogues and of the Torat Hayyim, Hayyei Olam, Etz Hayyim, and Beit El *yeshivot*.[86] Between 1967 and 1975, two more religious institutions were renovated (Ramban and the Sephardic complex; see below). A few other renovations were completed after 1975, including the Warsaw Rabbi MiKalish synagogue of Polish Jewry, the Moroccan Rabbi Tzuf Dvash synagogue and residential complex, the Karaite courtyard complex and synagogue, the Menachem Zion synagogue near the ruins of the Hurva, and Porat Yosef Yeshiva. All of these were local institutions, intended to serve the needs of particular religious groups. Their potential as religious centers or for heritage tourism was not taken into consideration, except perhaps for two institutions—the Sephardic Synagogue Complex and the Or HaHayyim synagogue, part of the Old Yishuv Court Museum complex.

At least 13 religious institutions were destroyed and not rebuilt. Residential buildings, shops, and a parking lot took their place. Repeated attempts by the endowment to rebuild the magnificent Tiferet Yisrael synagogue failed. Other synagogues had been part of a complex to which a new function was relegated. For example, the Bikkur Holim hospital, including the hall that had served as a synagogue, became a dormitory and later, a youth hostel. The Company sold Michael Roitman's house, formerly his residence, a community hostel and a synagogue, to a private household. Most of these institutions had left few oral or written chronicles, such that historical and cultural oblivion followed that of the physical.

Two new *yeshivot* were founded: HaKotel Yeshiva (discussed above) and Kol Yehuda, founded by Rabbi Yehuda Zvi Brandwein of the Histadrut (General Workers' Union in the Land of Israel), Israel's most powerful labor union. Unfortunately, Rabbi Brandwein passed away a few months later. His family continues to maintain the *yeshiva*, but it has not played a decisive role in development of the Jewish Quarter, nor is it any longer affiliated with the Workers' Union.

Ramban Synagogue

Of the few historic religious institutions renovated by 1975, the seven-hundred-year-old Ramban Synagogue was the only one directly renovated by the Ministry of Religion. In a letter to his family, Rabbi Moshe Ben Nachman (known as Ramban or Nachmanides, for whom the synagogue is named) describes his renewal of the Jewish community and establishment of a synagogue in Jerusalem in 1267, following almost two hundred years of warfare among Crusaders, Ayyubids, Mamluks, and Mongols, during which almost no Jews lived in Jerusalem. The synagogue he describes is strikingly similar to what is known as the Ramban Synagogue today.[87] In any case, this likely was the main Jewish synagogue of Jerusalem for both Ashkenazi and Sephardic Jews from the 14th century until 1586, when it was closed by Ottoman decree (Cassuto 2009, 328–29; Cassuto 1976, 122–26). For almost four hundred years, it lay buried and forgotten beneath the site of the Hurva Synagogue. Part was destroyed, and the rest served as storehouse, stable, cheese factory, and so on. In 1967, archaeologists rediscovered the synagogue, and in 1968, festive services were conducted there on Israeli Independence Day.

Architect Dan Tanai identified the site of the Holy Ark on the eastern wall and began renovations. Several of the synagogue's ancient features, such as its water cistern and a missing pillar, were discovered. One of the pillars bears an ancient Hebrew inscription, further evidence that the building was used as a synagogue. Because it had been buried for so many years, and because it had not originally been either an Ashkenazi or Sephardi synagogue, no group claimed title to the synagogue. Upon completion of renovations in 1972, it was designated central Ashkenazi synagogue of the Jewish Quarter (Tanai 1973, 286–300).[88] It is open for prayer and Torah study all day long. Tourists and visitors are welcome. However, despite its historical and archaeological importance, no attempt has been made to develop the synagogue as a heritage site. In the 1980s, a one-page flyer was distributed to visitors, explaining the synagogue's history and significance, but this was a one-man initiative that was eventually discontinued. The few visitors who do enter the synagogue depend on the knowledge and good will of their guides to convey its unique Jewish history, architectural features, and current usage.

The Sephardic Synagogue Complex

The Sephardic Synagogue complex contains four adjacent synagogues built from the beginning of the 17th century and on. The oldest and largest are the Eliyahu Hanavi and Rabbi Yohanan Ben Zakkai. Two other synagogues were added over the centuries as the Jewish population grew. The Istanbuli Synagogue served the Turkish Sephardic community, and the Emzai or Middle Synagogue was just that—an inner courtyard that became a fourth synagogue when the three others were overcrowded. In 1837, Ibrahim Pasha gave permission to erect stone roofs and to renovate the four synagogues. Towards the end of the 19th century, a *yeshiva* and elementary school, Metivta Tiferet Yerushalayim, were founded south of the synagogues. Adjacent were the Sephardi Chief Rabbi's home and housing for the aged (Cassuto 1976, 122–23; Tanai 1976, 124–26). The school had its own kitchen, dining hall, and workshops for the teaching of trades. Students helped with the cooking and built furniture in the carpentry. During the battle in May 1948, the synagogues served as shelters for about 1,000 of the residents.

The Sephardic Community Council was one of the oldest and wealthiest Jewish charitable organizations in Jerusalem. Of its many properties, the four Sephardic Synagogues and the Metivta Tiferet Yerushalayim (Sephardic *yeshiva*) had been damaged, looted, and filled with refuse, but not destroyed. Under Jordanian rule, they became goat pens filled with garbage. Eliyahu Eliashar, President of the Sephardic Community Council, described having to cover his face with a handkerchief because of the stench, and having to climb through a window in order to enter the synagogue in 1967.

> Thousands of visitors tour the Jewish Quarter of the Old City of Jerusalem daily, and see the destruction caused to the synagogues…. Many…cannot get into the synagogues because the Arabs closed up all the entrances….[89]

The Council was eager to begin renovations immediately, and to renew religious and educational activities. At an emergency meeting on June 18, 1967, it decided to transfer a branch of the (West Jerusalem) Sephardic Yeshiva to the Jewish Quarter in order to renew the institutions that had existed there for many generations. Despite these public declarations, months passed and nothing happened. In September 1967, Eliashar turned to Yehuda Tamir and to Dr. Ya'akov Herzog, presidential advisor, to request approval to begin clearance of the three-meter high piles of garbage and the goat pens and horse stalls in the synagogues. Eliashar succeeded in getting the support of the Rothschilds and other donors, and of Mayor Teddy Kollek. With the aid of the municipality, the synagogues were cleared of rubble and architect Dan Tanai began renovations. Most of the walls were intact, but doors, windows, roofs and flooring had been torn out. All the synagogue furnishings, such as the Holy Ark, had been plundered or burnt.

The renovations took five years, and were carried out by the Sephardic Community Council, with the aid and support of donors and personages such as President Zalman Shazar, Mayor Kollek, future President Yitzchak Navon, Eliyahu Eliashar, Sephardic Chief Rabbi Yitzchak Nissim, Dr. Ya'akov Herzog, and others. The organizations involved were public and semi-private: the Sephardic Community Council, the National Parks Authority, the Jerusalem Foundation, Yad Avi HaYishuv Foundation, the Company, and the Israel Foundation for Research and Education Grants. The Ministry of Religious Affairs was not officially involved.

By 1968, the Sephardic Yeshiva had already begun two different educational programs. Plans were to expand these programs into a full-scale spiritual and educational center for hundreds of students from Israel and from abroad. The council also called on the government to build a neighborhood in the quarter for veteran residents.

By 1972, renovations were completed, with three of the four synagogues in regular use by different Jewish ethnic groups. Tanai called this the most beautiful architectural complex in the Jewish Quarter, and one of the most beautiful in all of Israel. His approach to the renovation stemmed from the realization that in this case it was impossible to recreate the past. These synagogues had been built, damaged, and repaired over the centuries by different artisans and in different situations. These did not work according to strict guidelines, but rather used stone in secondary usage, fitting the style to the limitations of the particular time and place. Tanai chose to emphasize interesting details that indicated stages of construction and renovation over the years, causing a multiplicity of styles and clear asymmetry. In cases where the original could not be renovated (as in the case of the Holy Ark), Tanai worked with modern Israeli artists. Some articles, such as the 16th-century wooden renaissance Ark, were imported from Italian synagogues abandoned in World War II (Tanai 1973, 217–37; Tanai 1976, 124–26; Cassuto 2009, 331–32).

He explained his approach to conservation of the complex: "[W]e began gathering all the literary sources relevant to the synagogues, as well as drawings, photographs, and the like" (Tanai 1976, 124). He also drew on oral testimonies and personal memories to provide as complete a picture as possible of the past. His aim was to restore the traditional atmosphere, without being totally committed to replication, especially if the original was completely missing, or if it was necessary under current conditions (such as constructing a smaller dais in order to make room for more worshippers). He was careful to follow the first synagogue architects' example of not letting the synagogue stand out from the surrounding buildings.

Tanai was interested in the literary and the physical history of the synagogue's development. He held that restoration should not concentrate on one particular phase, or on a future vision, but rather on the historic heritage of development and adaptation over the years. Ignoring the dominant place of religious institutions in the Jewish Quarter's urban fabric, or replacing them with new, modern institutions would completely change the character of the quarter, even if the general architectural lines were preserved. Nonetheless, it was clear to all that it was impossible to preserve every single religious institution.

Tanai and his colleagues saw in the synagogues not only religious heritage, but also national, social, and architectural markers of the Jewish Quarter:

> John Ruskin was right when he said that good architecture is an expression of national life and character. It stems from strong longings for beauty. Is there any more faithful, more moral, more beautiful expression of our original architecture? Is there any more faithful expression of our national life and character than the synagogue? (Tanai 1975, 300–301).

As for the renovation of the Jewish Quarter:

> The urban and architectural nostalgia for the past should not blindly glorify the Jewish Quarter, but rather show it in its true light, as it really was, for good and for bad. It is impossible to explain the synagogues that I am renovating if the difference between Jewish and non-Jewish houses in the Old City is not understood.... Arab houses were principally...houses for one family, while Jewish houses even then were multifamily complexes.... From the middle of the 19th century on, decorations began to appear on synagogue facades only—to distinguish them from private homes.... The many synagogues and yeshivot, built during even the most difficult periods, destroyed, and built anew, were the principal urban Jewish markers. They gave it its true character. Although the synagogues were low and sunk underground, in accordance with non-Jewish law, they upheld and sustained the eternal values of the Jewish People beyond their physical limitations (Tanai 1973, 222).

Figure 16: Middle Synagogue desecrated, 1968. Source: Government Press Office.

Figure 17: Middle Synagogue renovated, 2007. Source: Tamar Hayardeni, via Wikipedia.

The Sephardic Community Council summarized its approach thus:

> We have a rich program of activities [planned] in the Ben Zakkai Synagogue.... The legacy of Sephardic and Oriental Jewry is not local heritage. It belongs to the whole nation of Israel. The "cradle" of Jewish activism during the Ottoman Period was here, in the Jewish Quarter.... We will make every effort to restore its former glory.[90]

To this day, the Ben Zakkai Synagogue is officially the main synagogue for Sephardic Jewry in Israel. Despite its small size, it is here that every Chief Rabbi is inaugurated.

In the late 1970s, Rabbi Aryeh Grayevsky launched one of the first museums in the Jewish Quarter, exhibiting photographs of the synagogues of the Old City before 1948, the destruction in and following 1948, and relics of the synagogues salvaged from the ruins. The museum still exists and is open daily, as are the synagogues, for an admission fee. The synagogues are open for prayer gratis.

The Debate over Renovation of the Hurva Synagogue

The other side of the coin was the opportunity to create something new, representing the rejuvenation of Jerusalem. Shabtai Shapiro, a fifth-generation Jerusalemite, wrote to Mayor Kollek:

> The other nations of the world have left their mark on Jerusalem in the past generations.... We were not empowered to do so, but now suddenly we have achieved the right and the obligation to make a dominant architectural mark on our city. It is appropriate to renovate the Hurva as soon as possible and as magnificently as possible....[91]

Others expressed similar sentiments. For example, architect Ari Shem-Or suggested the establishment of an international Jewish religious center that would be no less magnificent than Christian and Muslim holy sites in the Old City and environs. To do this, most of the old structures in the Jewish Quarter should be cleared away. In their place, Shem-Or proposed a central synagogue for 5,000 worshippers in the middle of the Batei Mahse Square, opposite Rothschild House. Northeast of it, he proposed erecting a "Religious Enclave" (counterpart of the Vatican), which would include the palace of the Chief Rabbinate, the Rabbinate High Court, a religious university, a Jewish library, a museum, and other institutions. These would occupy about a quarter of the Jewish Quarter. The rest would be for housing and for tourist and commercial use. This proposal was not accepted, but it does epitomize the desire for something new aroused by the unification of Jerusalem.

Should settling a small community of two to three thousand residents in the quarter, keeping its traditional Islamic–Middle Eastern character, be the fulfillment of our dreams of a unified Jerusalem? This small community in a modest quarter will not do much to transform the character of the Jewish Quarter or to raise Jewish status in the Old City.[92]

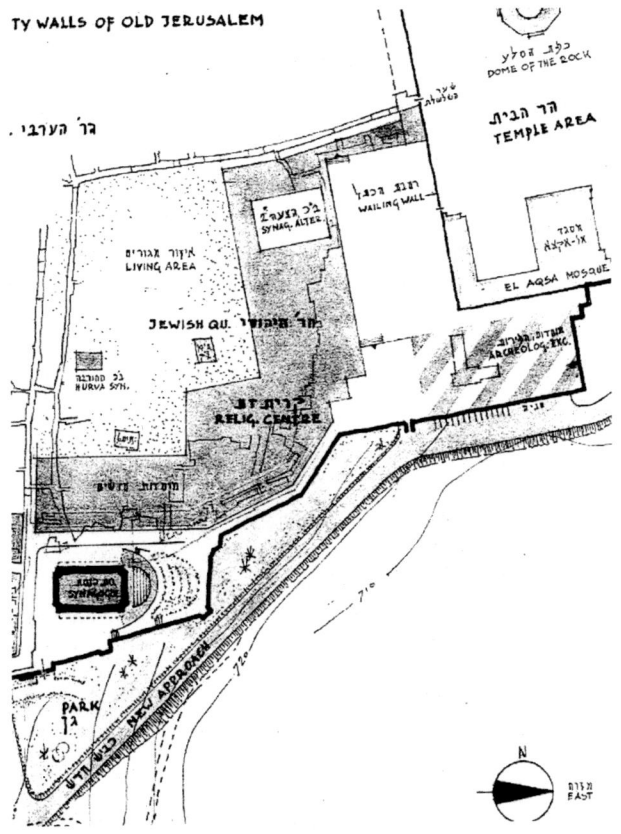

Plan 7: Shem Or's proposal. Source: JCA.

The strongest representation of this quest may be found in the debate over the Hurva synagogue, first built in 1864 on the ruins of an earlier Ashkenazi synagogue that had been destroyed in 1720 and had lain in ruins for a century. The synagogue was popularly dubbed the "Hurva" (meaning ruin), although its official name was Beit Ya'akov Synagogue, after Jacob (Ya'akov) de Rothschild. Its classical architecture and imposing height made it a landmark symbolizing the rejuvenation of the Jewish Quarter. Pictorial representations of the Hurva were a popular design element on souvenirs and documents, alongside traditional images such as the Western Wall or the Tomb of Rachel.

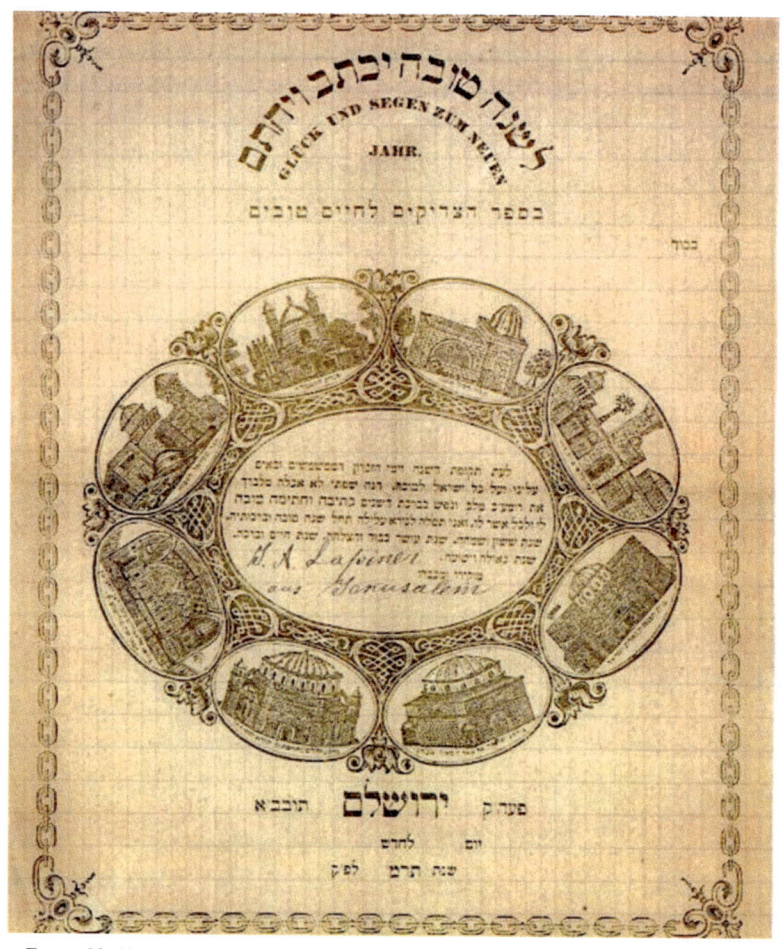

*Figure 18: New Year's greeting card depicting the Hurva and Tiferet Israel Synagogues.
Source: Old Yishuv Court Museum.*

Many important historic events took place in the Hurva, among them Herzl's visit in 1898, and the presentation of the Jewish Brigade flags at the end of World War I. In 1920, when British Lord High Commissioner Herbert Samuel first arrived in Jerusalem, he attended Sabbath services in the Hurva synagogue. In 1921, Rabbi Avraham Isaac HaCohen Kook was inaugurated there as Chief Ashkenazi Rabbi, and he frequently spoke in the synagogue. The main prayer service following the first news of the Holocaust was held in the Hurva. In 1948, the surrender of the Jewish Quarter followed immediately after destruction of the Hurva synagogue. In the explosion, the dome and much of the walls were destroyed, but total obliteration of the synagogue took place later under Jordanian rule. Discovery of this caused much anger in Israel after 1967.

Figure 19: Ruins of the Hurva Synagogue, 1967. Source: Government Press Office.

The "Ashkenazi Courtyard" complex included the Hurva synagogue and two smaller synagogues (Menachem Zion and Sha'arei Zion), Etz Hayyim Yeshiva, the Ashkenazi Rabbinic High Court, and a small apartment for Jerusalem Chief Rabbi Shmuel Salant (in the late 19th century). The Hurva and Sha'arei Zion were completely destroyed, but the other structures were only damaged. However, each institution had its own plans and conducted separate negotiations with the Company, despite the fact that renovation plans for each one would affect the others.

It was no coincidence that the Jewish Quarter surrendered less than 24 hours after the destruction of the Hurva. Its importance derived not only from historic events symbolizing the awakening of Jewish national aspirations at the end of the 19th century, but also from the fact that it was deliberately and almost totally destroyed by "our enemies, who viewed this particular building as symbolizing Jewish life within the Old City. Perhaps this is also the reason…that the question of its reconstruction… has become the central issue in the renewal of the Jewish Quarter" (Tanai 1973, 234).

In August 1967, lawyer Ya'akov Solomon was appointed to represent Minister of Religious Affairs Dr. Zerach Warhaftig in planning the renovation of the Hurva. He issued an international call for plans. The renowned American architect Louis Kahn contributed a plan for a monumental modern structure to be built adjacent to a memorial garden in which the ruins of the historic Hurva synagogue would be preserved. The new synagogue would be 25 meters high, faced with stones the size of the largest stones in the Western Wall (about 1.5 meters high), and able to accommodate 1,000 worshippers. The plan was modular, so that during ordinary weekdays, individual units in the synagogue hall, tailored to dozens of worshippers, could be used. "Prophets' Boulevard" (equivalent to Netzer [Menczel] and Ya'ar's Pilgrims' Route) would lead from the Hurva past the Tiferet Yisrael and Karaite synagogues to the stairway leading to the Western Wall Plaza.

Figure 20: Kahn's sketch for a new Hurva Synagogue. Source: David Cassuto.

חורבת רבי יהודה החסיד, מרכזי הראשון של עזחיים,
בירושלים העתיקה. שנחרב בחדש אייר

Figure 21: Hurva Synagogue complex as depicted on a 1935 Etz Hayyim calendar. Source: Bracha Slae.

This plan aroused much public debate. Both the bold architectural plan and the idea of replacing the old and traditional with something so different and modern were controversial. The Israel Museum held an exhibit of Kahn's model alongside other alternatives. A public symposium was also held in the winter of 1968 (Cassuto 1970). There were three options:

1. Build anew a copy of the "Old Hurva"—duplication.
2. Build a completely new synagogue in place of the old or alongside it, according to Kahn's or any other plan.
3. Preserve the destroyed Hurva as a memorial of the destruction and desecration wrought by Jordan.

Those who favored duplicating the 19th-century Hurva explained that it had been one of the most magnificent synagogues in the world, arousing and inspiring visitors and worshippers, both in its exterior and interior. In order to impart meaning to the present day Jewish Quarter, its built heritage must be preserved and reconstructed in its former location. The present must continue the past.[93]

Those who favored a new modern synagogue saw the need for a structure that properly represented the modern State of Israel, and whose architecture would provide the proper setting for both large and small groups of worshippers. Some favored erection of a new synagogue at a different site in the Jewish Quarter, instead of replacing the Hurva. Even among those who favored new construction, there were critics of Kahn's plan as too grandiose, one that would not blend in with the urban fabric of the Old City. Some saw it as competing in height and scale with the Dome of the Rock; others saw in it an attempt to become a replacement for the Holy Temple. Still others saw it as competing with the Western Wall. There were also fears that its grand scale might arouse antisemitism.[94] Others were enthusiastically in favor of Kahn's plan, which was esthetically pleasing, well planned, and flexible. It would also influence the spatial character of the Jewish Quarter by delineating a main route that would serve as its backbone.[95]

A third group saw primary importance in the preservation and memorialization of the Jordanian desecration. Dan Tanai suggested leaving the Hurva in ruins, but renovating the adjacent Ramban synagogue to serve as the central Ashkenazi synagogue of the Jewish Quarter.

Kahn's innovative and generous proposal to erect a new monument in the rejuvenated Jewish Quarter, offered as a donation to the State of Israel, could not be refused without starting a diplomatic and political crisis. On the other hand, it was clear that brilliant as it was, even to those who wished to break with tradition, Kahn's proposed synagogue would not be appropriate at that site. Time passed, the debate continued, until in 1973, Kahn agreed to begin by designing a commemorative garden around the existing ruins of the Hurva. Unfortunately, he passed away in 1974, before he had completed the plans.

Then the debate began anew and more plans were submitted. Finally, in the late 1970s, a new commemorative arch was raised above the ruins of the Hurva, and an open plaza built around it, leading to the tourist route to the Western Wall Plaza.

North of the Hurva stood the Etz Hayyim Yeshiva, the largest and most important Ashkenazi *yeshiva* in Jerusalem in its time. It had been damaged but not destroyed. The *yeshiva* administration claimed to hold the property rights both to their building and to the Hurva. They were not willing to allow the area of the Hurva to be expanded at their expense, contradictory to Kahn's plans. The *yeshiva* wished to repair the damage and return to its original location. However, it received no support from either the municipality or the government. On the contrary, despite the fact that renovation of the Hurva was at a standstill, Etz Hayyim Yeshiva was ordered to stop the renovations they were doing at their own expense and to vacate the building. A few years later, the *yeshiva* returned to its present location in West Jerusalem. Today, a branch of Etz Hayyim uses part of the premises and residents of the Jewish Quarter have renovated Menachem Zion Synagogue for local use.

Reconstruction of Tiferet Yisrael Synagogue

Facing the Temple Mount and Mount of Olives were the ruins of Tiferet Yisrael, the magnificent 19th century Hassidic synagogue destroyed in and after 1948. Besides the synagogue proper, this Hassidic center had had a modern heated ritual bath, a *yeshiva*, library, and study halls, the Hassidic high court of law, as well as several apartments for rabbis. It was known for its many Torah Scrolls and priceless Judaica. The rooftop had a magnificent view, and in 1948, it was one of the strategic military outposts for the Jewish Quarter's defenders. After the Quarter surrendered, the synagogue was looted and blown up, leaving only remnants of the graceful western and southern walls with their arched gates and windows. Attempts by the Hassidic community to rebuild the synagogue and re-establish a Hassidic neighborhood nearby failed, but the Company did minimal preservation of the ruins.

Figure 22 Tiferet Yisrael Synagogue, ca. 1940. Source: JCA.

Figure 23: Destroyed façade of the Tiferet Yisrael Synagogue, ca. 1968.
Source: Jewish National Fund Archive.

Over the decades, it had become clear that attempts to preserve the Hurva and Tiferet Yisrael Synagogues as ruins and memorials of the war were a failure. People wanted to see the originals rebuilt. Finally, in 1997, the Israeli government decided on replication of both the Hurva and Tiferet Yisrael Synagogues as national heritage sites that would be rebuilt by the State of Israel, and not by any particular NGO.[96] A detailed survey and archaeological excavations were conducted at the site of the Hurva, and then the synagogue was reconstructed using modern technology. Air-conditioning, elevators, and other modern amenities were installed while keeping everything else as similar as possible to the original. First and Second Temple Period and Byzantine ruins were rehabilitated and put on display underground.

Not until 2012, two years after the rededication of the Hurva Synagogue, was the outline plan for reconstruction of Tiferet Yisrael Synagogue approved. The plan includes authentic replication of the original synagogue, along with excavations and an archaeological museum in the lower stories, a lookout on the rooftop, and restoration of the ritual bath, with provisions for use of the building both for prayers and as a tourism heritage site. Work is still in progress.

Had the Hurva and Tiferet Yisrael been rebuilt decades ago, their reproduction would undoubtedly have been less successful. The research and technological capabilities of the Antiquities Authority today are many times greater than in the 1970s, and enable them to integrate modern technology such as elevators and air-conditioning without damaging authenticity. They also are able to preserve archaeological remains underground without undermining the stability of buildings.

These two monuments appear in all the panoramic representations of the Jewish Quarter from the 19th century until their destruction in 1948. Pictures of both appeared on greeting cards, wall posters, holiday decorations, and so on, even after their destruction, all over the Jewish world (Milstein 2010, 158). It is interesting to note that the most powerfully symbolic sites, such as the Temple Mount, the Western Wall, the Hurva and Tiferet Yisrael synagogues, Rachel's Tomb, the Cave of Machpela, and the Tomb of Joseph, are also those that have aroused the most debate regarding their renewal and conservation after 1967.

Porat Yosef Yeshiva

The Porat Yosef Yeshiva was the only new Jewish construction in the Old City under the British Mandate. It had its beginnings in the early 20th-century pre-Mandate Period, but World War I delayed its completion until 1923. The large Sephardic yeshiva campus included a study hall, synagogue, library, free soup kitchen and dining hall, rabbinical seminary, dormitory, and apartments for the staff. From the windows and rooftops one could see the top of the Western Wall, Mount Moriah (the Temple Mount), and the Mount of Olives in the background.

Studies continued uninterrupted from 1923 until 1948. With the increasing hostilities in 1947 following the UN partition vote, the British took over the buildings, whose strategic location ensured control of the Western Wall, the road leading down to it, and the southern corner of the Jewish Quarter. As soon as the British left, the Hagana moved in, setting up their headquarters and shelters for Old City residents, and later a temporary hospital after the demolition of the nearby Misgav Ladach Hospital. Jews left Porat Yosef as it was being blown up, room by room, by Arab forces turning cannons on them from a position below Al-Aqsa Mosque on the Temple Mount compound (Bier 2010, 111–13).

Immediately after the 1967 War, the Sephardic leadership began to clear away the rubble left from the original buildings destroyed in 1948. In 1970, renowned architect Moshe Safdie was commissioned to design a new modern building on the site. Safdie attempted to design something that would fit in with the fabric of the Old City, using modern techniques and materials such as fiberglass and cement (Safdie 1972, 93–95; idem 1998, 17–18). Both Porat Yosef and HaKotel Yeshivas are built over the Wohl Archaeological Museum Herodian Quarter. These excavations delayed construction of both *yeshivot* until the 1980s, following restoration and preservation of the Second Temple Period mansions underground.

SLAE & KARK | 89

Figure 24: Porat Yosef Yeshiva before 1948. Source: Wikimedia Commons.

Figure 25: Ruins of Porat Yosef Yeshiva at the top of the new staircase leading to the Western Wall Plaza, ca. 1970. Source: JCA.

Figure 26: Campus of Porat Yosef Yeshiva today. Source: Hillel Shalev, 2006.

The Karaite Synagogue

Probably the oldest synagogue of all is the Karaite synagogue. The Karaite community is an eighth-century offshoot of mainstream Judaism that does not accept Rabbinic law or interpretation. Consequently, Karaites observe only those aspects of Judaism explicitly written in the 24 books of the Bible. The Hanukah festival, for example, is not mentioned in the Bible, and therefore is not observed. Karaites have their own calendar, their own traditions and rabbis, and have maintained their own distinct entity for twelve centuries. Among the outstanding attributes of this community is their love and devotion to Zion.

According to Karaite tradition, their leader, Anan Ben David, founded this synagogue in the eighth century. However, according to modern scholars, its architectural style dates it somewhere between the tenth and the twelfth centuries, the "golden age" of the Karaite community of Jerusalem. Like the Sephardic synagogues, this structure, too, was built below ground level. It too was destroyed and desecrated in wartime. Although the ruins were cleared immediately after the 1967 war, renovations took more than a decade and restored only a small fraction of the original area of the synagogue and courtyard. A small museum on Karaite history and traditions is adjacent to the synagogue. As Karaite law regarding ritual purity and sanctity differs from that of mainstream Judaism, non-Karaites are not welcome in the synagogue, but can view it from a window in the museum.

Always "lovers of Zion," two Karaite families remained in the Jewish Quarter until 1948. They participated in Israel's War of Independence and earlier military operations, and were taken as prisoners of war along with the other survivors of the battle over the Jewish Quarter.

Figure 27: Destroyed façade of the Karaite Synagogue, ca. 1970. Source: World Karaite Jewry Archive.

Figure 28: Restored interior of Karaite Synagogue, 2006. Source: World Karaite Jewry Archive.

Muslim and Christian Holy Sites in the Jewish Quarter

There are a number of archaeological sites, but no Christian holy sites in the Jewish Quarter proper. Important churches west of Habad Street were registered as part of the Armenian Quarter: the Cathedral of Saint James, St. Toros Church, the Syriac Orthodox Church, and the Armenian Patriarchate and Museum.[97] There are also Armenian religious institutions on Mount Zion and in the Christian and Muslim Quarters. In addition, there are more than forty Muslim and Christian religious institutions in the Christian Quarter, including the Mosque of Omar. As noted, the Via Dolorosa runs through both the Muslim and Christian Quarters. The most important Muslim holy sites are on or near the Haram al-Sharif (Temple Mount): Al-Aqsa Mosque, the Dome of the Rock, and the Dome of the Ascension. Numerous small mosques are scattered all over the Old City.

There are two mosques in the Jewish Quarter: Sidna Omar Mosque, adjacent to the Ramban Synagogue, was built under Ottoman rule in the 16th century, and was the primary cause for closure of the synagogue in 1586. After 1967, the mosque was renovated, but not reopened. King Hussein of Jordan built the Nebi Daud Mosque on Habad Street at the juncture of the Jewish and Armenian Quarters in the 1950s, but never completed it. In the mid-1970s, the State of Israel completed its construction as a monument. Isolated Muslim tombs and prayer rooms situated on and near the Street of the Chains were registered as part of the Muslim Quarter.

For centuries, there have been Muslim residents and religious institutions in the Christian Quarter, while the Christian Via Dolorosa runs through the heart of the Muslim Quarter. Division of the Old City into four quarters on a religious-ethnic basis is a geographical oversimplification that does not reflect the demographic, historical, or legal aspects of the quarters.

Figure 29: The Byzantine Cardo in front of the Habad Synagogue. Seen in the background: the Hurva Synagogue arch and the Sidna Omar Mosque. Source: Government Press Office, 1984.

These examples illustrate the influence and interdependence of heritage sites upon national, religious, and communal identity, both in past and in present. They mirror Israeli society and the changes it has undergone since 1967. The numerous religious institutions of the Jewish Quarter from the 19th century until its surrender in 1948 represented a diverse multicultural community. However, these institutions played a marginal role in the reconstruction of the quarter after 1967. Only a handful of them have been rebuilt, and even less have been developed as heritage sites. Unlike postwar reconstruction of heritage symbols in other parts of the world, Jewish Quarter reconstruction has not given renewal of these institutions high priority. Re-establishing a residential neighborhood and developing tourism and archaeological attractions have come first. Replication of the Hurva and Tiferet Yisrael Synagogues today may signify a change in collective identity. The questions remain: What heritage is presented in the Jewish Quarter today? Are there other heritage narratives that do not find expression? Who profits from this heritage presentation? Does transformation of places of worship to tourism sites contradict their original designation or the religious needs of the local population today? Was the replication successful or should new modern religious institutions designed to fit today's needs have been built?

The Development of New Institutions

Instead of rejuvenating former institutions, new ones were established in an attempt to create new cultural and religious connections to Old Jerusalem as part of its heritage and tourism development.

Aish HaTorah Yeshiva is a unique outreach yeshiva for those with little or no Jewish background. It was established by Rabbi Noah Weinberg in 1974 and mainly attracts young English-speaking visitors to Israel, offering everything from short seminars on the basic principles of Judaism to advanced programs for rabbinical candidates. Today the yeshiva has branches in all parts of the world and a very popular website.

Although Aish HaTorah is a young organization, its campus is built on the remains of ancient structures. According to research published on its website, the newly renovated complex on the eastern ridge of the Jewish Quarter, facing the Western Wall, is built upon the remains of a Crusader-period Eastern Orthodox church. In the 19th century, the American doctor and missionary James Barclay established his mission on the site, as indicated clearly on his 1856 map of Jerusalem. In 1881, according to Aish research, the property was acquired by wealthy Bulgarian-born Yeshaya Bechar Shmuel. Yeshaya's Courtyard, as it was known, became a center of Jewish prayer, security, community, and charity, especially since the complex included a synagogue overlooking the Temple Mount. During the armed Arab resistance from 1936–1939, Jewish families left for safer dwellings, and Arab families moved into the building, thus saving it from destruction during the 1948 war. In the 1980s, the Jewish Quarter Development Company transferred ownership of the building site—constituting 40 percent of the frontage facing the Western Wall—to Rabbi Noah Weinberg and Aish HaTorah. In December 2009 the refurbished complex was dedicated as the Aish World Center.[98]

Bar Ilan University: In 1969, the university submitted a formal request to establish several research institutes in the Jewish Quarter to study the history of Jewish communities in the land of Israel, and to study Jewish history in Islamic countries. For this purpose, it leased a historic building from the Company, probably the former site of the Yemenite Succat David Synagogue (Izrael 1983, 47).[99] Bar Ilan University used the building until the 1990s, but today it serves as an elementary school.

Beit Ha-Sofer (Writer's House) opened in a historic, newly-renovated building in Batei Mahse Square in 1969 as a library and cultural center for literary activities for children and adults, centered on the theme of Jerusalem. It was planned to become a national and international center for Israeli prose and poetry but did not live up to expectations. After being active for about twenty years, the institution left the Jewish Quarter.[100]

The *Ben-Zvi Institute* was founded by Yitzhak Ben-Zvi (later second president of the State of Israel) in 1947 to explore the history and culture of Jewish communities worldwide. The Rachel Yanait Ben-Zvi Center for the Study of Jerusalem Youth Branch was founded in 1969 in the Jewish Quarter and ran the first teachers' courses on the history of Jerusalem. Today it continues with educational programs for all sectors and ages. In time, it also opened Ariel Museum of the First Temple Period in the quarter. The courses and the museum are still active today.[101]

Isaac Kaplan Old Yishuv Court Museum: This is the only museum planned during the first years of renewal of the Jewish Quarter, and the only recognized ethnographic museum to portray life in Jerusalem during Ottoman and Mandate Periods. The building itself dates back to the 16th century or earlier. At the beginning of the 19th century, Rabbi Shlomo Pach Rosenthal, a disciple of Rabbi Elijah of Vilna, acquired the courtyard and passed it on to five generations of descendants. In 1967, Rivka Weingarten, eldest daughter of Jewish Quarter *Mukhtar* (mayor) Mordechai Weingarten and granddaughter of the Rosenthal family, decided to establish the Old Yishuv Museum in her family residence in order to illustrate Jewish life in 19th- and early 20th-century Jerusalem. She attempted to recreate the tangible and intangible heritage of the variegated ethnic groups, lost in rebuilding and modernizing the Jewish Quarter. The museum includes a constantly expanding archive of written and visual material on the Jewish community of the Old City.

Unlike some of the other small museums in the Jewish Quarter, the Old Yishuv Museum is one of the recognized museums of the State of Israel, and an active member of the International Council of Museums (ICOM) and ICOM Israel. It is constantly developing and introducing new exhibits. According to tradition, the Holy Ari [Rabbi Isaac Luria], founder of Lurianic *Kabbala* (mysticism), was born in one of its rooms in 1534. That room served as a synagogue during the Ottoman Period and is now part of the permanent museum exhibition. In 1742, another famous rabbi and kabbalist, Hayyim Ben Attar [known as the Holy Or HaHayyim, from the title of his book] established a *yeshiva* and synagogue on the upper floor of the courtyard complex. Weingarten renewed the Or HaHayyim Synagogue, initiating the first prayer service there in the summer of 1967. It should be noted that this museum is located on a residential street, and not on the main tourist route (Perry and Kark 2017, 76-80).[102]

Figure 30: Left: Rivka Weingarten at the entrance to her family home, now the Old Yishuv Court Museum, June 1967. Right: Rivka Weingarten, Prime Minister Levi Eshkol, Central Command General Uzi Narkiss, and entourage tour the Jewish Quarter, 8 June, 1967. Source: Moshe Weingarten.

The *Sapir Institute for Jewish Heritage* was founded in 1972 by the General Workers' Union to inculcate Jewish values and a love for Jerusalem among Israeli youth through educational programs and tours. It also left the Jewish Quarter after two decades.

The *Misgav Yerushalayim Institute*: The Sephardic Community Council in cooperation with the Hebrew University of Jerusalem planned to establish a research institute to study the history and culture of Sephardic Jewry on the site of the destroyed Old City Misgav Ladach hospital. The institute was eventually established, but on the Mount Scopus campus of the university rather than in the Jewish Quarter.[103]

The *Siebenberg Archaeological Museum* is another museum established privately by Jewish Quarter residents. Theodore and Miriam Siebenberg were among the first to purchase a newly built apartment on the southeastern edge of the Jewish Quarter. Avigad's digs there had found nothing of importance, but the Siebenbergs decided to conduct their own excavations, revealing remains from the Iron Age, parts of a Hasmonean wall, a Second Temple period aqueduct and ritual baths, and a Byzantine water cistern. After years of negotiations with their neighbors, the Company, the Municipality, and the Jerusalem Fund, they succeeded in opening an impressive museum in the basement of their house.[104]

The Jerusalem Foundation renovated ruins of the Crusader period *Church of St. Mary of the Germans, and its Hospice and Hospital.* Today it is an open archaeological park overlooking the staircase from the Jewish Quarter to the Western Wall Plaza.

Former Jewish Quarter resident and veteran of the 1948 War, Hayyim Zelniker, was instrumental in the establishment of a small museum, *Alone on the Ramparts*, and a memorial site commemorating the battles and the fall of the Jewish Quarter in 1948.

The *Burnt House* and the *Wohl Archaeology Museum* are two archaeological museums exhibiting Second Temple period remains. The First Temple Period *Broad Wall* has been preserved and is on exhibit as an open archaeological site. The First Temple Period *Israelite Tower* was also excavated and opened to the public as a basement museum, but has been closed for the past decade for safety reasons.[105]

The last museum to open to date is the *Temple Institute*, a non-profit educational and religious organization founded in 1987. Its goal is to rekindle the flame of the Holy Temple in the hearts of mankind through education and thus to bring about the rebuilding of the Holy Temple. The Institute aims to raise public awareness about the Holy Temple and the central role that it occupies in the spiritual life of mankind. To this end, the Institute has begun to construct the sacred vessels for the service of the Holy Temple and to exhibit them in its museum. It also conducts research, holds seminars and conferences, and produces educational materials.[106]

In other parts of the Old City are the Tower of David Museum, the Christ Church Museum, Armenian Museum, Damascus Gate Museum, Church of Saint Anne, Terra Sancta Museum, Western Wall Tunnels and Heritage Foundation, Davidson Center, and other attractions. Suggestions for museums that did not materialize included an Islamic Art Museum (later opened in West Jerusalem), Shalom of Safed and other artists' galleries, Judaica exhibits, and so on. None of the museums were completed by 1975. The first, the Old Yishuv Court Museum, opened in 1976.

Preservation and Development of the Cardo

The Cardo—the "heart" or Main Street of Roman-Byzantine Jerusalem is the basis for the main commercial road of the Old City, running from Damascus Gate in the north to Zion Gate in the south. The street and shops of the earlier periods are buried beneath many later strata. Although it was not destroyed in war, much of the Cardo was decayed and incapable of rehabilitation. Planners decided to keep that part of the main commercial route in the Jewish Quarter (between Habad and HaYehudim streets) as an organic continuation of the Muslim and Christian Quarter markets. Much of the infrastructure and many shops were in ruins and in need of thorough reconstruction. Furthermore, no physical remains of the Byzantine Cardo had been found. The Department for Planning Policy in the Municipality, headed by British planner Prof. Nathaniel Lichfield and City Engineer Amikam Yaffe, advised the Company to hold an international competition to plan the commercial axis. Special attention was to be given to revealing ancient remains and to integrating new and old in the design.

The panel of judges, headed by Sir Nicholas Pevsner of Great Britain, chose four of the twenty-seven schemes they reviewed as worthy of a monetary reward. These were exhibited in the four Sephardic Synagogues in the Jewish Quarter, and later in Beit HaMehandes in Tel Aviv. Shlomo Aronson, Peter Bogod, and Esther Niv-Krendel received first prize for their design of a reconstruction of the Byzantine Cardo street running between Habad and HaYehudim streets. Although the Madaba Map that described the street in detail had been publicized about a century before, no remnants had yet been found at the time of the competition. The planners simply assumed that archaeological remains would be discovered on a lower level.

The main points of the plan were as follows:
1. Renewal of the Byzantine and Crusader Cardo, assuming remains would be found, and their integration into a rebuilt street connecting with Khan a-Zeit Street in the Muslim Quarter
2. Turning the Cardo into a covered gallery, whose roof would serve as an entrance to apartments and hotel rooms above it. The third story would be a garden promenade on the rooftops.
3. Integration with existing structures, their style and scale
4. Use of arches, but with modern technology, to create architectural unity
5. Creation of a dialogue between old and new

The original plan called for thirty-one apartment units (capable of being joined to the shops below), a hostel, three hotels, including one apartment hotel, all of which would have their own entrances from Habad Street. Entrance to the commercial area would be from HaYehudim Street, and would also serve as part of the pedestrian route to the Western Wall Plaza, and as part of the route from Zion Gate to Damascus Gate. On the assumed level of the original Cardo, two meters below HaYehudim Street, sixty new shops were planned. The covered street would have small open squares between its segments, and would connect up to the Hurva Square nearby.[107]

In 1976, about five years after the competition, work on the street was begun. The archaeological excavations uncovered substantial remains of the Byzantine and Crusader "shopping center," a 22.5-meter-long and 12-meter-wide paved road for pedestrians and chariots, with rows of shops on both sides. Along part of the road had been rows of 5-meter-tall columns supporting rafters to protect passersby from sun and rain (ibid.; see also Aaronson et al 1972, 96–102). Beneath this street were the remains of First and Second Temple Period city walls and towers. These excavations made the existing structures above unstable. In addition, a sizable number of the existing shops refused to relocate. Thus, significant changes to the original plans were necessary. The southern segment of the Cardo remained an open area, and no hotels or rooftop promenade were constructed at all. Only forty-three shops, a restaurant, and visitors' center were constructed in the roofed over section of the Cardo, and above that, thirty-seven residential units.

This was one of the most successful projects in the renovation of the Old City. Its integration of commercial facilities with archaeological exhibits is a great tourist attraction. The residents of the apartments above enjoy maximum privacy, as they have a separate entrance from Habad Street into their own private courtyard, so that they have no connection with the commercial and tourist area. Huge black concrete pillars support the modern residences above and contrast with the ancient stone pillars alongside them on the Byzantine road.

Figure 31: Preparations for a party in the Cardo, 2013.
Note the ancient and new pillars and paving stones. Source: unknown.

The approach here was entrepreneurial, and intended to preserve and present the remnants of the past, investing modern shopping experience with a fourth dimension—shopping and visiting Jerusalem in ancient times. This is in contrast to the religious, historical, social, and national values of the other projects already described. Preservation took precedence over possible financial profits that could have been reaped from building more shops and facilities instead of conserving and renovating as effectively as possible. However, the exciting historical background draws visitors who might have preferred to shop elsewhere had it not been for the unique experience of shopping in a Byzantine and Crusader mall.

Much archaeological and historical research preceded the actual conservation. The methods used, such as exhibiting a copy of the Madaba map on the wall at the entrance, contribute much to the successful result. They imbue a visit to the Cardo with a feeling of history, not only of aesthetics and of architectural experience. The reconstructed remnants of the past are easy to understand, and their presentation does not interfere with the functioning of the shops.

Several entrepreneurs wished to renovate old courtyards and to erect new hotels, particularly near the planned terminal. Debates and negotiations continued over many years, but no hotels were opened. Other tourism-based projects such as galleries, workshops, and restaurants also took many years to develop, and many never passed the planning stage.

The Terminal and the Amphitheater

Archaeologist Professor Michael Aviyonah had expected to uncover the Roman amphitheater and theatre described by Josephus Flavius in his excavations south of Batei Mahse Square. Instead, he found the Byzantine Nea Church and important Muslim and Crusader remains. Nevertheless, Teddy Kollek laid foundations for an amphitheater in the archaeological park there, and it is in use today. This was the planned site of the terminal, but a final decision regarding preservation and construction in this area has not yet been reached. Meanwhile, the area has been in use as a public park, and is currently (2017) undergoing renovation.

Accessibility is the first pre-condition for successful tourism. Before unification of the city in 1967, there had been no motor accessible roads into the Old City from the south (Zion Gate) and southeast (Dung Gate). Ehud Netzer planned a new terminal consisting of underground parking with a commercial center, hotel, school, and residential buildings above it in the southwestern corner of the Jewish Quarter. Entrance into the Jewish and Armenian Quarters would be either through a new gate in the city wall or through a tunnel under the wall near Zion Gate, leading to an underground parking lot.[108] Meanwhile a "temporary" parking lot in the empty space left after destruction of the Karlin Yeshiva and other buildings was erected. To this day (2017) the new entrance, terminal, and parking lot have not been built. This greatly interferes with daily life and with tourism in the Jewish Quarter.

Chapter V
Preservation and Development of Historic Cities in Israel

The British Mandatory Government was the first to introduce modern scientific methods for the preservation of holy sites in Palestine, including documentation and repair of damage caused by warfare and natural catastrophes such as earthquakes. When the State of Israel was established in 1948, it adopted and continued many British policies and legal frameworks. However, the Israeli government in its first decade had to provide housing and employment for hundreds of thousands of new immigrants. It established a central planning authority, charged with dispersing the population throughout the country in new and existing rural and urban settlements, developing agriculture, industry and transport infrastructure, and providing education, culture and health services (Kark 1995, 461–94).

From the beginning, the Planning Department, headed by architect Arieh Sharon, intended to develop parks and recreation areas for both local and foreign tourism purposes. It recognized and endorsed conservation and development of archaeological and heritage sites of all religions and all historical periods (Sharon, radio lecture, 2 Aug. 1949). However, Israel was still relatively isolated from developments in conservation practice in other western countries. It lacked expertise, did not include full preparatory documentation and surveys, and did not have the necessary budgets or statutory regulations to do more than adequately secure structures and ensure inhabitants' safety (Schaffer 2009, 39–40).

Archaeologist Shmuel Yeivin was Director of the Israeli Department of Antiquities, founded on July 26, 1948, and held that position until 1961. He established an interdepartmental committee to research and recommend development and conservation policy for the new Israeli government. Based on the committee's recommendations, the Department for the Improvement of Landscape was established in the Prime Minister's Office in 1955. In 1963, it became the National Parks Authority. The department provided a framework for the preservation of a wide range of natural and historic sites and was authorized to establish tourist infrastructure (Fuhrman-Naaman 2008, 99). (Prime Minister Eshkol originally entrusted the planning and development of the Western Wall Plaza to this department in June 1967. Two months later, authority over the Plaza was transferred to the Ministry of Religious Affairs.)

By the 1960s, preservation had become a popular movement throughout the western world. The Venice Charter of UNESCO in 1964 and the U.S. National Historic Preservation Act of 1966 are two examples of the prevailing approach. These documents present preservation as an end in itself, didactic and non-profit in purpose. However, approaches to heritage conservation worldwide gradually changed, due to changing historical and economic circumstances and to improved methods and accumulated experience.

In Israel, the Planning and Construction Law of 1965 was the first comprehensive attempt to create a uniform obligatory legal framework for physical development, requiring planning approval before construction. One of the principles of local outline schemes was "preservation of every building or site of architectural, historic, or archaeological importance," but the law allocated to local authorities the right to decide on criteria for preservation. In addition, the law had no "teeth" to enforce preservation. There were different approaches to planning, conservation, and development of ancient cities. The one considered the most fitting for Acre and other Middle Eastern cities was the "Moroccan model," isolating the old from the new by a green belt and city walls, and freezing the old by keeping modern transportation, building and industry out of the historic center (Fuhrman-Naaman 2008, 65).

Academic studies of the Land of Israel and the many important archaeological discoveries in the first two decades of statehood raised awareness of the historic and architectural treasures scattered throughout the country. Between 1948 and 1955, dozens of archaeological, historical, and ethnographic museums were erected in Israel. These were followed by a wave of historical museums focusing on the history of modern Jewish settlement, particularly at agricultural sites. In many instances, these museums were located in early buildings of the settlements, which were restored and preserved for this purpose (Fuhrman-Naaman 2008, 63; Perry and Kark 2017, 34–37).

All of these made an imprint on Israeli conservation practice. When planning the rehabilitation of Jerusalem's Jewish Quarter, planners expected preservation to turn it into a tourism and pilgrimage center, but they did not have the tools to implement this goal. The choice of sites to be preserved and the ideological, religious, and political bases for these choices were similar to those made in Israel's historic and ethnographic museums, and to the didactic approach prevalent then in the United States (Hall 2002, 264; Perry and Kark, 2017).[109]

Since 1955, there had been a Department of Antiquities and Museums within the Ministry of Education and Culture, a continuation of the Mandatory Department of Antiquities. The Antiquities Law prohibiting illegal construction and destruction was not passed until 1978. This law applied to structures and artifacts predating the year 1700; only later was the Council for Conservation of Heritage Sites founded to protect post-1700 historic structures. In 1990, an independent Israel Antiquities Authority was formally established, greatly influencing conservation methodologies and policies throughout the country, especially in Jerusalem. Furthermore, a special department was established within the Antiquities Authority capable of carrying out large-scale preservation projects.[110] Progress in methodology and technology changed preservation and development activity in Israel dramatically, making it increasingly professional. One reason for this progress was the massive immigration to Israel from countries in the former Soviet Union, which brought experts in both historical architecture and in conservation methodologies. In addition, the restoration of ancient sites came to be recognized as a profitable tool for increasing tourism. This led to the opening of academic and training programs related to conservation. Private NGOs also took a more professional approach to conservation of their historic structures. Conservation groups from Egypt and Jordan and professionals from the European Union have also contributed expertise for projects in Jerusalem (Schaffer 2008, 240–45).

The Council for Conservation of Heritage Sites in Israel was founded in 1984 as part of the Society for the Protection of Nature in Israel, in response to the destruction and damage inflicted on historic heritage sites in Israel. On January 1, 2008, the Council was registered as an independent non-profit organization. Its aim is to locate and preserve authentic remains of historic processes in Israel from the year 1700 and onward. Moreover, it has taken upon itself educational and cultural responsibilities in an effort to raise awareness and promote conservation activities among all sectors of Israeli society. It is responsible for development and operation of selected sites for visitors and offers a wide variety of tours, publications, and educational projects for all—from schoolchildren to academic interdisciplinary studies. It is responsible for the conservation of 150 sites in Israel, and with the help of a widespread volunteer network, is always ready to protect threatened heritage throughout the country. The Council has greatly influenced Israel's built heritage, both in physical preservation and in inculcating preservation as part of the public dialogue. It has teamed with the Jewish National Fund in preserving agricultural and military sites of importance to Israeli history. It has also teamed with the Antiquities Authority in preservation of multilayered sites, such as the Ottoman Fortress and British Mandate prison built on the foundations of the medieval Hospitaller Fortress of Acre (Regev 2016, 150–211).[111] (see below).

In Jerusalem, it is chiefly the Antiquities Authority that has been involved in preservation of the Jewish Quarter and the other quarters of the Old City, despite the fact that the fabric of the Old City today, in all four quarters, is primarily 19th-century Ottoman. The entire Old City, including the Jewish Quarter, is classified as an archaeological site. In contrast, the Council for Conservation of Heritage Sites has concentrated on historic areas in the New City dating from the 19th century and onward. Surprisingly, the Council has not been involved in conservation of individual 19th-century monuments and landmarks such as the Rothschild House or the Hurva and Tiferet Yisrael synagogues.

In greater Jerusalem, there has been a spurt of preservation and development of historic, post-1700 sites over the past decade, with an average of one new preservation plan deposited every two weeks. Muallem theorizes that this increase in preservation practice in Jerusalem and other major Israeli cities is due to economic considerations, and not only to geo-politics. In recent years, significant incentives have been awarded to developers, such as added building and tenancy rights and the right to modify historic properties and their vicinities. These economic incentives may be particularly effective in an urban environment such as Jerusalem or Jaffa, where private owners and developers constantly seek ways of boosting their investment in historic properties. In peripheral and smaller townships, economic incentives may not be sufficient to offset increased costs incurred in developing a historic property (Muallem 2016, 629–34).

The latest and greatest preservation project in Israel is "Landmarks," established in 2010 by Prime Minister Netanyahu as a branch of the Ministry of Jerusalem Affairs and Heritage to strengthen, rehabilitate, and preserve Israel's national heritage for the coming generations. Landmarks works together with all other preservation agencies in Israel and deals with all eras—from biblical to modern, and with a wide variety of ethnic and religious heritage sites in Israel. Along with physical work on the various sites, efforts are being made to create online educational resources to transmit the history of important sites in an exciting way.[112]

Jerusalem has been recognized by UNESCO as a World Heritage Site since its nomination by Jordan in 1981. It is the only city on UNESCO'S list whose nationality is not listed, and which was nominated by one country whereas the actual preservation has been carried out by another (Israel). In 1999, Israel and UNESCO began a new era of coordination and positive relations, and several outstanding historic and nature sites were added to the World Heritage list. However, UNESCO'S recent decision not to recognize any connection between Jewish history and the Temple Mount has antagonized Israel and world Jewry (Baker 2016). That said, UNESCO's international recognition generally increases public interest worldwide in cultural heritage and impacts local preservation policy (Muallem 2016, 637). Acre, a World Heritage Site recognized by UNESCO, will be discussed below.

Guidelines are still needed regarding reconstruction and authenticity in cases where postwar or disaster reconstruction is considered critical. There is a need for better guidance and greater clarity about what reconstruction means, when it is admissible to carry it out in a style or form reflecting so far as possible what has been lost, how it should be done, and what authenticity actually means (Bold and Pickard 2013, 105–28).

Examination of preservation and development of three ancient and historic cities in Israel over the last five decades may shed light on Israeli preservation and development approaches and how they have changed over time.

Jaffa

In Israel, the first historic town to be successfully renewed as a cultural and tourist center was Old Jaffa—almost a decade before work began on the Jewish Quarter of Jerusalem.

Until the mid-19th century, Jaffa was a small port with an ancient fortress protected by a wall, ramparts and moat. No construction was allowed near the wall. Following the Ottoman reform (1841–1876), the port became a major commercial node, competing with Acre and Beirut as an entrance gate to the Middle East. (Tel Aviv and Haifa developed later, in the 20th century.) To foreign eyes, Jaffa was a typical Oriental city. Until 1869, it had only one gate, and it was locked at night. With the improvement of security, Ottoman authorities built a new gate and assisted in tearing down segments of the wall. Within a few years, the eastern, southern, and western walls facing the sea had disintegrated or been dismantled. The moat was filled in and became a broad street. At the time, this process symbolized progress. There were no second thoughts about preserving the wall, gates, and citadel.

On the eve of the First World War and during the war, Hasan Bey al-Basri al-Jabi, the Ottoman governor of Jaffa, initiated a number of development projects in the city, including paving Jamal Pasha Street and transforming it into an attractive boulevard. In the heart of town, he razed old buildings and a market in order to open new streets and broaden existing ones. North of the Old City near the shore, he erected a new mosque that still bears his name. Jaffa's population reached 40,000 to 50,000, making it the second largest city in Palestine (Kark 1990, 49–64; idem 2010, 29–37).

In April 1936, the Arab leadership in Palestine declared a countrywide strike in an attempt to paralyze the economy and pressure the mandatory government to halt Jewish immigration. The strike began in Jaffa Port—the symbol of Arab resistance. Rioting was so violent that British military forces lost control. Jaffa's Old City, with its maze of homes, winding alleyways, and underground sewer system, provided an ideal escape route for rioters fleeing the British army. In May, municipal services were cut off, the Old City was barricaded, and access roads were covered with glass shards and nails. In June, British bombers dropped boxes of leaflets in Arabic advising inhabitants to evacuate that same day. On the evening of June 17, 1936, 1,500 British soldiers entered Jaffa and a British warship sealed off escape routes by sea. The British Royal Engineers blew up homes from east to west, leaving an open strip that cut through the heart of the city. On June 29, security forces implemented another stage of the plan, carving a swath from north to south. Mandatory authorities claimed the operation was part of a "facelift" of the Old City, but aerial photographs taken at the time illustrate the damage done to the city fabric by this military action (Gavish 1989, 316–19).

Figure 32: Aerial photo of Jaffa destruction, June 1936. Source: Dov Gavish.

*Figure 33: Cutting new road through Old Jaffa, 1936.
Source: Whiting Collection, Library of Congress, Washington, D.C.*

Israel destroyed additional houses during the 1948 war and early in 1949 in an attempt to minimize the largely Arab population of Old Jaffa. Of Jaffa's largely Arab population of 100,000 in 1947, only 3,900 remained after the 1948 war. Of these, 1,800 lived in Old Jaffa.[113] In 1950, Jaffa was annexed to the Tel Aviv Municipality, which, together with the Israel Lands Authority and the Custodian of Absentees' Property, began to plan the demolition of the rundown Old City of Jaffa. For almost a decade, destruction of Jaffa progressed from the coastline towards the city core. However, artists were attracted to Jaffa's picturesque streets and old houses, and public figures began to lobby for conservation of the historic core. The first was archaeologist Shmuel Yeivin, head of the Antiquities Department. Second was architect Eliezer Brutzcus, head of the National Planning Department, and third was architect and artist Marcel Janco (Paz 1998, 134–95; Alfasi and Fabian 2009, 141–42). Brutzcus in particular insisted on preserving the city's unique fabric, not only its monuments.

Although their heritage and architectural value were recognized, many buildings were in such poor condition that they warranted being condemned. After eighteen people were killed in the collapse of one of Jaffa's older structures, Israel appointed a committee of inquiry that recommended that all old buildings be examined and either repaired or destroyed. A public outcry followed, particularly by the architects and artists' guilds, demanding that the government preserve and renovate at least a part of Old Jaffa, allocate housing and studios for artists and for museums, and preserve all religious institutions. The government accepted these recommendations and stopped demolition of Old Jaffa in 1951, but did not actually begin renovation until the 1960s (Paz 1998, 97–105).

Meanwhile, Jaffa was included in Tel Aviv Outline Plan 606. This plan restricted almost all construction in the 130 dunam historic core, with many open spaces dedicated to archaeological exploration and public parks. Any new construction required approval from a special professional committee. Excavations were conducted in the mound at the top of the open space, and extraordinary finds, such as the 3,500-year-old Ramesses Gate, were discovered, preserved, and displayed. However, it was also during these years that the residential areas suffered from neglect, decreasing public safety, increasing crime and drug abuse, along with deterioration and abandonment of many buildings and monuments (Strul 2010, 41–51).

The Company for the Development of Old Jaffa—a joint profit making venture of the Ministry of Tourism and the Municipality, was founded in 1960. It aimed to turn Old Jaffa into a cultural and tourism center through gentrification and restoration of picturesque buildings as art galleries and workshops, coffee houses, hotels, and restaurants, while preserving the ancient, oriental atmosphere, as well as religious and archaeological sites (Alfasi and Fabian 2009, 145). This follows the paradigm described above of heritage conservation and development by local and national authorities. The architectural and historical significance of Old Jaffa was recognized and preserved, but the goals were gentrification of the neighborhood for economic and socio-political gain. Support came from the artists and merchants who stood to profit from the project, rather than from the local population. The company succeeded in compensating and relocating "undesirable" residents and in leasing much Armenian and Greek Orthodox Church property, thus allowing renovation of the neighborhood.[114]

This project was very successful at first, and served as a model for the renewal of the Jewish Quarter of Jerusalem.[115] However, the renewal project referred only to the 130 dunams of Old Jaffa, and made no effort to renew the surrounding areas, also plagued by poverty, crime, and drugs. Old Jaffa of the 1960s had only about 200 households and less than 100 commercial ventures, not enough to draw large numbers of visitors and tourists or to create a vibrant community. The gap in standard of living between renewed Old Jaffa and the surrounding areas was glaring. As a result, many of the artists' galleries and homes remained vacant, and this caused further deterioration in the city fabric.[116]

Efforts to explore, preserve, and develop Old Jaffa's ancient sites continue today. Since 1947, more than eighty excavation permits have been issued, but no systematic publication of past and present archaeological excavation has yet been undertaken. In 2007, the Israel Antiquities Authority joined with the Old Jaffa Development Corporation, the Jaffa Museum of Archaeology, the University of California in Los Angeles, the Johannes Gutenberg University of Mainz, and individual Israeli research associates to form the interdisciplinary Jaffa Cultural Heritage Project (JCHP) of archaeological research, outreach, excavation, conservation, and publication of Old Jaffa's cultural heritage. Since Jaffa is a large and complicated archaeological site within a living town with a diverse cultural heritage, the coordination of these efforts is a monumental task (Peilstocker and Burke 2010).[117] The JCHP is also involved in development of the Jaffa Visualization Project at UCLA, which will contribute to both on-site and online presentations of Jaffa's archaeological and architectural remains. The JCHP also hopes to attract volunteers, particularly students, and to engage in public education projects.

One of its latest projects was supervising and coordinating salvage excavations together with the Israel Antiquities Authority. The city was badly in need of new infrastructure (communications, electricity, water, etc.), but Israeli law requires conducting "salvage excavations" in areas designated as archaeological sites before any new construction is begun. The urban archaeology carried out in Jaffa went down to bedrock in many cases and provided much valuable information to the research community in Israel and abroad. Although excavating within a busy urban milieu was very difficult, an enormous amount of archaeological information was generated. Moreover, working processes developed during this project have since been applied to other excavations in Israel (Ajami 2010, 33–36). Israel has come a long way since the first excavations of Old Jaffa and of the Jewish Quarter of Old Jerusalem.

Among the main attractions of Old Jaffa is its 4,000-year-old *tell*—Gan HaPisga (the Summit Garden)—with its restaurants, galleries, art and Judaica shops, and unique atmosphere; the seaside promenade and walls of the old city; the visitors' center in the old courtyard; and the fishing port. There are also several important Christian sites in Old Jaffa such as the 17th-century Church of Saint Peter, the house of Simon the Tanner, and the tomb of Tabitha. One of the most interesting phases of settlement in Jaffa was the Ottoman period, during which it was Palestine's principal port (Kark 2010, 129–37). Today the port serves as a tourist attraction, as do the 17th–19th-century winding cobblestone streets, the flea market, ancient cemetery, synagogues, churches and mosques.

There is a tremendous difference between renovation of Old Jaffa and of Old Jerusalem's Jewish Quarter in their economic, political, and religious aspects and in the aims of rehabilitation. In Jaffa, preserved and rehabilitated buildings compete with modern skyscrapers in the burgeoning real estate market. Jaffa's archaeology and history, its low skyline and proximity to the sea all serve to generate profit (Strul 2010, 41–51). Old Jerusalem, on the other hand, is a vital part of Israel's contested capital city and a most holy city to the three monotheistic faiths. Its national and international significance makes it much more sensitive and challenging.

What the two cities do share are some problematic phenomena. In both, significant areas allocated for public or institutional use instead became residential or commercial areas and vice-versa. In Jaffa, shops closed and part of the renovated area became a ghost town. Historic buildings have been "developed" to serve as exclusive residential or hotel units. In the Jewish Quarter, apartments were turned into dormitories and classrooms, and shops into small vacation units and offices. In both cases, attempts "from above" to control land usage and population have failed. Additionally, attempts to renovate "islands" within historic cities in other areas of the world have led to renovation of the surrounding areas (Fitch 1990). Not so in Jaffa or in the Jewish Quarter, where the renovation has served to sharpen differences between each quarter and its surroundings. Permanent administration by a government corporation has not been overly successful, not insofar as local residents are concerned, nor insofar as economic and tourism development are concerned.[118]

Acre (Akko)

The UNESCO World Heritage site of Acre is a 4,000-year-old port city with continuous settlement from the Phoenician period until today. As the capital and chief port of the Crusader Kingdom of Jerusalem, it was one of the most important ports in the world, with an estimated population of around 40,000—larger than London in the 12th century. Today, the remains of the Crusader city, dating from 1104 to 1291, lie almost intact, both above and below today's Ottoman-period street level, providing an exceptional picture of the layout and structures of the walled capital of the Latin Kingdom of Jerusalem.[119] According to architect Alex Kesten, who mapped and surveyed the ancient city from 1959–1961, Acre is unique in that a Medieval Christian city plan served as a foundation for an important Muslim city center at a time of fierce struggles between the two powers (Kesten 1962).

After the Mamluk siege and conquest of Acre in the 13th century, it declined in size and importance, but retained its military significance. In 1799, Napoleon put siege to Acre in an attempt to wrest control of the Middle East from the Ottoman Empire, but he was repulsed. Towards the end of the Ottoman period, with the industrial revolution, Haifa began to replace Acre as the chief Middle Eastern port, and the city declined both physically and economically (Waterman 1975, 107–16).

During the British Mandate, Haifa continued to grow while Acre declined. British plans for developing Acre included expansion of the new city outside of the walls for residence, commerce, and industry, along with preservation and development of tourism in the Old City. Acre is similar to Jerusalem in that both boast a magnificent past with unusually well preserved medieval and "oriental" features, making them potentially profitable candidates for preservation (Fuhrman-Naaman 2008, 38–41). In addition, Jerusalem and Acre were the two most important cities of the Christian Crusader Kingdom of Jerusalem, and it is common knowledge that the British saw themselves as a continuation of the Crusaders. However, while Jerusalem became the capital city of the British Mandatory government, Acre lost its status as a major port to Haifa, and its population declined to 10,000. As in Old Jerusalem, preventing modernization of Old Acre led to even further decline.

110 | JERUSALEM'S JEWISH QUARTER

Figure 34: British Mandate photos of Old Acre, ca 1940.
Source: Israel Antiquities Authority Historic Archive.

The 1929 Acre Report, "Preservation and Reconstruction of Acre," called for a study of the city's history and architecture, a population census before rehabilitation of the city walls and buildings, and improvement of accessibility in order to encourage tourism. Little of this was actually carried out (Fuhrman-Naaman 2008, 9). G. F. Lowick summarized the history of Acre for the British Antiquities Department, describing its walls, fortifications, and monuments. He also added details on taxes levied, land ownership, and the legal status of property. Apparently, one of the issues preventing reconstruction of Acre during the Mandate was Muslim *Waqf* ownership, including *Waqf* claims to remains of the Crusader Citadel and the Ottoman fortress and prison built upon it.[120]

McLean's 1918 plan for Jerusalem aimed "to ensure the proper restoration and preservation of the Old City within the walls so that its mediaeval aspect may be maintained...." Similarly, Henry Kendall in the 1940s drew up an outline plan for Old Acre, designating it an area for conservation, ordering new construction to be faced with stone, prohibiting construction close to the city walls, and surrounding the Old Town with a green belt, as in Jerusalem (Fuhrman-Naaman 2008, 8). Percy Winter, in his comprehensive archeological survey of Acre in 1944, wished to give visitors to Acre a medieval experience. He called Acre "probably the most beautifully situated town in Palestine and…one of its finest architectural and archeological monuments.… Acre should gain new importance as an outstanding attraction for tourists" (Fuhrman-Naaman 2008, 40–43).

At the same time however, the survey and other reports emphasized that much of the Old City was an overcrowded slum. The water supply and sewage system were sources of contamination: "the health of the population is at risk… leakage of sewage into the water supply resulted last year in a severe epidemic of typhoid fever."

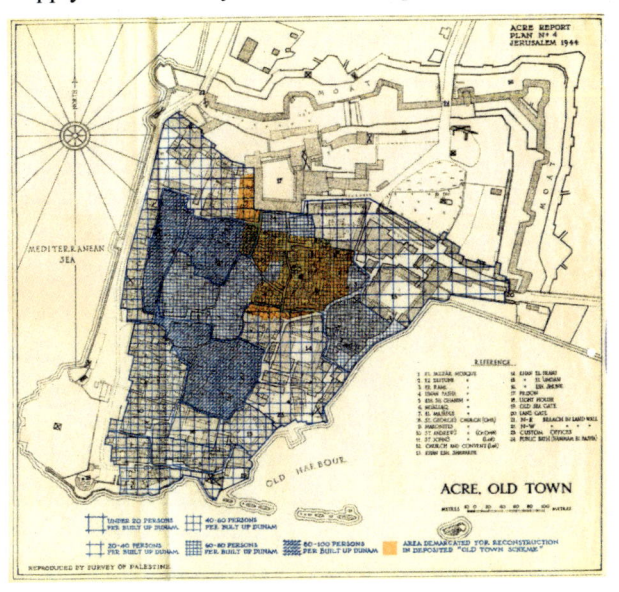

Plan 8: Old Town Report Plan no. 4, Monuments and Population Density, Published in Jerusalem 1944. Source: Israel Antiquities Authority Online Historic Archive.

In 1945, a committee was appointed to discuss Winter's report and make recommendations. The committee proposed conducting an archaeological survey of Acre detailing monuments and sites of historic and architectural value from the Crusader Period to the 19th century. It estimated there were some seven monuments from the Crusader Period and twenty of later date, plus about a dozen private dwellings characteristic of Acre street architecture, but a sizable staff and budget would be necessary for implementation. The Acre Reconstruction Committee of September 5, 1945 recommended beginning with a number of limited but valuable projects to redeem the city's architectural treasures and monuments. A list of "Works Required for Acre Monuments," and a request to establish an Acre Reconstruction Office was submitted, but it was rejected because of lack of funds. Thus, while Winter's survey and recommendations were welcomed, the project could not proceed.[121]

Acre has always been a heterogeneous city in which different ethnicities, religions, and cultures coexisted, similar to the Old City of Jerusalem. During the Mandate, only a few hundred Jews resided in Acre. When the Mandate ended and war broke out, Acre fell to Israeli forces together with all of Western Galilee as early as May 13, 1948. Thousands of Jewish immigrants to the new State of Israel soon joined the remaining Arab inhabitants in the Old City. Acre did not suffer war destruction, but was still badly in need of rehabilitation, as noted in the Mandate report. As Jewish residents gradually moved to newer areas, thousands of poor Arabs from neighboring villages moved into the Old City.

In 1949, Shmuel Yeivin, the first director of the Israeli Department of Antiquities, established an inter-departmental committee to decide on preservation policy in the new state. In its second meeting, it appointed a special sub-committee for Acre and Safed that recommended conservation of the ancient city fabric along with modernization of the interiors of apartments and infrastructure to allow residents a higher standard of living. Façades and monuments were to be rehabilitated and new uses found for them when necessary. Old Acre and Old Safed were to be "nature preserves" surrounded by a green belt, while the new city was to be constructed as a modern city, separate from the old. Not everyone agreed with this approach. For example, D. Levinson of the Tourism Ministry claimed that tourism could only develop if Old Acre were made accessible by development of transportation infrastructure (Fuhrman-Naaman 2008, 55–59).

During the first years of Israeli statehood, planning authorities recognized the value of conserving archaeological and historic sites for two purposes: strengthening national identity through anchoring it to the past, and reaping economic benefits from tourism. The question of Acre was not resolved. How much of the city should be preserved—monuments only, or the entire city fabric? Should Crusader or Ottoman sites take precedence? What should be the relation between the old and new cities? Whose heritage should be preserved, whose stories presented, and from whose point of view? How should planners relate to current residents in developing heritage tourism?

Local politicians in Acre wished to develop the historic city as a tourism center by building new boulevards, erasing the city walls, and modernizing the harbor and promenade. Professionals from the Antiquities Department, however, preferred to follow British policy and keep the Old City a "museum town" (Paz 1998, 123–28). Yeivin emphasized the importance of conserving the ancient city and developing it as an international tourist attraction, especially in light of the fact that Old Jerusalem, the only other city with comparable monuments, was not at that time within Israel's borders.[122]

The entire city's lack of development as an urban center, and the Old City's low socio-economic status and primitive living conditions made creating a major tourist attraction on a shoestring budget almost impossible. Neither were there activists, as in Jaffa, who could influence the future of the Old City. Tours spent a few hours at best in Acre on their way from Haifa to Tel Aviv. This had also been the situation during the Ottoman and Mandate periods (Waterman 1969, 10–15).

According to Fuhrmann-Naaman, an examination of the Israeli Planning Department's treatment of Old Acre shows that it was not given national priority, since its heritage was non-Zionist and non-Jewish (Fuhrman-Naaman 2008, 71). In fact, had there been more motivation to preserve and develop Acre, Jewish heritage could easily have been integrated into the narrative. Acre was an important city on the northern boundary of the Land of (Eretz) Israel in Byzantine and Early Muslim Jewish literature. Under the Crusaders, it was one of the main ports of the Middle East. Nachmanides, one of the most influential rabbis of all times, made Acre his home in the 13th century. Elchanan Reiner, in his discussion of Jewish pilgrimage literature during the Medieval Period, notes, "All the itineraries are circular, beginning and ending at Acre…. [O]ne large circle goes as far as Jerusalem and Hebron, then returning to Acre" (Reiner 2002, 13). Furthermore, the eminent Kabbalist Rabbi Moshe Chaim Luzzato chose to reside in 18th-century Acre, "the port of entry to the Land of Israel." His synagogue in the Old City is designated for renovation as part of the World Heritage Site.

In April 1959, the Department for the Improvement of Landscape established an office for planning Old Acre, headed by architect Alex Kesten. In 1962, he published results of the thorough survey he had carried out: *Acre—the Old City: Survey and Plan*. This served as the basis for the Master Plan that was approved in 1965. Kesten recommended excavation and restoration of Crusader Period structures, even at the expense of conservation of Ottoman-period architecture. Fuhrmann-Naaman notes that the fact that the plan was prepared by the Department for Improvement of Landscape and not by municipal or regional planning authorities shows that Old Acre was considered a "nature preserve" and tourist attraction, not an integral part of the city. Kesten refers to Old Acre as a "monument," in the spirit of the Venice Charter of

1964. However, he makes no mention of the socio-economic aspects of conservation and tourism development— neither of the difficulties, nor of the potential benefits for its inhabitants (Fuhrman-Naaman 2008, 72–84). Most residents of Old Acre were newcomers and unfamiliar with the unique historical, cultural, and architectural heritage of their city, but no effort was made to involve them in conservation or tourism development. Because of its outstanding value as a Crusader and Ottoman-period city, Kesten recommended preservation without modernization, leaving residents to adapt to life in an ancient city or to leave (Kesten 1962, 27). This approach was a direct continuation of Mandatory policy.

In 1966, Israel established the Company for the Development of Old Acre. Architect Dan Tanai, who specialized in planning and preservation of ancient cities and monuments, was chosen to head the planning and development committee. He strongly opposed Kesten's plan for a "museum city" with emphasis on restoration of the Crusader capital. Instead, he proposed planning Acre "as a mixed Jewish-Arab city, conserving its historic sites and ancient atmosphere…including the Jewish history of the city." To Tanai, "the charm of an ancient city lies in its gradual development over the ages, combining many different civilizations and values, and culminating in one harmonious whole." He predicted that Acre would become a bi-level center, with an extensive underground Crusader city underneath the living city from the 18th century to the present (Fuhrman-Naaman 2008, 93–94).

However, from 1967 on, Acre took second place to Jerusalem's Jewish Quarter as a tourist and archaeological attraction. The Kesten and Tanai plans were not implemented for two more decades. This turned out to be a blessing, as the Crusader city buried underground was not excavated until the 1990s and was thus saved from both the deterioration and the development that were the fate of so many historic centers during the 20th century. Meanwhile, the physical and socio-economic condition of Old Acre's residential neighborhood continued to deteriorate.

In January 2000, Israel signed the World Heritage Charter, obligating preservation and presentation of heritage to the coming generations. In 2001, UNESCO declared Acre a World Heritage Site. In its decision, UNESCO emphasized the following criteria:

1. The Old City is exceptional in the manner in which significant remains of Crusader structures are preserved beneath the Moslem Ottoman city that itself dates from the 18th and 19th century.

2. The remains from the Crusader period in the Old City, which are on and below the level of today's living city, provide an extraordinary picture of the urban structure and organization of the Crusader Kingdom of Jerusalem of the Middle Ages.

3. The present-day Old City is an outstanding example of a walled Ottoman city that includes the typical functional urban structures such as a fortress, mosques, inns (khans), and a preserved bathhouse, built upon the remains of Crusader structures.[123]

At the same time, work began on a new outline plan for Old Acre, one that would combine tourism development with urban rehabilitation, and concentrate on the city aboveground rather than on Crusader sites not yet excavated (Fuhrman-Naaman 2008, 13). Architect Arie Rahamimov's outline plan is based upon ICOMOS Washington Charter on the Conservation of Historic Towns and Urban Areas of 1987, and combines global, multi-ethnic values with national Jewish ones (Fuhrman-Naaman 2008, 26–28).

Figure 35: Cannons on the city wall. Source: Alexander Dvorak, Acre Visitors Center, 2006.

Figure 36: Crusader dining hall in restored Hospitaller complex. Source: Alexander Dvorak, Acre Visitors Center, 2005.

Today, the total population of Acre is 47,500, of whom only 10 percent live in the Old City. Only about 25 percent of greater Acre's population is Arab, but 95 percent of Old Acre is Arab. The city was intended to become a commercial and industrial center for the northern part of Israel, but has remained a relatively unimportant and underdeveloped urban area, serving as a regional center for small Jewish and Arab villages nearby (Waterman 1969).[124] Haifa is the commercial and industrial center of northern Israel, and Nahariya is the resort center.

Old Acre still looks much as it did in the 18th and 19th centuries—narrow winding alleyways, mosques, khans as small strip-malls, market streets, and small traditional workshops, surrounded by the new modern city. Acre may also serve as a model for joint development of ancient (pre-1700) and historic (post-1700) sites: For example, Bedouin Sheikh Daher al-Umar built the Acre Prison on the remains of the Crusader Hospitaller Citadel. During the Ottoman period, Al-Jazzar Pasha (Governor) restored the site as a palace, a government house, and a military camp. Under the British Mandate, (1917–1948), it served as a maximum-security prison where Jewish underground fighters were jailed and subsequently executed. On May 4, 1947, the IZL (National Military Organization) launched an attack on the Acre fortress, freeing twenty of their comrades and hundreds of other Jewish and Arab prisoners in what was called the "greatest jail break in history." After 1948, Acre's prison became a hospital for the mentally ill. In 2007, the site was converted into the Underground Prisoners Museum and integrated into the tourism route of Crusader and Ottoman monuments (Ben Solomon, *Jerusalem Post*, 28 Mar. 2013).[125]

For the first time since the establishment of the state, a residential quarter has undergone rehabilitation and conservation in Old Acre. The Israel Antiquities Authority and the Old Acre Development Company, in cooperation with the Israel Lands Administration, initiated the Old City's rehabilitation and conservation in 2001. The quarter, containing 250 occupied apartments, was selected as a national pilot for determining criteria regarding the conservation, rehabilitation, and rebuilding of historic urban fabrics while safeguarding their residential, commercial, and tourism functions. The residents' participation in the rehabilitation, conservation and maintenance processes was also emphasized, aiming to create a sense of belonging and obligation to the place and an awareness of its value. It is hoped that this will aid official bodies in maintaining the city at a proper level of conservation.[126]

The Western Galilee College in Acre is an independent accredited academic institution, offering the only B.A. program in conservation in Israel. Due to the College's geographic location and its close relationship with the city and its residents, it emphasizes conservation of buildings and monuments in Old Acre.[127] In coordination with UNESCO, the International Conservation Center Città di Roma was also established in Acre in 2005. It is Israel's premier institute of technical conservation and historic preservation, and serves as a living laboratory for researchers, students, and emerging professionals from Israel and abroad, providing them with unrivaled hands-on conservation experience and field work together with the Israel Antiquities Authority. Other programs feature Acre's rich cultural heritage and encourage economic development for the city's residents.[128]

Acre is a good example of a historic city whose economic base rests upon tourism development, concomitant to preservation of its authenticity and sensitivity, to the limits of sustainable development, and to the needs and involvement of the local population. Great efforts have been made to create a partnership between the Company for the Development of Old Acre, the Antiquities Authority, the Municipality, Israel Lands Development Authority, and the Israeli Government Tourism Company, aiming to improve the quality of life of the local population and to create the infrastructure for economic development of heritage tourism. To date, all profits of the development companies have been ploughed back into further projects, increasing the number of festivals, hotels, and attractions in the area.[129] Residents are encouraged not to "sell out" to gentrification, but rather to develop their own commercial and tourism services in the spirit of Old Acre, and to preserve the ethnic and cultural mix that characterizes the city today.

Safed

Safed is an ancient city built upon three steep hills in Northern Israel, and dating back to the Bronze Age. It was called "the key to the Galilee," as it controls the road connecting Acre on the Mediterranean to the Sea of Galilee. The Crusaders built an exceptionally large and important walled fortress on Mt. Safed hilltop in 1103. Surrounding it on the slopes was the residential area of the city. Mamluk Baybars captured the fortress in 1266, and he made it his capital in Galilee.

In the 16th century, under the Ottoman Empire, Safed became a gathering place for many great Jewish thinkers and poets who had been expelled from Spain in 1492. Their teachings and those of their students greatly influenced Judaism throughout the ages. Even today, the city is steeped in the heritage of the sacred literature and poetry of these great Jewish philosophers and mystics. Safed was the spiritual and physical center of Jewish life in Israel from the 16th until the mid-19th centuries, and one of the four holy cities (Jerusalem, Hebron, Safed, and Tiberias) in Jewish tradition. Even today, pilgrims flock to the graves of illustrious religious and communal 16th century leaders, among them Rabbis Isaac Luria (the Holy Ari), Yosef Karo, Moshe Alsheikh, and Shlomo Alkabetz; their legendary synagogues still serve as spiritual centers today. Even Safed's architectural heritage sheds light on its illustrious past.

Safed saw many ups and downs. It is estimated that 13,000 people lived in Safed in the 16th century, about half of them Jews. In the Ottoman period, Safed's Jewish community was the largest in Israel, but then suffered heavy losses from earthquakes in 1759 and in 1822. A decade later, in 1837, another earthquake caused massive destruction and a death toll of thousands. This and local violence caused many of the survivors to relocate to Jerusalem, and the Jewish community shrank to about 1,000 (Wilson 1847, 154–55). The city gradually revived, but World War I brought another crisis, and the Jewish population again declined sharply. According to a census conducted in 1922 by British Mandate authorities, Safed had a population of 8,761, of whom 5,431 were Muslims, 2,986 Jews, and 343 Christians and others.[130]

Figure 37: Old postcard of Safed, general view. Source: unknown.

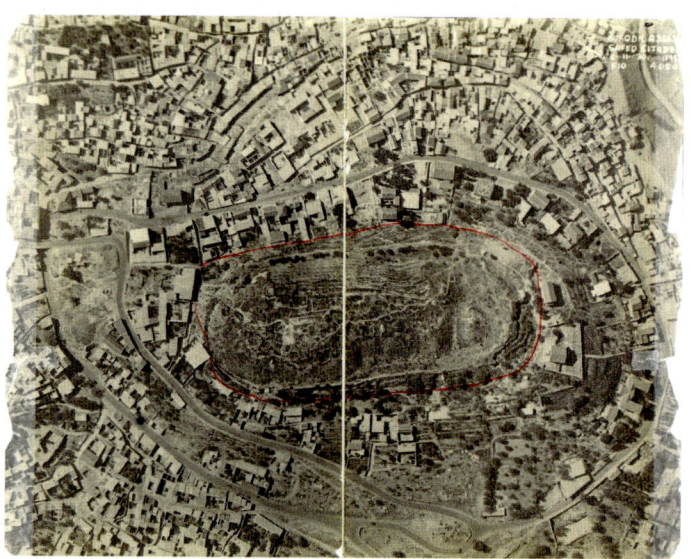

Figure 38: Aerial view of the Safed Citadel and Old City, ca. 1930. Source: Israel Antiquities Authority Historic Archive.

Situated on a mountaintop in the Northern Galilee, its refreshing air and inspiring landscape made Safed a favorite resort site from the Mandate period and on. Hotels and tourism were the main financial resource of both Jews and Arabs in Safed, despite the Arab-Jewish conflict, lack of security, lack of basic modern infrastructure such as water and electricity, adequate roads, and employment opportunities.[131]

Nevertheless, it remained the central town of Upper Galilee, surrounded by Jewish, Circassian, Bedouin, Druze, and Arab agricultural villages who depended upon its services. In 1944, Safed's population was almost 12,000, of whom 80 percent were Muslims and 16 percent Jews, with a few hundred Christians, Bahais, and others. By the 1948 census, the Jewish population had declined to only about 12 percent, or 1,600 Jewish residents, alongside 12,000 Arabs (Abbasi 1999).

Unlike in Acre, the Mandate Department of Antiquities showed little interest in Crusader and Mamluk Safed. The Safed Castle, as it was called, was described thus by Antiquities Inspector Makhouly:

> Safed Castel is believed to have been built...about 1140.... The sides are steep and between their summit and the final ascent to the top of the mound are the remains of a moat. Except for the citadel at the south end, now only a large mound of concrete, the fortress at the present day merely consists of a large grass covered mound with a few shapeless masses of concrete sticking out at wide intervals. Not a single facing stone remains, which is explained by the statement of Guerin that some of it was being taken away daily at the time of his visit (c. 1870), that it served as a quarry for the inhabitants of the city. There is now nothing left to save.[132]

Another British document states that the medieval castle was mostly destroyed in earthquakes of 1759 and 1837, and current remains are of the comparatively poor work of Dahar al-Umar who dominated the Galilee earlier in the century.

> Almost all the well-cut masonry above the surface has been carted off...but everywhere below the surface, the remains of the earlier buildings may be found. A thorough excavation of this site would be of undoubted interest... [The Castle is an] "asset of great archaeological importance, and of high potential value as an attraction to visitors and tourists."

However, instead of conducting excavations, and despite its legal status as British government property, the site was fenced with barbed wire by the agriculture department and treated as a forest preserve. "The trees planted by Agriculture Dept. are growing now into a thick forest, so all masonry remains are hidden from sight and disfigured."[133]

There were still visible remains of the moats and water cisterns. In the 1930s, the Jewish National Fund offered to buy half of the property to build new housing, but the offer was refused. Other "neighbors" attempted to use the cisterns as reservoirs and to destroy parts of a wall and use the stones, but were stopped by the Antiquities Department. Various government departments were involved in plans for the Castle area, and even the High Commissioner was involved, but funds were scarce and nothing concrete was accomplished. Only on 10 June 1947 at the 27th Meeting of the Galilee District Building and Town Planning Commission was an outline town planning scheme for Safed drawn.[134] Henry Kendall, Government Town Planner, was involved in composing the scheme. Handwritten on a 1948 report is a request from Antiquities Inspector N. Makhouly to young archaeologist Michael AviYonah to transfer the following monuments [using the English transliteration done by Makhouly] to the Town Plans, and confirmation by AviYonah that he had done so.

1. Qal'at Safad (Castle)
2. Maqheret Banat Ya'coub (Tombs)
3. Zaiviyah Banat Hamid (Tombs within Mamluke Building) [Zawiya – Islamic Sufi lodge and monastery]
4. Jami'el Ahmer (Al-Ahmar Mosque)
5. el Qaisariyeh (Medieval caravansery)
6. Sheikh Ni'mah (Moslem shrine)
7. 'Ain en Nayim (An old wall with a thick arch sheltering a small outlet through which water out of a weak spring pours) ['Ain — spring].

George Hamilton, Mandatory Director of Antiquities, asked to make proposals concerning certain monuments. In addition, the Palestine Exploration Fund issued frequent reports on antiquities in the region, generally Arabic architecture and inscriptions from the Middle Ages. Interestingly, not one historic Jewish site is mentioned, although the existence of the ancient cemetery and synagogues must surely have been known to the authorities. It may be because Safed's Jewish population at that time was small and poor.

In 1945, the Company for the Development of Safed was founded, headed by Moshe Pedatzur, later to become Safed's first Israeli mayor. The Jewish National Fund, the Histadrut Workers' Union, the Sollel Boneh building company and others initiated and supported projects such as enlarging the electricity supply of the city, establishing and supporting industrial and commercial initiatives, increasing the city's Jewish population, land acquisition and construction of buildings and roads (Abbasi 1999, 146–49).

Israeli forces captured Safed in 1948, and most of its Arab population left the city. As in Acre and Jaffa, European and Middle Eastern immigrants moved into vacant apartments. In the 1950s, Safed's Mayor Moshe Pedatzur established an artists' colony in abandoned houses in the former Arab section of the Old City. As in Acre, most of the physical degeneration of the Old City was due to natural causes, rather than to the war. The Municipality attempted to conserve and develop the Old City on an inadequate budget and with limited success. About a third of its houses were still in need of serious renovation in 1986 (Lichfield and Schweid 1986).

Nevertheless, Safed's artist-residents included some of the foremost talents of those days. Safed's spirituality and physical beauty made it a popular vacation spot during the 1950s, 1960s and early 1970s. Then, as in Acre, restoration and development of post-1967 Jerusalem led to a decrease in tourism and pilgrimage to Safed.

Population growth was slow and by 1983, Safed's population was less than 16,000. Today, its population has grown to 35,000.[135] That is 15,000 fewer than Acre today, and less than the population of Jerusalem's one-square-kilometer Old City.[136] Less than 4,000 people live in Safed's Old City. Even today, most Safed residents earn much less than the national average, and less than half of those who finish high school are eligible to go on to college. It is estimated that 45% of Safed's residents received welfare aid from the Municipality in 2011. In 2016, the mayor announced that the city would receive additional financial aid after publication of the statistics on Safed's low socio-economic status.[137]

The Municipality and NGOs have recently begun projects to promote Safed's economic and social well-being, such as adding more industry and educational institutions. In 2011, Bar Ilan University opened a medical school affiliated with Ziv regional hospital. Safed Academic College is a rapidly growing public college located at the gateway to the historic city. Originally an extension of Bar-Ilan University, it was granted independent accreditation by Israel's Council of Higher Education in 2007.[138] Safed Academic College not only grants a bachelor's degree in various professions, but also encourages volunteer programs advancing urban renewal and new technologies. Its campus is situated in two preserved and restored historic landmarks: The first, known today as Bussel Home, was originally built in 1904 by the Templer architect Gottlieb Schumacher as a British Mission hospital run by Dr. Walter Henry Anderson. As in Jerusalem, the London Association for the Promotion of Christianity among Jews (London Jews' Society) offered free medical care to the city's Jewish population as the basis for its missionary activities. A competing Jewish institution was founded nearby in 1910, the Rothschild-Hadassah Hospital. This was the main Jewish hospital until 1934. After a large regional hospital was established, the Rothschild-Hadassah Hospital served as a tuberculosis ward, then a maternity hospital and so on, until it was sold to Safed College at the beginning of the 21st century.

Meanwhile, the Mission hospital functioned until World War I, when the Ottoman army took it over. In 1922, it was sold to the Scottish Mission and served as a multi-ethnic school. In 1943, it was acquired by the Jewish National Fund and turned into a convalescent home named after Yosef Bussel. Recently, the college acquired the Bussel Home complex and is planning to conserve and rebuild it as part of its campus, including a library, auditorium, cafeteria, and medical center. It is very proud of the rich heritage embodied in its modern campus, which serves the Jewish, Muslim, Druze, Bedouin, Circassian, and Christian population of Galilee today (Har Noy and Giladi 2016, 119–26).

In 2002, the Israel Antiquities Authority Conservation Department, the Safed Municipality, and Project Renewal of the Ministry of Housing began preservation and restoration of several historic synagogues. The oldest synagogue in Safed is the 14th-century Sephardic Ari Synagogue. Tradition attributes it to the Holy Ari himself, as well as to the prophet Elijah. It was severely damaged in the 1759 and 1837 earthquakes but subsequently rebuilt. From 1990– 2005 the IAA together with the synagogue's directorate has carried out various restoration projects, but there is still much work to be done.

As recorded above, the Ottoman fortress built upon the Safed Citadel ruins was destroyed in the earthquake of 1837, and stones from the site were freely taken for secondary construction. Excavations from 1980 and after by the Israel Antiquities Authority have uncovered one of the three largest Crusader fortresses of Israel, with Mamluk and Ottoman remains as well. Visitor paths and signs were installed in the surrounding garden during 2001–2007.[139] There is a lookout point from which visitors can view the lake of Tiberias, Mount Hermon, Mount Meiron, and Safed's hilly surroundings. A recording also recalls Safed's military history during the 1948 war.

No comprehensive plan has yet been developed for conservation and tourism in Safed. The Interior Ministry, the Municipality, IAA, and other bodies are working on a comprehensive plan, but so far, all projects have been piecemeal. Meanwhile, individual homeowners and entrepreneurs have taken the initiative in renovating old buildings on their own, often very successfully. The IAA and others hope to found a conservation center in Safed similar to that in Acre, and to employ students in field work on local projects (Kislev interview 2016; Hillman to Slae 2016).

The first Israeli Outline Scheme 552 for Safed was composed in 1962, before enactment of the Planning and Construction Law of 1965,

> to ensure preservation of its unique architectural character ... and to safeguard its panoramic scenery, both because of the city's sanctity and its national significance, and in order to develop it as a tourism and vacation center....

Restrictions were placed on building height, and new construction was allowed in stone only, in conformity with the architectural style of the neighborhood.[140] However, these instructions were not detailed, and had no mechanism for enforcement.

In 1978, architects Ora and Ya'akov Ya'ar prepared Outline Scheme #1698 for the Old City of Safed as part of scheme #1697 for the whole city. This plan was based on scheme #552 and reiterated its goals: Preservation and enhancement of historic, religious, and architectural values, development of tourism attractions through renovation of old buildings, removal of harmful additions, new building where possible and necessary, improvement of pedestrian and motor accessibility and of underground infrastructure. Historic, architecturally outstanding, and holy sites fall under the authority of the Antiquities Department. The Ari Synagogue in particular must be preserved and developed. A representative of the Antiquities Department would also participate in the Preservation and Development Committee of the Regional Planning Committee. Here too, the goals are clear, but there was neither an official list of sites to be preserved nor binding legal restrictions. In addition, no financial sources or implementation mechanisms existed.

The latest outline scheme, composed in 2013, attempts to be more specific. For the first time, it directs planning authorities to compile a documented list of sites to be preserved, and to abide by instructions including restrictions on the height of new buildings. It requires new construction to be environmentally friendly and approved by an architect and by the regional planning committee.

A number of projects are underway by individual NGOs and public-private partnerships: One of the most ambitious is the Landmarks Project for renovating Beit Hakahal. On October 30, 2011, the Israeli Government designated a 16th-century ruin in Safed a National Heritage Site, part of the Prime Minister's Office plan to establish a series of heritage sites and routes throughout the country. The 700-square-meter site, in the heart of the city's ancient Jewish Quarter, is owned and operated by Livnot U'Lehibanot (To Build and Be Built), a non-profit educational institution. Livnot conducts educational programs, volunteer excavation and renovation projects, and other activities to connect Jewish youth from around the world to their heritage, strengthening their Jewish identity through experiential learning and hands-on restoration. It is rebuilding the "Kahal"—a 16th-century series of old structures, communal areas, underground rooms and crawlspaces that had been buried by earthquakes in the 18th and 19th centuries. Livnot plans to establish an interactive learning center for all ages, with musicians and actors in period costumes. The Israeli government is participating in the restoration of the site with matching funds. Ultimately, the goal is to transform Safed into a UNESCO World Heritage Site.

Figure 39: Artistic rendering of the Kahal site. Source: Livnot U'Lehibanot.

The Municipality and the Antiquities Authority have initiated another unique project called "Conservation Trustees for the City of Safed." In essence, the aim of this heritage project is to increase community awareness of the city's rich past and to build a team of residents who are committed to heritage conservation. This group cooperates with organizations working for the preservation of the heritage of Old Safed. Another goal is to promote a process of dialogue between residents and government authorities of Safed's Old City regarding the city's future.[141]

Although Safed has a mixed Jewish-Arab population, most of its historic and religious sites are uniquely Jewish and Israeli, and its cultural heritage more national than universal. In addition, it is less motor accessible than Jerusalem, Jaffa, or even Acre. Despite its rich Jewish heritage, picturesque architecture, and beautiful scenery, Old Safed is still part of a city on the periphery, waiting for massive investment and renewal of its cultural, religious, national and architectural heritage. Since conservation techniques have improved so much in the last decades, it may be to Safed's advantage that conservation of the city was delayed for so many years.

To sum up, Israel today is making efforts to apply the lessons learned and to carry out intensive preservation and development of Acre, Safed, Nazareth, Lod, and other historic cities in Israel. Surveys are being taken, outline schemes are being drawn up, and alternatives for administrative, technical, and economic management of the programs are being examined, based on Israel's experience in Acre and other sites. Gentrification through "compensation and relocation" is no longer considered proper practice. All over the world, neighborhoods are being renewed not only physically, but also socio-economically, by helping the local population raise their standard of living and improve their living conditions with the aid of voluntary organizations. Preservation policy aims to inculcate heritage values in the residents as a means of motivating them to participate in efforts to preserve their historic neighborhood (Fitch 1990). The Company for the Development of Old Acre is using this approach today in renovation of Crusader and Ottoman-period architecture in the old city. A comparison of the approach taken in the renovation of Old Jaffa in the 1960s with the renovation of Old Acre from the 1990s and after illustrates the social gains that may be achieved through preservation, and the mutual influence of communal and tourism gains.

Post War Reconstruction and Politics

In Old Jaffa, wartime destruction by the British led to erasure of Arab neighborhoods and to modernization. Along with the pre-1948 structures, Arab heritage in the form of street names, monuments, and the traditional population also disappeared. The newly founded State of Israel continued this destruction and modernization while at the same time beginning its first preservation efforts. When Israel decided upon neighborhood renewal and conservation of Old Jaffa, its motivation was both commercial and political. Those who benefitted most from the renewal were artists and others who replaced the local population. Today, with the rise in real estate, great efforts are being invested in systematic exploration, renovation, preservation, and at the same time, modernization and development of Old Jaffa and its surrounding areas. Some of these are private entrepreneurial projects, such as the Andromeda gated housing project. A most recent one to be mentioned is a new boutique hotel market house that opened in 2017 in the old building of the *kishle* (the Ottoman prison and later police station) (https://www.atlas.co.il/heb/market-house-tel-aviv). Others, such as renewal of the Jaffa Port and Clock Tower Square, are municipal. How many local inhabitants will benefit has yet to be seen.

In the Old City of Jerusalem, the situation is much more complicated. No other historic city core is as densely populated, and no other is divided into "quarters" according to ethnic group. It is also unique in that only the Jewish Quarter was destroyed in wartime. The other three quarters have simply deteriorated over the centuries.

The Christian population has been decreasing since the 1980s, and is probably no more than 5,000 today. The Muslim population has increased to about 28,000, and the Jewish population to about 4,000, of whom about a quarter live in the Muslim and Christian Quarters. In addition, there are some 2,000 students in Jewish educational institutions throughout the Old City. (These numbers are approximations based on Choshen and Korach 2009, 120–40; Glass and Khamaisi 2007, 3). Outside of the Jewish Quarter, the population is economically and socially weak and much of the housing substandard. The southern section of the Muslim Quarter has a density of almost 100 persons per dunam, one of the highest in the world, and even the Jewish Quarter has a density of almost 20 persons per dunam, compared to 5.4 in the rest of Jerusalem. This does not include small hostels, hotels, B&B, or dormitories. About 6,000 households inhabit 5,000 housing units, most of the overcrowding being in the poorer areas of the Muslim Quarter (Glass and Khamaisi 2007, 11-14).

Muslim and Christian public bodies do not recognize Jerusalem's status as the capital of the State of Israel, and the Israeli government has chosen not to force the issue. Nevertheless, noteworthy improvements in infrastructure have been carried out recently by government agencies such as the Jerusalem Development Company and the Company for the Development of East Jerusalem. These include making the streets of all four quarters wheelchair accessible, cleaning and restoring Hezekiah's Pool, improved garbage disposal methods, awnings and street coverings, cleaning of medieval arches and renewal of air vents in the covered market streets. The *Waqf* has renovated its Mamluk edifices on Iron Gate Street, two Hamams (bathouses) adjoining the Temple Mount–Haram al-Sharif, and private dwellings all over the Muslim Quarter. The UN Development Program has also been involved in restoring the Goldsmiths' Market and residential apartments in East Jerusalem. No matter who has sponsored the work, the Israel Antiquities Authority is authorized to approve and supervise all renovation projects of ancient structures. This has led to a serious reduction in illegal construction (Meitav interview 2017).

Since the beginning of the 21st century, NGOs based in the Middle East, Europe, and Turkey, in cooperation with the Jerusalem *Waqf* and the UN, have tried to take the place of Israeli government conservation and renovation of the Muslim Quarter. Over the past two decades, they have invested millions of dollars in rehabilitation of ancient Crusader, Mamluk, and Turkish structures and holy sites, in particular those on or surrounding the Temple Mount–Haram al-Sharif. Large sums of money have also been expended on much-needed social, health, and welfare projects in these areas.[142] Some of these projects have been carried out in coordination with the Jerusalem *Waqf*, who owns most of the property. These actions are political in nature, but do aid in the preservation and restoration of religious, historic, and architectural treasures. Although these programs discuss the urgent need to decrease the Muslim residential population, no practical steps have been taken for political reasons.

The Report on the Socio-Economic Conditions in the Old City of Jerusalem plainly states:

It is clear to both the Palestinian population and the Israeli authorities that there are too many people living in the Old City, and the situation is not conducive for the inhabitants and is harming many structures of historical significance (Glass and Khamaisi 2007, 24). "Along with overcrowding, the Old City, including the Jewish Quarter, does not have a firm economic base...The taxes collected directly in the Old City from its residents and its enterprises are insufficient to provide the necessary level of services for the well-being of the resident population, the security of the residents and visitors, and the maintenance of the physical infrastructure...." (Glass and Khamaisi 2007, 30). "Despite the importance of the Old City as a magnet for millions of tourists... [it] is an economic engine which benefits the rest of the city...." (Glass and Khamaisi 2007, 32).

The same may be said of the old cities of Acre and Safed. This is exactly what Ashworth and Tunbridge described in their seminal work on *The Tourist Historic City* (1990, 25–30; see Introduction above).

Modernization, Reconstruction, or Preservation

Was modernization or preservation of the historic city cores the consequence of planning or did it "just happen?" It appears to be a combination of the two; each city has its own unique history. The process of modernization of old cities began at the end of the Ottoman period in Jaffa and Jerusalem. In general, the more important the city, the greater the modernization. Only in Jaffa and Acre did the modernization allow for at least partial motor accessibility. In Old Jerusalem and Safed, the infrastructure has been renewed, but the narrow alleyways are for pedestrians only. Today, small electric vehicles have come into use for residents' needs.

Even in Acre, along with modernization came limited conservation. Acre's historical heritage narrative was appreciated by Mandatory town planners, and a town plan prescribing preservation was drawn up, but the city was poor and run down. The new town was modernized, but there were insufficient funding or motivation for preservation and rehabilitation of the old, especially when it became clear that the days of the Mandate were limited. In 1948, Acre did not suffer wartime destruction and therefore was not in need of consequent rebuilding. The population did change several times, but each time, only the weaker elements remained in the Old City. Throughout, Old Acre remained a poverty stricken area.

Decades later, as a World Heritage Site, resources have enabled its systematic exploration, planning, development, and preservation. The old city's heritage narrative has basically remained the same, with emphasis on its architectural and historical values. In keeping with modern approaches to heritage development, much effort is invested today in educating and involving local residents, and in sharing economic, tourism, and cultural benefits with them.

Safed too did not suffer wartime destruction nor benefit from postwar reconstruction. In the 19th and early 20th centuries, earthquakes wreaked havoc on the older neighborhoods, and the Jewish population decreased sharply. Under the Mandate, Safed was a predominately Arab city with obvious ruins from the Crusader period and on, but not so promising as to attract resources for research, excavation and renovation as a heritage site. During the 1948 War, much of Safed's Arab population fled and was replaced by Jewish immigrants. An artist's quarter was established in the former Arab quarter, thus conserving and renovating a small number of ancient buildings. Modernization was almost non-existent, thus allowing de facto conservation of the ancient built environment still existing today.

The Old City of Jerusalem underwent limited modernization at the end of the Ottoman period. However, British Mandate planners were careful to prevent any modernization or change in its "Biblical", Oriental heritage narrative. This led much of its Jewish population to move to new "Jewish Jerusalem." During and following the 1948 War, extensive destruction and desecration of Jewish national and religious monuments in the Jewish Quarter occurred. There is no parallel to this ruination anywhere else in Israel, just as there is no parallel to the symbolic importance of Jerusalem in Jewish collective identity. Likewise, there is no parallel to the Israeli government decision in 1967 to rebuild and repopulate the Jewish Quarter.

Especially striking are the differences in guiding principles regarding local residents. Today, conservation authorities in Acre make every effort to retain and to educate and involve local residents in their work. In Safed, the local residents themselves have initiated and carried out preservation and heritage development, often without any governmental intervention or supervision. In Jaffa, according to City Building Plan 606, not only was a special committee including artists involved in planning and development, they also decided who would be privileged to live in the renovated city core—no one but artists and people in related professions. This made Jaffa a ghost town with few young families and children. The streets were empty and even the galleries often closed. The fact that it was not a residential neighborhood meant that it had fewer services and attractions for both residents and tourists. In contrast, the Jewish Quarter was rebuilt as a residential neighborhood with a small but significant population and accompanying services.

Luckily for Old Jerusalem in 1967, and for Safed and Acre today, maintaining a lively residential neighborhood has had high priority from the very beginning of development efforts in these cities. As already mentioned, both Old Jaffa and Jerusalem's Jewish Quarter are surrounded by slum areas. Aside from the need for neighborhood renewal for its own sake, these slum areas imprison the quarter in the heart of a hostile neighborhood. Today, there are large scale development projects for both Jaffa and Old Jerusalem that will hopefully make a difference.[143]

During the British Mandate, efforts were made to preserve the Old Cities of Jerusalem and Acre as medieval cities. Little was done regarding other ancient cities, and in Jaffa serious damage was done to parts of the Old City. During the first years of the State of Israel, planners and conservators followed the British model, including preference for Crusader Acre over Ottoman Acre as the dominant heritage narrative. In fact, renovation and development of Old Acre actually began only recently, at the end of the 20th century. It is propelled by Acre's recognition as a World Heritage Site, and by the involvement of international conservation institutions in the city. Renovation and development of old Safed is also just gaining speed now, at the beginning of the 21st century. In this case, much of the development has come from NGOs and private initiatives rather than from comprehensive municipal or national planning and investment. The Academic College of Safed is one of the most active players in revitalizing Safed, both the local community and its heritage sites. In Acre, institutions of higher education, particularly in the field of conservation, play a prominent role in heritage development. However, as in the Old City of Jerusalem four decades ago, policy determination and implementation are still centralized under the Antiquities Authority, Interior Ministry, Tourism Ministry and its subsidiary companies, and the Municipality. Community involvement in policymaking and in planning is still minimal. Only in Safed is heritage development still largely a private initiative.

Compared to European cities, and even more so to American cities, Israel lacks the involvement and initiatives of private and voluntary organizations. There is as yet only a limited entrepreneurial approach to heritage development through education and through the media, or involvement of the local community. Heritage development in Old Jaffa, on the other hand, is part of the gentrification and increased real estate value of the neighborhood. Examination of heritage conservation and development of these ancient cities has illustrated three very different patterns that have developed over the past half-century: Jerusalem is the most extreme case of governmental involvement and of selective renewal, as well as geo-political and religious sensitivity. Jaffa is economically the most promising neighborhood for gentrification. Acre is the focus of international development and cooperation. Safed has the least economic potential, accessibility, and universal appeal, and this has slowed its development. Hopefully, its natural beauty, unique built environment, and rich Jewish heritage will provide the necessary foundation for its development as a vibrant heritage site.

Chapter VI
Middle Eastern and European Cities

Each historic city is a world of its own. No less than human beings, each city has a physical expression and a character of its own. The historic Israeli city cores discussed in the last chapter share much common history, geography, culture, and architectural features. A closer look at their renovation over the past sixty years has highlighted the uniqueness of each one, and the changes in approach to its conservation and development over the years. Comparison of Jerusalem's Old City to other historic city cores in the Middle East and in the Western World is a prodigious challenge and beyond the scope of this book. However, a limited examination of certain key facets of conservation and development is possible.

Cairo

Unlike Old Jerusalem, Beirut and Warsaw, Old Cairo did not suffer war destruction. Nevertheless, comparison of its problems and possible solutions with those of Old Jerusalem can be quite enlightening. Despite the obvious differences between Old Cairo and the Old City of Jerusalem, such as size, particular heritage, spatial characteristics, and climate, they have much in common. Jerusalem's Old City is built upon 4,000 years of Canaanite, Jewish, Roman, Byzantine, Early Muslim, Crusader, Mamluk, and Ottoman rule. Historic Cairo is built upon the remnants of Roman fortifications, early Christian and Coptic sites, previous non-Muslim cultures such as the ancient city of Fustat, and a 9th-century Jewish neighborhood containing the Ben Ezra Synagogue.[144] The Muslim walled city of Cairo was built in 979 as the palace city of the Fatimid dynasty. It developed organically as a Muslim center of religion, learning, and commerce over some 1,300 years under successive Fatimid, Abbasid, Ayyubid, Mamluk and Ottoman rules. Today it is home to the largest collection of Islamic monuments in the world.[145] Likewise, in Old Jerusalem, the number and variety of religious institutions that served the community in its heyday are unparalleled. The visible Old City of Jerusalem of today is primarily composed of Mamluk and Ottoman period structures, some of which are strikingly similar to their Egyptian counterparts.

The beginning of the processes of modernization began during the conquest and rule of Muhammed Ali between 1831–1841 (Shamir 1986, 138–58). Mohammed Ali's rise to power in 1805 brought about a drastic change in Egypt's development. He introduced reforms in the political, military, and administrative systems, and began to develop a new economy based on European culture and technology. Modernization and a steep increase in population led to the creation of a "new city" to the north and west of the old walled city. Modern technology, European culture, education, and architecture made the new city flourish economically and culturally. As noted previously, Muhammed Ali's rule in Palestine also ushered in an era of unprecedented growth for Jerusalem.

The old walled cities with narrow convoluted lanes and inadequate access roads were too insulated and unfit for a modern way of life. This led to a population shift in which the wealthier residents left the core to the poor and unemployed. Both urban decay and population density increased gradually in the old city. Under Mohammed Ali's grandson and successor Ismail Pasha, Greater Cairo expanded further and was split socially and functionally between the old and the new. The new was "westernized" while the old was neglected and crowded. In both Cairo and Jerusalem, historic city cores that had once been central commercial, religious, and national hubs with exceptionally rich heritage, gradually suffered decline and destruction to the point of becoming almost irrelevant to the modernization taking place all around them.

In 1881, as part of Egypt's modernization, a Committee for Ancient Monuments was founded, patterned after western models of preservation instruments. It drew up a list of 800 relics and monuments in Cairo to be preserved. These came under the ownership of the Committee, but the endowments intended to provide for their financial support remained in the hands of the Waqf council (administration of Islamic endowments). Meanwhile, municipal town planners did their best to knock down all projecting balconies, straighten all bends, and impose a modern rectangular order upon the city (Nasser 2000, 251–69).

In 1882, Britain invaded the Suez Canal Zone and seized military control of Egypt. However, the country officially remained a part of the (enemy) Ottoman Empire until the outbreak of World War I in 1914, when Britain proclaimed Egypt a protectorate. In 1952, seventy years after the British invasion, the Free Officers, a military group led by Col. Gamal Abdel Nasser, toppled the monarchy, ousted the British, and established a centralized socialist nationalist government. Thus, both Israel and Egypt were under British control until they became independent states several years after the end of World War II.

Figure 40: Street scene in Cairo, 1934. Matson Collection, Library of Congress, Washington, D.C.

Until then, most public buildings, philanthropic, religious and educational institutions in Muslim cities had depended on the institution of *waqf* ("perpetual charity," pl. *awqaf*) for their construction and maintenance (Barnes 1987, 45–49; Papasthatis and Kark 2016, 264–82).[146] This institution is an important feature of Muslim religion, culture, and law. A property may be irrevocably donated to charity, and all its revenues earmarked for charitable purposes. Other than a prohibition against selling the property, the donor of the *waqf* could make any rules he saw fit regarding its governance. The dedicated asset could be used to provide revenue for specific benefit to society (education, health, charity to the poor), or it itself could be dedicated to serve public or private interests. A common feature among all historic Muslim cities is indeed the dedication of a huge share of the real estate and agricultural lands as *waqf* (Nour 2012, 42). The purpose of the endowment was to help the local community or to maintain culturally significant public institutions. Rigid *waqf* property laws protected the fragmentation of land and the change of land usage, inhibiting the application of traditional patterns of Islamic inheritance and the subsequent subdivision of land parcels. Thus, the institution of *waqf* preserved plot patterns and land usage to a great degree. However, the mechanism of *istibdal* allowed exchange of one property for another should it become necessary for financial reasons. Once a *waqf* was exchanged for another asset, the previous property became open to redevelopment.

In Egypt, Nasser concentrated all *awqaf* properties under a central national authority, divesting the *waqf* institution of most of its powers. In 1953, the government created the Egyptian Antiquities Organization within the Ministry of Culture and transferred to it the functions of the Committee for Ancient Monuments. Instead of being maintained and preserved by the private religious sector or by the Committee, historic structures came under the jurisdiction of the Ministry of Culture. This later became the Supreme Council of Antiquities (SCA) (Williams 2001–2002, 591–608). Mamluk and Ottoman heritage was considered "foreign," not Egyptian, and emphasis was placed on preservation and restoration of "authentic Egyptian" monuments such as Abu Simbel and the temple at Philae at the expense of the heritage monuments characterizing Old Cairo. Important historic monuments were destroyed to make space for modern housing projects (Nour 2012, 117–18; Reiter 1990, i–ii). Put simply, the historic and religious heritage of Mamluk and Ottoman periods was not the heritage Nasser wished to develop under his socialist regime.

When Anwar Sadat came into power in 1973, his reforms included a master plan for all of Cairo including the Old City. He stressed the need for pedestrianization, restoration of monuments and their surroundings, and the removal of polluting activities. In 1974, his successor, Muhammad Anwar al-Sadat opened Egypt's doors to foreign visitors for the first time since the socialist revolution of 1952. Heritage tourism—which had become popular worldwide in the 1960s—now reached Cairo. Public interest reached its peak in 1979 when UNESCO inscribed historic Cairo as a World Heritage site of outstanding universal value with the direct support of the Egyptian First Lady. However, despite UNESCO's efforts, it took the earthquake of 1992 to awaken the Egyptian government into finally taking concrete conservation steps (Nour 2012, 122). Even this was insufficient, and in 2001, UNESCO declared historic Cairo an endangered site.

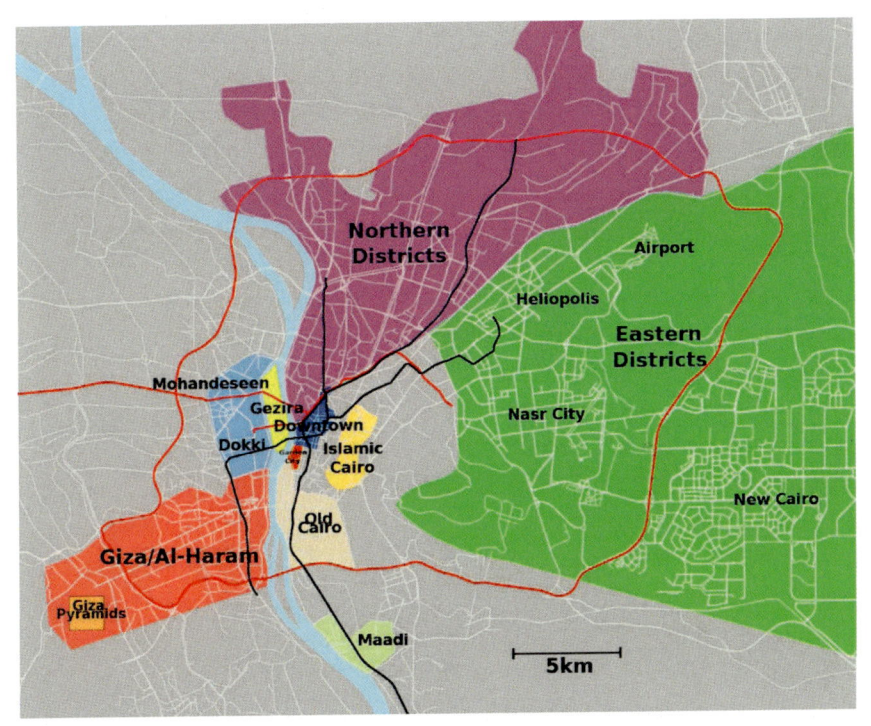

Map 8: Cairo map by regions. Source: Wikivoyage.

One of the challenges facing Old Cairo is the integration of development goals with conservation aims through a complex interdependence between the various urban components. In today's context, conservation, restoration, development, and maintenance are in the realm of the Supreme Council of Antiquities and the Ministry of Planning, fueled by the desire to profit from tourism development. However, the Ministry of *Awqaf* still owns 95% of the listed monuments in the walled city and is mainly concerned with renting real estate (Nasser 2000, 305, 360; idem 2007, 89; Sutton and Fahmi 2002, 82). Rehabilitation has been slow, hampered by bureaucratic barriers between the SCA in a restoration role and the Ministry of *Awqaf* as landowners. Currently, the SCA's goals are in conflict with those of the Ministry of *Awqaf* regarding the purpose of rehabilitation—for tourism and economic gain, or to empower and involve the local community, bringing back traditional crafts, way of life, and religious observance (Nour 2012, 67).

Practical proposals for sustainable tourism together with protection and preservation of heritage have been offered by many, including Sutton and Fahmi. They advocate revitalizing the community surrounding the monument while simultaneously restoring it and adding economically profitable services. There is no doubt that community use of a monument brings it to life, and that this continued interaction between the monument and the community is a part of the living heritage. In Old Cairo today, most mosques are still used for prayers, and the caravanserais in the area still play a prominent economic role. Small-scale manufacturing and trade once depended on transit trade; revival of these traditional commercial complexes may profit today from tourism. Preventing the use of such monuments is harmful and may even cause a threatening change in lifestyle.

Cairo still suffers from a lack of conservation expertise, problems of urban decay, congestion, poor infrastructure, and accessibility. The ideas are there but the will power, organization, and funding are lacking. The challenge is to develop tourism without it contributing to the deterioration of the unique features that attracted tourists in the first place, and to enable residents to enjoy the historical and cultural environment as well (Sutton and Fahmi 2002, 73–93; Nour 2012, 140).

A parallel institution to the *waqf* exists in Jewish communities—the *hekdesh*—dedication of property to a religious or philanthropic institution. Communal and religious institutions in the past were usually *hekdesh*, rather than private or government property. In many cases, the revenue from shops and living units belonging to a *hekdesh* was dedicated to the specified institution. Both *waqf* and *hekdesh* dedications are perpetual and irreversible. In Jerusalem sometimes a building belonging to a *yeshiva* was *hekdesh* (possibly but not necessarily the *yeshiva* itself). Sometimes, the *yeshiva* owned another building whose apartments were *hekdesh*. Rent and other fees then went to the *yeshiva*. For example, in 1883 Moshe Wittenberg dedicated a large courtyard he owned as *hekdesh* whose profits would support orphaned and poor students in specific Ashkenazi educational institutions (Zecharia 1985, 90). This system guaranteed the preservation and maintenance of these institutions over the centuries. It served as an alternative to today's western preservation movement in that it guaranteed the continued use and maintenance of historic buildings deeply embedded in the daily life of the local community. Most public services such as education and healthcare were founded and maintained at least partially by *waqf* or *hekdesh* institutions. Of course, ownership and management rights over so much valuable property gave these institutions a great deal of power and influence over development of a city, and as such were often politicized (see Reiter 2001, 14, 158–59; idem 1991, ii–iii; Assi 2008, 380–85).

Today's challenge in Cairo is to improve the built environment and bring it into modern use by safeguarding its historical qualities and cultural identity in the face of pressures from tourism that could ultimately lead to gentrification and change land uses and values (Nasser 2000, 295). In the Jewish Quarter of Jerusalem, this has already happened. The Israeli government expropriated a substantial amount of *hekdesh* property in the quarter after 1967, without attempting to document the Quarter's history in depth or to restore traditional property uses. Gentrification prevented many old-time residents from returning to the Quarter. Many of the *hekdesh* organizations could not meet the challenge of renewing their property there. Most notably, the Hurva and Tiferet Yisrael complexes were not rebuilt by the original *hekdesh*, but rather by the Company as a national heritage project. It was clear from the outset that Jerusalem's newly rebuilt Jewish Quarter could not support the many synagogues and *hekdesh* institutions that had existed before 1948. However, research and presentation of the Quarter's history in situ in cooperation with these institutions could have enriched the lives of both residents and tourists. As for the conflict of interest between tourism development and traditional functions, a balance was reached in the Hurva and Sephardic Synagogues, whereby they are open for prayers at specific times, and serve as revenue collecting tourism attractions at others. A similar arrangement is in effect in some of the mosques of Cairo.

There is a significant ideological and practical difference between the Western concept of conservation as nostalgia for the past and appreciation of aesthetic value, and the principles of Islamic and Jewish religious law and value of charity upon which the *waqf* or *hekdesh* institution is based (Nour 2012, 169–70). According to the UNESCO World Heritage Convention:

> Cultural and natural heritage is among the priceless and irreplaceable assets, not only of each nation, but of humanity as a whole. The loss, through deterioration or disappearance, of any of these most prized assets constitutes an impoverishment of the heritage of all the peoples of the world. Parts of that heritage, because of their exceptional qualities, are of "Outstanding Universal Value" and as such worthy of special protection against the dangers that increasingly threaten them.... To ensure, as far as possible, the proper identification, protection, conservation and presentation of the world's heritage, the Member States of UNESCO adopted the World Heritage Convention in 1972... The Convention aims at the identification, protection, conservation, presentation and transmission to future generations of cultural and natural heritage of Outstanding Universal Value.[147]

However, nowhere in the Convention is there mention of any continuation of the original or traditional use of the heritage site. Modern concepts of heritage consider a historic building to have intrinsic value even if it presently serves no (or a different) function (Nour 2012, 57). On the contrary, it is then a candidate for "development" as a tourist attraction. Structures such as mosques, khans, sebils (water fountains), and madrasas (religious schools) have become the heritage tourism attractions of today because of their exceptional architecture and meaningful history, rather than because of their current religious, cultural, or national values.

The 1987 Washington Charter for the Conservation of Historic Towns and Urban Areas and the Burra Charter for Places of Cultural Significance, revised in 1999, suggested reforms in the way heritage is considered. Historic areas must be functionally integrated into the modern city. Residents of those areas as well as people for whom the place has meaning or who have social, spiritual, or other cultural responsibilities for the place must be involved in both the decision-making and the management of conservation plans. Accordingly, the conservation process is not an aim in itself but rather an integral part of more comprehensive and coherent policies of socio-economic development and of urban and regional planning. Both the physical elements and the values of the local community should be well-defined, understood, respected, and used as driving forces for the conservation process. In that framework, international institutions such as UNESCO may afford technical assistance but may never define value (Nour 2012, 174–77). Unfortunately, UNESCO itself has been politicized, as its recent proclamations regarding Jerusalem have shown.

Figure 41: Ayyubid Wall, Al-Azhar Park, Cairo, 2006. Source: Blazei Pindor. Wikimedia Commons.

Comparison of *waqf* performance in Jerusalem and in Cairo is also relevant. Yitzhak Reiter researched the *waqf* in Jerusalem during the Mandate period, and concluded,

> The traditional image of the waqf as an institution whose properties are neglected and inefficiently administered...is not supported by the Jerusalem Sijill [the Muslim sharia court records] during the Mandate.... There are numerous instances of waqf properties being renovated and maintained, of new construction.... (Reiter 1990, ix–x).

After 1948, "[t]he Jerusalem *Waqf*, whose properties from public and family endowments include most of the Old City...was a positive factor in the economic development of the city during the Jordanian period" (Reiter 1991, iii).

Following the reunification of Jerusalem, most church and *waqf* properties in Jerusalem were not expropriated. On the contrary, faced with the Muslim community's lack of recognition of the State of Israel, Israel retained a low profile and allowed the Waqf council to administer its many properties in the Old City without interference. Today,

> The Waqf serves the Arab population as a substitute for governmental institutions, and its economic resources have been mobilized for the political struggle...strengthening the Arab population's attachment to Islamic institutions, to the local leadership that administers them.... It would seem that waqf property be fated for stagnation and degeneration. However, various mechanisms have developed in Islam facilitating the preservation and perhaps, even the economic development of these properties.... (Reiter 1991, i–ii).

Unfortunately, the politically-motivated Waqf council has encouraged the doubling of the Muslim population of the Old City since 1967, without renovating properties to allow tenants a minimum standard of living.[148] Nevertheless, Reiter concludes optimistically: "The findings indicate that the Jerusalem *Waqf* is an institution of great economic flexibility.... This contrasts with the prevailing image of the *waqf*...." (Reiter 1990, ix–x).

To sum up, the cases of Old Cairo and Jerusalem illustrate possible alternatives to the western approach to preservation.

Beirut

Beirut is another Middle Eastern capital often compared to Jerusalem. Both Beirut and Jerusalem are mentioned in the ancient Egyptian Tell el-Amarna letters, dating to the 15th century B.C.E. Recently, during reconstruction of the city center, significant remains of the Phoenician settlement of 5,000 years ago were excavated and displayed. Both Beirut and Jerusalem are built upon Hellenist, Roman, Byzantine, Muslim,

Crusader, Mamluk, and Ottoman remains. Both became the capitals of new states in the 1940s. Both are multi-ethnic and multi-cultural cities with internal conflicts.

Aside from a rich archaeological heritage, Beirut's tourist attractions include its spectacular hilly landscape, beaches, and port, its open cosmopolitan society, and financial resources. Religious and national heritage, so important to Jerusalem, play second fiddle to Beirut's role as the financial capital of the Middle East and to its commercial importance as a port city. Since the Crusader Period, Beirut has been a major port and international financial power.

During the Ottoman period, its population rose and fell according to circumstances, from about 6,000 to 15,000. Among other factors, civil wars in the mountains between Druze and Christians led to a large wave of Christian refugees into Beirut. From the nineteenth century on, Beirut developed close trade and cultural connections with the United States and with European powers, particularly France, making the city even more metropolitan. After World War I, Armenian refugees from southern Anatolia joined Beirut's Maronite and other Christian population, along with Shi'ite and Sunni Muslims. This highly mixed population remained under French Mandate until achieving independence in 1943, with Beirut as the capital of Lebanon. Beirut's population grew from about 160,000 in 1920 to 400,000 in 1950, when it had become one of the leading financial centers in the world. In 1970, Metropolitan Beirut's population reached more than one million. It was considered the most open, pluralistic society in the Arab world, the "Switzerland of the Middle East" as a commercial hub and "Paris of the Middle East" as a tourism and cultural center (Yahya 2004).

For centuries, Beirut functioned as a multicultural heterogeneous city where religious groups coexisted but lived in separate enclaves, with few mixed neighborhoods. As the population expanded, violence erupted over socio-economic and ethnic differences. A devastating Lebanese civil war from 1975 to 1990, and two wars with Israel during that same period, destroyed much of Beirut and fractured the commercial and governmental infrastructure, perhaps even more seriously than it caused physical damage to the city and its residents. The civil war led to the creation of the Green Line, a long demarcation line between the predominately Muslim West and Christian East Beirut. The CBD (central business district) of the city, previously the focus of commercial and cultural activity, became a desolate "no man's land." Attempts at reconstruction continued throughout the 1980s simultaneously with recurring violence and destruction. Towards the gradual end of violence, Rafik Hariri, a billionaire businessman turned politician, established Solidere, a private land-holding and development company, to rebuild the Bourj', site of Beirut's CBD, parliament, municipal headquarters, religious edifices, transportation terminals, *souk* (*suq*, market) and shopping, culture and entertainment, financial institutions, the place where everything came together (Khalaf 1993, 96–98). Rafik Hariri was assassinated in 2005, but rebuilding the CBD and the Bourj' continue to this day (Sarkis and Khalaf, in Khalaf and Khoury 1993; Nasr 2008, 1116–41).

Figure 42: "Good Morning from Beirut" 1958. Source: http://www.lebanoninapicture.com/.

A review of some of the latest literature on postwar Beirut shows that the very same characteristics that provoked violence were the factors behind Beirut's economic and political strength: its intergroup proximity and multiethnic contacts (Bollens 2013, 187). From the beginning of the civil war, fear of the other, rather than a physical wall, has divided the different confessions and ethnic groups, a profound sociological change for the worst. Separation fosters distrust, hostility, prejudice, and stereotypes. Fear of recurring violence has led to physical partition–a measure of the failure of the municipal government. Walls are cheaper than are effective police. They solve a profound longstanding problem in a superficial, temporary way (Calame and Charlesworth 2009, 1–5). This raises important questions: How can spatial planning of postwar reconstruction encourage diverse religious and ethnic groups to live together peacefully and productively? (Khalaf and Khoury 1993, *xii–xvii*; 11–62). Is physical separation a just and effective tool to reduce conflict? What does it do to the city?

According to Scott Bollens, the common reaction of separating populations in situations of ethno-national conflicts is faulty and not in the interests of the urban populations involved. Alleviations of violence through separation and bounding may work short term, but they harm the long-term capacity of cities and divided societies to encourage pluralistic activities and attitudes (Bollens 2013, 11). "Reconstruction is not just about buildings but about the values by which we live and how communities may survive and prosper" (Bold and Pickard 2013, 118). Furthermore, contemporary planning interventions in divided cities do not address the root causes of division. Hence, incorporation of "difference" as a prominent feature of the city to its plans is not addressed as it should be in these special cases (Caner and Bolen 2011, 139–56). The challenge is to rearrange space to offer opportunities for hostile groups to mix in open common spaces (Khalaf and Khoury 1993, 55–56).

Khalaf and Khoury confirm this pragmatically: Despite all the traumas Beirut residents have undergone, and despite the tendency to withdraw to family and confessional circles, land values in mixed areas tend to be higher than in segregated ones, all other factors disregarded. More than twenty years ago, they asserted that postwar reconstruction must not only restore the physical destruction but also correspond with demographic changes and the spatial, socio-economic, and cultural damage done to the social order (Khalaf, in Khalaf and Khoury 1993, 56). It must be recognized that decisions to reconstruct are political (that is, subjective) rather than scientific (objective). Sometimes, reconstruction might be considered destruction and an attempt to rewrite history (Bold and Pickard 2013, 117). When reconstruction is the result of warfare, these questions become even more pressing.

Figure 43: Beirut downtown seafront, 2011. Source: A. K. Khalifa, Wikimedia Commons.

When populations are disrupted by the loss of their familiar landscape or by "exile" to new surroundings, they lose not only their physical homes, but also their self and group identities and pride (Khalaf 1993, 96). Many postwar-related questions have arisen: Should physical damage be preserved in situ as a reminder of the conflict or should it be erased by new construction? Is the most successful tourism narrative erasure or embellishment of war scenes? For example, the city of Dubrovnik was hard hit by the post-Balkan war that began in 1991. As Wise and Mulec concluded: "Future work seeks to draw comparisons to the erosion of cultural heritage and local concern regarding overdevelopment by making comparisons with local efforts to preserve heritage during the period of war" (Wise and Mulec 2012, 57–69). How should we treat cultural heritage symbolizing the identity of the different parties involved in the conflict? What will this do to present collective identity? All of the above are relevant to both Beirut and Jerusalem and to many other cities. In many places in the world, people learn to live with tolerable conflict between diverse communities and with people of different ideologies, without resorting to formal separation lines or physical violence.

Another issue concerning both Beirut and Jerusalem is the role of municipal development in a national capital. What is the logic of postwar reconstruction that prescribes an international role for the city rather than a process of reconciliation that turns the city inwards, onto its own territory? (Yahya 2004). According to Lebanese law, electoral separation only divides the country on a national level, but this has seeped down to the municipal level and unbalanced Beirut's proper functioning. National power struggles have shaped Beirut's development and governance (Bollens 2013, 49). The imperative of Lebanon's postwar reconstruction drive and specifically the rebuilding of the city center was identified at the onset by the Prime Minister at the time, Rafik Hariri, as the need to recapture Lebanon's place as an international financial capital and thus reinsert Beirut into the global narrative. Similarly, Beirut's historic core is described as the "national heart" of the country, thus linking the rejuvenation of both economy and nation to the rebuilding of the center of the city (Yahya 2004).

In contrast, reconstruction of Vienna following World War II aimed to develop a functional, pleasant metropolis, but not to restore the city's former status as a "world city." The monuments on the Ring were restored, but very little additional or innovative construction was attempted (Diefendorf 1993, 1–19). As for Jerusalem, national and international concerns have significantly influenced the development of its Old City, including the Jewish Quarter. Lack of international recognition of Jerusalem as the capital of the State of Israel and refusal to acknowledge Israel's authority in the Old City have hampered its development.

Warsaw

The story of Warsaw's rehabilitation after World War II is an outstanding example of the significance of heritage as an indicator of victory or defeat in war.

Warsaw has been the cultural capital of Poland since the early 14th century. Its buildings are representative of nearly every European architectural style and historical period since then. Having restored independence in 1918, Poland immediately began to identify and conserve its heritage. A Ministry of Culture and Arts responsible for the conservation of historic monuments was established in 1918. Ten years later, in 1928, the Polish national legislature adopted a remarkably comprehensive statute protecting landmarks, their surroundings, parks, gardens, monuments, and historic districts in urban areas. This is the earliest modern preservation statute to recognize the significance of protecting entire historic neighborhoods. It predates the special zoning statutes of both Charleston (1931) and New Orleans (1932) in the United States, as well as those in Paris, London, Amsterdam, Rome, and Vienna. The latter had formulated national preservation laws long before Poland but had not empowered conservation authorities to restrict the development of whole urban areas (Tung 2001, chapter 4).

In 1939, Germany invaded and conquered Poland. Here too, Warsaw (and Poland in general) was unique in that it resisted the invasion on two fronts: physical and ideological. The famous Jewish uprising of the Warsaw Ghetto took place in 1943, followed by a general uprising in 1944 by the Polish resistance Home Army to liberate Warsaw from Nazi Germany. Together with earlier damage suffered in the 1939 invasion of Poland and the Warsaw Ghetto Uprising in 1943, the Germans had destroyed over 85% of the city by January 1945 (Murawsky 2009, 14). A parallel war was fought on the cultural level: German architects singled out historic, architectural, national, and religious monuments—buildings of great symbolic importance as part of Warsaw's seven hundred year cultural inheritance. These buildings were carefully analyzed, and just enough explosives were detonated to destroy them and to defeat the spirit of resistance among the Polish people (Tung 2001, chapter 4).

*Figure 44: Destroyed Warsaw, capital of Poland, January 1945
Source: Life Magazine online archive at Google.com.*

Warsaw was not the only historic city to be singled out, and Germany was not the only nation to intentionally or unintentionally destroy important cultural, political, and religious landmarks. The Allies bombed the historic cities of Dresden, Hamburg, and Berlin, for example. More recently, Sarajevo, Mostar, Dubrovnik, and other historic cities have suffered similar destruction. Now it is the turn of Iraq, Iran, and Syria to wreak havoc and destroy important heritage sites as part of their war tactics in the Middle East (Tung 2001, 16-17).

To counter the German cultural attack on Warsaw, an underground resistance movement of architects and city planners arose while the war was still raging. It covertly documented the city's architecture, conserving past surveys, photographs, and maps, and drawing up new plans for reconstruction after war's end. Among those involved in this clandestine operation were members of the faculty of architecture of Warsaw Technical University. Professors and over 150 students of the defunct Department of Town Planning, while pretending to do mechanical drafting exercises, secretly developed plans for the rebuilding of Warsaw (Tung 2001, chapter 4; Gliński 2015).

Reconstruction of Warsaw in 1945 was the first attempt in history to reconstruct not only individual monuments, but also to recreate the entire historical tissue of a city. At the time, it was doubtful that the enterprise would be successful. Warsaw had become the capital of communist Poland, and accordingly, was conceived as a model Socialist city. Professor Jan Zachwalowicz, head of the Office for the Reconstruction of the Capital (BOS), argued in favor of replication and reconstruction at the expense of authenticity (Gliński 2015). This followed the principles of Stylistic Restoration, as laid out by the French architect Eugene Emmanuel Viollet-le-Duc [1814–1879]. According to Viollet-le-Duc, the purpose of restoration is to bring the monument to architectural perfection, even if it was not originally so. In order to achieve this goal, it is permissible to use new modern building materials in place of the original imperfect ones (Fuhrman-Naaman 2008, 29).

Zachwalowicz reconstructed a replica of the city center, but not a one-on-one reproduction, despite the fact that extensive sketches and photographs of prewar Warsaw were available to the architects. In many instances, they chose to reproduce the buildings and streets as depicted by the 18th-century Venetian artist Bernardo Belloto. His paintings were thought to be a purer form of architecture, not tainted by the capitalist 19th and 20th-century excesses. The prewar form of Warsaw's Old Town was known, but the communist regime attempted to rebuild the environment to fit its socialist philosophy. For example, in the Nowy Swiat district, tall surviving buildings were reduced to three-story height and lower ones heightened to produce an "egalitarian" skyline (Murawsky 2009, 14–15).

Figure 45: Castle Square in Old Town Warsaw. Source: Olaf, 2007. Wikimedia Commons.

Many late 19th-century and early 20th-century tenant houses that had survived the war were pulled down, although they were the most outstanding feature of Warsaw's prewar character. To facilitate the reconstruction effort, the Communist regime introduced the so-called Dekret Bieruta (Bierut's decree). Declared in November 1945, Dekret Bieruta stated that all land within the prewar boundaries of Warsaw was to be nationalized. Today, many historians believe that without nationalization, the rebuilding of the capital on this scale would not have been possible (Gliński 2015). Here too, the parallel with Israel's expropriation of Jerusalem's Jewish Quarter, and the centralized planning and development are quite striking, and possibly related to the socialist nature of Israeli government in its first decades. The nationalization of Warsaw enabled planners to treat parts of the city as a tabula rasa, another shared characteristic of Jerusalem and Warsaw.

As the popular Socialist slogan went, Warsaw was (re-)built by the whole nation, with donations and volunteer workers coming from all over Poland. The widespread enthusiasm, as caught on newsreels from the period, cannot be dismissed as merely Communist propaganda. In fact, it just might have been a prerequisite for success of the rebuilding project (Gliński 2015). Here, too, there is a striking similarity to the reconstruction of the Jewish Quarter in Jerusalem.

In the Jewish Quarter of Jerusalem, unlike Warsaw, replication was seen as both technically impossible and culturally undesirable. Preservation of war-destroyed ruins as such was also largely rejected. In Warsaw, socialist ideology succeeded in adopting and modifying its national heritage to its own time and place. In Jerusalem, however, conflicting narratives competed with each other, presenting problems of managing the heritage of non-conforming definitions of Israeli identity and heritage and discordant heritage messages. This is similar to the oscillation between national and supra-national roles of recent heritage interpretation in Hungary. It also shows how political, social, and economic aspects of heritage usage become inextricably related (see Ashworth and Tunbridge 1999, 105–16; Calame 2005, 40).

The pioneering and unique effort of reconstruction in Warsaw was proclaimed in 1980, when Warsaw's Old Town was selected as part of UNESCO's World Cultural Heritage list. Later, in 2011, the Archives of BOS were recognized as one of the most valuable examples of human documental heritage, and enlisted on the Memory of the World list.[149]

York

We can briefly chart the changes in approach to revival of historic city centers in the western world by documenting the heritage tourism development of York, England, one of the most successful in recent years. Local authorities, central government departments, and locally and nationally organized preservation groups have been working together since the 1960s to make the most of York's heritage as a major asset for its growth and development. In so doing, their approach has evolved from one of preservation to conservation to commodifying and "selling" various narratives.

The walled Roman city of Eboracum, later to become York, was founded in 71 C.E. In the Middle Ages, York became a major trading center, as well as a religious and political center. From the 18th century on, it was an important port as well as an upper class resort city. In the 19th century, York became a hub of the railway network and a confectionery-manufacturing center with a largely blue-collar population.[150] At the same time, York was a popular vacation center for the wealthy, with its annual horse races and cultural activities.[151]

In 1942, the Luftwaffe heavily bombed its strategic targets—the railway line, the station, the carriage works, and the airfield. However, York's famous medieval cathedral, the Minster, was not harmed. Across the city, houses were destroyed, schools wrecked, the Guildhall and St Martin-le-Grand Church burnt out. The Bar Convent collapsed, and huge craters scarred the streets and Clifton airfield. Nevertheless, that same morning the city went back to work. As the *Daily Mail* put it: "The gates of York still stand high, like the spirit of its people who, after nearly two hours of intense bombing and machine-gunning, were clearing up today."[152]

In the 1950s and 1960s, York's place as an industrial center declined, unemployment rose, and the historic city core degenerated to the point where it was threatened with destruction. Redevelopment of cities in those decades generally entailed demolition of historic buildings and enforced movements of local populations out of residential areas. Proposals for the revitalization of York included destruction of architecturally outstanding Georgian structures in order to construct a ring road around the ancient walled city. At this time, the Minister of Housing and the City Council commissioned a report on five historic towns, including York. The Esher Report, published in 1967, proposed alternatives to the ring road and recommended conservation of the inner city. The local population enthusiastically supported it. Additionally, the Civil Amenities Act of 1967 granted local authorities the power to conserve much of the historic town. As noted above, preservation of historic sites was under governmental jurisdiction, and public participation in renovation of historic European city centers was quite rare (Meethan 1996, 322–40). Nevertheless, the residents themselves led the movement to preserve York. In 1971, they formed "York 2000," a citizens' group to fight construction of the ring road and to preserve historic York. In addition to public grants of over two million pounds Sterling, the private sector contributed 10 million, thus saving the historic buildings and the picturesque narrow winding streets of the walled city.

Esher recognized the dangers motor vehicles posed to the city's historic fabric and recommended that access be restricted or closed in historic areas, except for residents' cars. Four multi-story car parks were to be built outside the walls, so that visitors might "park and ride." Much of his vision was put into practice. In 1968, the entire historic core of York was designated a conservation area.[153] Stonegate became York's first "foot-street," cars being banned from it in 1971. In the 1980s the city's other main shopping streets were pedestrianized. This lack of traffic in the city center, together with its architectural quality, have been the key to the city's unusual character and hence its popularity.[154]

The initial preservation of the historic city center by the authorities took place in the 1960s and 1970s. Until 1972, city council policies tended toward modernization. During the 1970s they shifted to conservation and "allowed" tourism if it would not harm conservation efforts. During the 1980s they worked together with public institutions such as the York Civic Trust and the York Archaeological Trust to maximize the social and economic gains from tourism while enforcing conservation policies. Today, York's approach to heritage development has changed to one of public-private partnership for the benefit of both residents and visitors. It involves the private sector in the planning, renovation, development, and presentation of heritage for tourism. This has led to the creation of the York Tourism Bureau, the Tourism Strategy Forum, the National Railway Museum, and the Jorvik Center (a shopping center and archaeological site). From the end of the 20th century, stress has been placed on empowerment of local consumers and citizens. The Tourism Forum has reformulated the tourism strategy for York to maximize economic and employment benefits, managing the environmental and social impacts of tourism to enhance the quality of life for both residents and tourists, imbuing local citizens with appreciation of the benefits of tourism for York, and so on (Bahaire and Elliot-White 1999, 260–64).[155]

Perhaps what really sets the city apart is its gradual recognition that its greatest asset is its history. York is also one of the few heritage tourism oriented cities whose population has remained stable over the decades and whose self-identity is intrinsically York. Residents are proud of their city and its heritage, in addition to the economic and social benefits of the booming tourism industry.[156]

Figure 46: Etching of Micklegate Bar, York showing the ruined barbican still in place.
Etching by S. Noble from a drawing by William Westall, in
The Architectural Antiquities of Great Britain, vol. 4 (1814), by John Britton.
Source: Wikipedia public domain.

These benefits are significant: "The processes that gave rise to the production of the townscape of York…have now become subsumed and revalued under the production of a national and local heritage in which the processes of history are commodified and organized as narratives of objects and spaces for leisure consumption…. Although a reflection of national trends, the growth of heritage as entertainment, spectacle and mass consumption…" emphasizes the fact that both tourism and shopping in a tourism-historic city involve consumption of space and time (Meethan 1997, 333–42).

Figure 47: York City Center. Source: Wikimedia Commons.

In contrast to York, the seeds of public-private partnership in the development of the Jewish Quarter of Jerusalem are just beginning to sprout. The government-owned Company for the Reconstruction and Development of the Jewish Quarter in the Old City of Jerusalem Ltd. retains exclusive rights on property, accessibility, parking, commercial activity, educational and public institutions, and tourism initiatives. It also serves as a government housing company, and in this capacity, it handles real estate and asset registration, the reassignment and transfer of rights, lawsuits relating to expropriation, ownership claims, illegal building, evictions and the management of land registration ledgers. Since the residential areas are fully renovated, the Company now concentrates on tourism development. It has recently begun to work together with residents and community organizations on planning and quality of life issues, and this, along with other changes noted above, may be the beginning of a new era for the Jewish Quarter and the whole Old City.

Similarly, the development of Old Jaffa is centrally planned and administered by the government Company for the Development of Old Jaffa. A recent development is the formation of the interdisciplinary Jaffa Cultural Heritage Project (JCHP) in partnership with the IAA and academic institutions in Israel and abroad. Time will tell if this is successful. Neither did the Company for the Development of Old Acre alone succeed in realizing Acre's heritage potential until its declaration as a World Heritage Site by UNESCO. Then, in conjunction with the IAA and the Israel Lands Administration, serious excavations, conservation and rehabilitation began, Recently, new local academic institutions have augmented these conservation activities and are building a world conservation center in Acre. Only in Safed is there as yet no centralized government planning and no approved outline scheme. Recent activities by the Safed Academic College and by the NGO Livnot aim to change this and to put Safed on the heritage tourism map. Here too, the extent of their success remains to be seen.

The Jewish Quarter was planned, from the beginning of its reconstruction, as a living Jewish residential, cultural and religious center, at the same time conserving and presenting multiple heritage narratives. Two of these narratives were preferred: First and Second Temple Period finds such as the Broad Wall were preserved at the expense of partially destroyed 19th-century (religious) institutions above them. In addition, built heritage significant to Israel and to the Jewish world was developed more intensively than ancient Christian and Muslim sites. However, much depends on the heritage preferences of the groups and their guides. Jewish, Christian, and Muslim religious heritage, medieval, Turkish, British and Israeli history, the unique architectural fabric of the quarters—are all narratives fitting for a tour of Old Jerusalem. Similarly, visitors to Beirut, Cairo, Warsaw, and York will hear heritage narratives whose subjective meaning will depend on each visitor's personal and collective identity.

The Armenian, Christian, and Muslim Quarters of the Old City have had a relatively stable population over the past two centuries. Only the Jewish Quarter's demography has changed abruptly, from Jewish to Muslim, to eviction (ordered by King Hussein), and back to Jewish within 70 years. No longer are Jews second-class citizens, as they were until 1967. Nominally, at least, the State of Israel governs Old Jerusalem. All inhabitants of Old Jerusalem must come to terms with these dramatic changes affecting each group's collective identity and their place in the larger context. It would seem that residents of the Jewish Quarter are more aware of their own collective heritage and of that of their neighbors than are Israeli citizens living in more homogenous areas of the country.

Both Jerusalem and Cairo share the history of conquest by Muslim and Christian empires and of absorption into their culture, both tangible and intangible. When conserving, a decision must be made as to which narrative is "authentic." We have discussed Jerusalem's heritage narratives above. What constitutes ancient Cairo's heritage—early Egyptian pre-Muslim society and architecture (as evidenced by the pyramids), or Mamluk and Ottoman Muslim heritage (mosques and madrasas), or both? What constitutes Beirut's heritage—ancient Phoenician and Roman remains, traditions, and tangible heritage of the varied ethnic groups, or the cultural heritage of France and Great Britain? The heritage narratives of Warsaw and York seem to be much more clearly delineated.

Another issue concerns the question of whether heritage should be inner-directed toward local inhabitants or outer-directed for financial profit. The pendulum has swung back and forth and not yet reached equilibrium. Related to this is the decision that must be taken regarding the large number of religious institutions in both Jerusalem and Cairo in a post-modern society. Should traditional usage continue, or should they be destroyed, preserved as relicts, modernized and their usage adapted, or preserved as museums? Cairo seems to be returning to an appreciation of its medieval buildings and to their use in more traditional ways, both for tourism and for local consumption and benefit.

Jerusalem and Cairo underwent the same split between "old" and "new" during the same period. The "old" was frozen and degenerated, while the "new" was built outside. In both, this was accompanied by a change in governance—religion lost its power to a more secular centralized government. Both Jerusalem and Cairo shared the system of religious endowments for caring for tangible heritage of religious, educational, medical and cultural institutions (*awqaf* and *hekdeshim*). In both Israel and Egypt, this unresolved tension between centralized government administration, and administration by traditional religious councils still exists, both in practice and in principle.

The city of Beirut was conquered and ruled by many of the same civilizations as Cairo and Jerusalem. It too came under strong European influence from the mid-19th and 20th centuries, culminating in the creation of the independent state of Lebanon with Beirut as its capital. However, its character is quite different, with emphasis on the modern rather than the traditional, and on the global rather than the local. Both in Beirut and in the Jewish Quarter, the debate continues regarding heritage oriented to specific ethnic, religious, and national groups. However, in contrast to Jerusalem and to Cairo, Beirut is not a religious center for Islam, Christianity, or Judaism. Like its neighbor Acre, its significance is primarily historic, strategic, and financial.

Beirut today has no ancient walled city as do Jerusalem, Acre, Cairo, and York. It was an important city in the Roman period, but was not fortified until the early 17th century, and has no typical ancient walled city core. Much of Berut's past has been discovered in excavations in the destroyed area of the Bourj', but systematic excavation, documentation, publication, and renovation have not yet been accomplished. As in Jerusalem, internal ethnic conflicts and external pressures have damaged valuable heritage and hampered development of heritage sites. Its civil war and wars with Israel have shaken Beirut's foundations, leading it to emphasize modernization and conservation of ancient and universal heritage rather than preservation of the city fabric reminiscent of its recent divisive history. Heritage tourism development is intertwined with the ability of each municipality and state to solve general social, economic, security, transportation, and other problems, but Beirut is still in the formative stage of both physical and social reconstruction. Of the cities reviewed here, Beirut seems to be the historic city most modernized and least preserved, both because of ongoing political and military conflict and destruction and because residents and visitors are attracted to its cultural and recreational opportunities more than to its history and heritage.

Historic Warsaw was rebuilt after World War II as the capital of a communist regime, and its historic architecture modified to fit communist ideology. After the fall of communism in 1989, Warsaw's metropolitan population increased to more than 3 million people. Within this metropolis, one of the Polish Republic's greatest achievements is in developing sustainable tourism. Due in part to the exceptional reconstruction of the Old Town and other heritage sites, Warsaw is the most often visited city in Poland.

The postwar reconstruction of historic Warsaw and of Jerusalem have often been compared, both in the purposeful destruction of their heritage during wartime and in the determination of both nations to restore that heritage. In both, the centralized government was essential for carrying out the renovation, and it also determined the character of the rebuilt environment. Nevertheless, the grassroots support, patriotism, and sense of collective identity were indispensable prerequisites for restoring both historic Warsaw and Jerusalem's Jewish Quarter. Both attempted to recreate a living city with residential areas along with reconstructed national and religious symbols. Both compromised authenticity to some extent, but in different parameters. Both succeeded in modernizing infrastructure as well as in preserving the traditional city fabric.

In Egypt, Lebanon, Poland, and Israel, the narratives chosen to present as heritage have changed as the societies changed (from religious to secular and vice versa, capitalist to socialist, inward or outward orientated (isolation or globalization), traditional or modern. York's population and orientation, in contrast, has changed very little in the past half-century. Because of its homogenous, stable population, fewer conflicts over cultural narrative seem to have been aroused. Thus, York has been free to modernize infrastructure and achieve a high standard of living for residents, along with capturing "the spirit of the past" for heritage tourism. Much effort is invested in making tourists feel welcome by residents and vice versa. Yorkers have "pride of place" and are aware of the social and cultural benefits of tourism, and not merely of economic gain. They actively participate in planning and maintaining tourism activities, an achievement residents of other historic cities, including Jerusalem's Jewish Quarter, can envy.

Chapter VII
Discussion and Conclusions

Our aim in this study was to use the framework and methodology of historical geography and of heritage studies to unravel the multitude of historical, geographical, and societal threads that combined together at the initial stage (1967–1975), to produce the renewed Jewish Quarter of Old Jerusalem. As unique as it is, Jerusalem has undergone the same processes as have other historic cities: modernization, wartime destruction and consequent rebuilding, changing heritage values and changes in heritage narratives from one period to another. The first part of this book proceeds chronologically, and zooms in from a "macro" history of Jerusalem to a "micro" examination of its Jewish Quarter, and then to relations between the Jewish Quarter and Greater Jerusalem, and to parallels or contrasts with restorations of other historic city cores elsewhere, and with current approaches and methodology.

❶ Four Sephardi Synagogues
❷ Hurva Synagogue
❸ Broad Wall — First Temple Period City Wall
❹ The Cardo
❺ "Alone on the Walls" Exhibition (1948)
❻ The Burnt House– Katros House
❼ Herodian Quarter–
   Wohl Archaeological Museum
❽ Reconstructed Temple Menorah
❾ Temple Treasures Institute
❿ Aish HaTorah Visitor Center
⓫ The Western Wall
⓬ The Israelite Tower
⓭ Ariel Center: Yad Ben Zvi –
   1st Temple Period Model
⓮ Rooftop Promenade
⓯ Old Yishuv Court Museum
⓰ Batei Mahase Square
⓱ Jewish Quarter Defenders Memorial
   and Battle Map
⓲ Ophel Archaeological Park
   and Davidson Center
⓳ Gan HaTekumah — Playgrounds
⓴ Stepped Pool (Miqve) – Info. Center
㉑ Jewish Quarter Defenders Monument (1948)
㉒ Beit El Synagogue
㉓ Nea Church

Map 9: The Jewish Quarter today.
Source: The Company for the Reconstruction and Development of the Jewish Quarter.

Throughout the process of rejuvenating the Jewish Quarter, heritage has been a key consideration. Debates over the international status of Jerusalem depend upon the priority given to Christian, Muslim, or Jewish heritage. Within Judaism, Jerusalem is central, but the weight to be given to its national and religious significance is still a matter of debate. Politically and strategically, the status of Jerusalem has been one of the most serious and hard to resolve questions of the last two centuries.

Other factors are critical, too. The map of the Jewish Quarter today is primarily a product of spatial factors existing in June 1967. Topographical factors and accessibility are of prime importance. The built environment, typified by narrow connecting lanes, living areas, and institutions juxtaposed one upon the other with little breathing space between, determines the carrying capacity for both residential and tourism development. At the same time, it is part of the heritage to be conveyed to coming generations. The professional capabilities of planners and contractors, advances in technology over the years, and economic capability are crucial to the success of the rebuilding. Another critical factor has been the centralization and organization of the bodies in charge. These, combined with public opinion and grassroots initiatives both determine and are expressions of collective identity. Much has also depended on the political, spiritual, and popular leadership of each given period. Important events such as the wartime destruction of 1948, the Yom Kippur War of 1973, the intifadas, and the remarkable archaeological discoveries of the 1970s have had unpredicted and decisive effect on renewal of the Quarter. Technological achievements such as recent improvements in accessibility thanks to the light rail, and the introduction of small electric vehicles for the residents' benefit have improved the quality of life. The reconstruction of the Hurva Synagogue is also a technological feat that could not have been accomplished half a century ago. All these continue to have a profound influence on heritage presentation in the Jewish Quarter of Jerusalem, and on its urban landscape.

The Jewish Quarter: Continuity or Opportunity for Change?

Ideas and practices often have a long life span, as in Israel's continuation of the British Mandate policy that separated the Holy Basin from Greater Jerusalem and limited the Old City's development in order to preserve the townscape and way of life of an ancient city. In the last century, Jerusalem has grown from a small town to a great metropolis, and modern society demands accessibility, communication capabilities, and sophisticated infrastructure—demands that are difficult to satisfy within the framework of current limitations upon development within the Old City. Its isolation and inaccessibility have tended to deter both residents and visitors. Half a century has passed and the planned terminal close to Zion Gate has not yet been built, nor has an additional gate been opened in the city wall and a motorway constructed. This greatly restricts accessibility and prevents a solution to the transportation and parking problem.

The center of the quarter was designed as an open space around the (remains of the) Hurva synagogue. From there, a wide "Pilgrims' Route" passes archaeological sites, museums, and renovated or destroyed synagogues, leading to the Yehuda HaLevy Stairs that go down to the Western Wall Plaza and the Temple Mount (Haram al-Sharif)—the foremost pilgrimage and tourism site. However, the height difference between the Jewish Quarter and the Western Wall Plaza is 23 meters (approximately 75 feet). This situation makes it impossible for people with disabilities to access the Western Wall from the Jewish Quarter and vice versa, severely limits the elderly population, and inconveniences families with baby carriages and children, among others. Expanding the Western Wall Plaza and making it accessible to vehicles through Dung Gate made it easier to visit the area without passing through the Jewish Quarter, something that had not been possible before. Thus, these have now become two separate spaces, no longer spatially connected.

The Western Wall and Temple Mount are visited by approximately 8 million people every year, among them many who require these sites to be accessible according to modern standards. Currently, two elevators are being planned from Misgav Ladach Street to the Wall, each able to carry 20–30 people at a time, along with public bathrooms and roofed open spaces where visitors can rest.[157] In the longer term, a cable car from the new city or the City of David and perhaps an underground railway from Tel Aviv are being planned. Meanwhile, the Jewish Quarter no longer necessarily reaps economic or other benefits from the millions of visitors to the Western Wall and Temple Mount. In addition, not one of the Old City gates leads directly to the Jewish Quarter.

Recently, the Company for the Reconstruction and Development of the Jewish Quarter in the Old City of Jerusalem (the Company) published a plan for urban construction over an 18,000-square-meter area close to Zion Gate that will include a combination of residential and commercial buildings, hotel, and other public spaces, to be built over a new underground parking lot sufficient for both residents and visitors. This project, now in its final planning stages, will be carried out in cooperation with the Jerusalem Municipality and the Jerusalem Development Authority.[158]

Opportunities to develop all four quarters as one integral unit were cramped by government policies as well as the lack of cooperation by leaders in the Muslim, Christian, and Armenian Quarters. Despite its being the oldest and most central part of Jerusalem insofar as its Jewish history is concerned, the Old City (including the Jewish Quarter) did not become a central area within today's capital city—aside from its value as a heritage site. Various proposals were made to erect major public institutions and official residences in the Jewish Quarter, but none were realized.[159] In the early stages of rebuilding the Jewish Quarter, personal security problems were a serious issue, leading potential residents to think twice about purchasing an apartment. Furthermore, the continuing struggle over international recognition of Jerusalem as the capital, or even part of, the State of Israel led to insecurity regarding the future of the Jewish Quarter, and of the Old City in general, making investment problematic. The gap between the vision of a gentrified Jewish Quarter, conserving and presenting religious and historic values in an aesthetic and tourist-friendly built environment, and the difficult social and physical conditions and potential for violence of the early years appeared almost impossible to bridge.

About a third of the Jewish Quarter was in complete ruins and another third in partial ruins, particularly in the center of the quarter, where there once stood at least twenty institutions for prayer and study, as well as Misgav Ladach Hospital. A comparison of the location of these institutions with the location of areas in ruins in 1967, and with excavation sites after 1970 shows significant overlap. Most of these destroyed synagogues and *yeshivot* could not be renovated as there was almost nothing left of them. At these sites, archaeological digs revealed significant findings from the First and Second Temple periods. These discoveries aroused great interest worldwide and in Israel, and led to heritage taking a turn, from emphasis on 19th- and early 20th-century Jerusalem to emphasis on First and Second Temple Period Jerusalem. In many cases, archaeological exhibits took the place of historic religious institutions and residences as heritage and tourism sites that strengthen the Jewish character of the quarter. This new-old heritage narrative placed renewed Israeli sovereignty in Jerusalem on a continuum with the city as the capital of Biblical, Hasmonean, and Herodian Jerusalem. Thus, two- and three-thousand-year-old heritage largely replaced the merely century-old heritage.

Synagogues in general were narrowly conceived as performers of traditional religious functions. These institutions had characterized the "Old Quarter" of the 19th and early 20th century, but were almost incidental in the renewal of the Jewish Quarter after 1967. A relatively small number were renovated, most of them for local use and not for the public at large. Despite official Israeli Government policy, a number of new religious institutions were established in the Jewish Quarter over the years. An opportunity was missed here to convey religious, historical, social, and ethnic heritage through the varied religious institutions.

There had been about fifty synagogues and *yeshivot* in the quarter, representing almost every Jewish ethnic group and religious sect. It would have been most appropriate to perpetuate this heritage by partial conservation, building signs, museum exhibits at appropriate sites, and so on. With the exception of small private museums erected later by the Karaite and Sephardic synagogues, commemoration of these religious institutions is minimal. As of today, there is not even a major synagogue in the Jewish Quarter large enough to be used for official ceremonies. The Sephardic Chief Rabbi is still inaugurated in the Ben Zakkai Synagogue, but only a small part of the congregation can actually be present inside. Those synagogues and *yeshivot* that were not rebuilt have been almost completely forgotten, and with them, the rich heritage of their past.

The reconstructed Hurva Synagogue serves as a living museum for the Ashkenazi community in the Jewish Quarter. It is expected that the rebuilt Tiferet Yisrael Hassidic Synagogue will complement and enrich this heritage presentation. Archaeological excavations under the synagogue ruins have revealed structures from the First Temple Period three thousand years ago, and from all subsequent periods up to the present. The synagogue itself, aside from its religious and historic significance, served as an important defensive outpost in 1948. And the magnificent view from the rooftop is unparalleled.

The relatively speedy renovation of the four Sephardic synagogues by the Sephardic Council may be attributed to a consensus among community members regarding the values, methods of conservation, and modern uses of the historic buildings and institutions. In this case, one specific type of heritage was rebuilt by its "owners" to their satisfaction, with the support of government and private philanthropy. Such consensus and leadership were lacking in the Ashkenazi community and the general Israeli public. The heated public debate over the Hurva synagogue was not simply about architecture or conservation principles, but also about the heritage values expressed in a physical construction.

A third heritage site, the less-known Batei Mahse, did not receive the attention and treatment it deserved. Heritage that could have served as an educational and tourist springboard was ignored. Had a museum been founded in the Rothschild House, telling the story of this historic neighborhood and its inhabitants, and of the 1948 War and the fall of the Jewish Quarter to the Arab Legion been commemorated, it would have lent an entirely different significance to this area and provided a much more meaningful experience. Likewise, the neighborhood originally was characterized by greenery and red-tiled roofs, in the style of a European village of that period. This backdrop was rejected by the architects in charge of restoration as not being in line with typical (Ottoman) Old City architecture. Instead, the Batei Mahse Square was paved with stone and restructured to form a "theatre." In front of Rothschild House, two enormous pillars from the Second Temple Period were placed. However, they were dug up at another site and have no integral connection to Batei Mahse Square. Perhaps a way can still be found to convey its historical and other heritage values, in addition to the aesthetic experience it provides to visitors today.

Two competitions were held for restoration of heritage sites: one for the Hurva Synagogue and the other for the Cardo. The first aroused a fierce debate that is still unresolved (even after the physical replication of the synagogue today; see

Chapter IV). The second was welcomed and led to completion of a very successful scheme that overcomes spatial limitations and combines a modern residential and commercial neighborhood with relicts of the past. The experience of shopping in a Byzantine and Crusader mall enriches and lends added value to the present day shopping experience.

Other aspects of heritage conservation and presentation were overlooked. Little attention was devoted to the history of the Jewish community and its various ethnic groups in the Medieval, Ottoman, and Mandate periods, nor to the siege and battles of 1948 and 1967, the desecration wrought upon the quarter under Jordanian rule, or to Jewish religious traditions and institutions. Christian and Muslim sites were excavated and conserved but did not become major attractions. Developing these different facets on site would have presented a much richer picture.

Figure 48: Aerial View of Old City and Temple Mount, 1979. Source: Palphot.

The Influence of Unforeseen Factors, Disparities, and Private Initiatives

A central and unforeseen barrier to major reconstruction of the whole Old City was the attitude of its large non-Jewish population. Israel did not anticipate the strong and unyielding Muslim and Christian opposition and refusal to recognize Israeli rule over Jerusalem. Unwilling to force the issue, the government did not enforce requirements for planning and building permits. This led to unsupervised construction, the doubling of the local population, and worsening slum conditions instead of gentrification. Of course, it also led to a very undesirable contrast of the three other sections with the Jewish Quarter. Problems of land ownership and tenants' rights, and proximity to areas heavily populated by Christians and Muslims prevented expansion of the Jewish Quarter. "Islands" of Waqf and Church property remained in the Jewish Quarter, so that even today much of its population is not Jewish. There is still a vast gap between the standard of living, infrastructure, employment conditions, cultural, educational, and health facilities between East and West Jerusalem, between the Jewish Quarter and the rest of the Old City.

In 1967, Minister of Religious Affairs Dr. Zerach Warhaftig proposed creating a new Jewish continuum of residence around the Old City walls, sending "fingers" south along Mount Zion to Silwan and the City of David, west towards Jaffa Road, and north, through the Muslim Quarter out to the Shimon Hatzadik neighborhood. He opposed the separation of different religious and ethnic groups and sought to join the holy and ancient with the new and modern. However, prevailing opinion to this day holds that the greatest danger to the ancient walls is modern building in close proximity.

Warhaftig's proposal was rejected, and all structures close to the walls, from Jaffa Gate to Damascus Gate, were removed. Geddes' and Ashbee's schemes were still the guidelines.[160] The Jewish Quarter of the ancient city remained isolated both from the modern metropolis and from most of the Old City. Had the whole Old City been treated as one integral unit, the result would have been quite different.

Ideologically, Mayor Teddy Kollek envisioned a Jerusalem of "mosaics"—a variety of separate areas for different socio-economic and ethnic groups, each in its own space. This remained municipality policy for several decades. However, Warhaftig's proposal to connect the Jewish population in the Jewish Quarter to other Jewish residential areas in and around the Old City has been happening slowly in any case, and seems to be an inevitable process. The Jewish Quarter alone and isolated is not a viable neighborhood. To survive, it must have a broader base and continuity with surrounding areas. This development has been encouraged by NGOs and private initiatives, rather than by official government or municipal policy. Hundreds of Jews live in the Muslim and Christian Quarters today. Recent archaeological excavations and renovation of the 150-year-old Ohel Yitzchak synagogue in the Muslim Quarter north of the Western Wall Plaza may perhaps be an indication that the Jewish Quarter is indeed expanding northward, as it did in the 19th century. Jewish neighborhoods have sprung up in the City of David, Silwan, and the Mount of Olives. Residents there use the cultural, health, commercial, and educational services of the Jewish Quarter.

All four of the historic Israeli cities mentioned above (Jerusalem, Jaffa, Acre, and Safed) have a mixed Muslim-Christian-Jewish population, a population that has changed a number of times in the past 200 years, primarily because of warfare and hostilities. In addition to the political and security implications, this situation is the source of serious legal problems regarding land ownership and tenancy rights. These problems have not yet been solved in any of the historic cities mentioned here. Further research in this area is necessary.

The problems of planning before conducting archaeological digs and before solving technical problems have already been considered. Among other things, this led to unnecessary differences in street level, staircases that made pathways inaccessible to the disabled and difficult for others, and discontinuity between adjacent areas. For example, Jewish Quarter Street, built about a decade before reconstruction of the Cardo, is on a higher level than the Cardo, simply because the Cardo had not yet been excavated when infrastructure for the street was laid.

Another example of the failure to plan in advance is the construction of residential neighborhoods adjoining the Hurva synagogue and around Batei Mahse Square. Residents must close all windows to escape from noise and disturbance during holidays and when events take place in the area. The educational institutions in the Batei Mahse Square also intrude on the privacy of the households. As noted, the attempt to separate residential use from commercial and institutional use (as in Bruges, Belgium) was only partially successful. This separation is necessary to preserve the urban fabric of the historic areas and improve the quality of residents' lives (Orbasli 2000, 267–71).

The Israel Antiquities Authority did not yet exist in its present state at the time that conservation and development of the quarter began. There was not yet a proper legal and planning system, nor did the Company have the knowledge or the staff to carry out conservation and development according to more recent standards. Renovations were tailored to then-current needs and economic and political orientation.

It is axiomatic that identity and collective memory are influenced by the manner in which heritage is presented. In the case of the Old City of Jerusalem, this heritage is contested both from within and without. Those who oppose the dominant narrative often attempt to change it by changing the physical expression of the heritage. Jerusalem is not the only historic city in which contesting narratives compete over one heritage site, but it finds exceptionally strong expression here.

Before and during reconstruction of the Jewish Quarter, there was a lively public debate on the plans: Some wanted to reproduce the "Old Yishuv" (the traditional Jewish community in Palestine) of the past century—physically poor but spiritually rich. They wished to re-establish the old religious institutions in their original form, and to populate the quarter with a traditional population who would constitute a kind of living museum. However, Shneur Peleg, Director of the Company for the Reconstruction and Development of the Jewish Quarter in the Old City of Jerusalem, stated, "Those in charge of renovation have done all they could to prevent this from becoming a densely populated, poverty stricken neighborhood again…. Time cannot be turned back" (Gotkind 1976). To this, some Jews responded that the quarter was "an architectural pearl...that will cause many tears in the future. Upon the site overlooking Mount Moriah (the Temple Mount), a neighborhood is being built with no spiritual criteria whatsoever.... It is almost off-limits for religious Jews" (ibid.).

Others sought a different, modern cultural profile, one that would bring gentrification and prevent former residents from reinstating their traditional life style. Still others were more extreme: the League for the Prevention of Religious Coercion wished to open a trans-ethnic center in the quarter. City planner Doron Klinghoffer thought that tourism could be stimulated by turning intimate spaces of ancient structures into nightclubs and bars, while others thought this was an appropriate opportunity to begin building the Third Temple.

The diversity of opinion concerning renewal of the quarter made planning and execution more difficult. Not only was Israel enmeshed in local politics and policies, it was also hesitant to awaken the wrath of the United Nations, particularly after its forced retreat from Sinai in 1956. The common denominator of all was the power assigned to the traditional old city townscape as capable of transmitting the heritage of the Jewish Quarter. Perhaps the replication of the architecture would somehow succeed in conveying heritage without actually spelling it out.

We have documented two opposing processes: one, the attempt to concentrate all planning and development in the hands of the Company for the Reconstruction and Development of the Jewish Quarter in the Old City of Jerusalem; and the other to decentralize by involving a large number of other bodies in policymaking and implementation. Concentration of power in the hands of the Company meant not allowing free market development of commerce and tourism, nor of the religious, cultural, and socio-economic character of the residential areas. This approach was characteristic of Israeli governance at the time, and quite different from current practice.

At the same time, various national and municipal agencies competed over authority and decision-making in the renewal process. These included the various planning agencies, the city engineering department, the Tourism and Housing Ministries, the Ministerial Committee for Jerusalem, the Company for the Development of East Jerusalem, along with the Company for the Reconstruction and Development of the Jewish Quarter in the Old City of Jerusalem and others. This resulted in an exorbitant number of public bodies involved in the development of East Jerusalem. For example, the Company for the Development of East Jerusalem, a subsidiary of the Ministry of Tourism, was responsible for the restoration of Yemin Moshe and Mishkenot Sha'ananim neighborhoods outside the Old City's wall, and facing the Valley of Hinnom. The Tower of David just opposite was repaired and restored by the Municipality, and the Valley of Hinnom itself by the National Parks Authority. Obviously, this multitude of agencies and approaches did not aid in unifying Jerusalem.

The decision was made to carefully preserve the unique architectural townscape when renovating the Old City, but dynamic leadership to develop its economic and demographic potential was lacking. Public interest was high, but was not channeled constructively.

The Company for the Reconstruction and Development of the Jewish Quarter in the Old City of Jerusalem had not been intended to make policy, only to implement it, but no other body met the challenge. This centralization of authority prevented developments perceived by the Company (and the government) as deleterious and encouraged others that did not necessarily prove wise in the years to come. Economic initiatives were not particularly successful, despite the optimistic estimates for large numbers of tourists. The Company failed to provide hotels and other tourist-centered services, to solve problems of accessibility, or to establish many heritage-centered initiatives during the first formative years. Today, the Company is deeply involved in developing tourism attractions, improving the quality of life in the Jewish Quarter, and in working in cooperation with the residential community. Of course, the long term effect of this change in policy cannot yet be evaluated.

As Ashworth has pointed out, the economic profits of tourism do not necessarily accrue to the tourist site itself (Ashworth and Tunbridge 1990, 25–30). So too here, thousands of upper-end hotel rooms were constructed after 1967, many of them a short walking distance from the Old City, but not bringing it any direct economic benefit. Almost no new hotels were built in East Jerusalem in the first ten years after the reunification, and those that existed were priced in the low to mid-range, attracting pilgrims rather than tourists who tend to be more affluent.

There were initially great hopes for economic benefits from tourism, and from hundreds of workshops, galleries, hotel rooms, restaurants, and shops that were planned, but not carried out. It was taken for granted that the "oriental *suq*" (market) of the Old City would be a big tourist attraction, including the street later known as the Cardo in the Jewish Quarter. Today, about ten shops cater to residents and only about thirty-five (mostly eateries and souvenir shops) cater to the thousands of visitors and students in the Jewish Quarter. There are eight archaeological and holy sites and museums that charge fees. This is quite a small number for some 2 million visitors annually.

The economic success of tourism depends on efficient planning, especially of infrastructure guaranteeing comfortable tourism (Page 2009, 12–14). In general, if a renewed historic city is a nice place to live, it will also be attractive to tourists (Orbasli 2000, 172–83). Since creating a comfortable space to live in was not one of the priorities of the Company (except for Gardi's residential planning), it was not planned as a comfortable space for tourists either. This, too, is gradually changing. In addition, the Company and the Municipality are making efforts to include Jewish Quarter residents in planning and in cultural initiatives.

The Company for the Reconstruction and Development of the Jewish Quarter in the Old City of Jerusalem was not intended to make a profit or to develop tourism, as was the Company for the Development of East Jerusalem. Although the Tourism Ministry and the Antiquities Authority were represented on its board, the Company had no education, culture, or tourism committees, while it did have a committee for population and another for relocation and compensation. Aside from designing Batei Mahse Square as an open air theatre, holding an international competition on the design of the Cardo, financial aid to the Old Yishuv Museum, and aid for the renovation of religious institutions, it is difficult to discern any serious attempts to develop heritage attractions in the Jewish Quarter in the early years. Mayor Teddy Kollek was one of the few who did actively promote such programs. Lately, the Company for the Reconstruction and Development of the Jewish Quarter in the Old City of Jerusalem has begun to develop and to administer several of the tourist sites. It is responsible for the reproduction and management of the Hurva and Tiferet Yisrael synagogues. However, even today administration of tourism attractions is allocated to several different bodies: Non-profit organizations, the Municipality, the Company for the Reconstruction and Development of the Jewish Quarter in the Old City of Jerusalem, the Jerusalem Development Authority, and other government agencies.

For the first ten years, while excavations and construction were ongoing, residents suffered from a lack of adequate medical, educational, and cultural services. In particular, parents worried about the potentially hazardous excavations and building sites that were everywhere—and liable to change from one day to the next. Infrastructure was often lacking and roads were unpaved. Motor access, even to the edges of the quarter, was impossible or difficult. The renewed Jewish Quarter was planned to fulfill all functions, but first and foremost to form a resilient community with a Jewish presence twenty-four hours a day. New institutions were established to populate the quarter quickly with maximum security and population density and minimum cost during the first years. The first wave of residents was quite aware that they were "making history."

In 1971, residents established a committee that successfully lobbied the Municipality to provide them with basic services. The residents of the Jewish Quarter and the committee they elected to represent them had no formal legal status, but did have a significant impact on the development of cultural and educational institutions in the quarter; they facilitated establishment of synagogues, a community center, educational facilities, libraries, and a civil defense system. Three museums—the publicly recognized Old Yishuv Courtyard Museum, and the private Siebenberg and Temple Institute Museums, were founded by residents. After years of untiring effort, Jewish Quarter residents and veterans of the War of Independence succeeded in achieving the cooperation of the Company to present the heritage of the 1948 battle over the Jewish Quarter through a small museum and a documentary film. Residents also founded educational programs for Hebrew-, Spanish-, French-, and English-speaking students, and opened galleries and shops catering both to residents (post office, grocery, electrical appliances) and to tourists (art, Judaica, restaurants).

However, attempts at community involvement in the planning and development carried out by the Company were rebuffed time after time, despite the fact that many of the residents held very responsible positions in public and governmental institutions in Jerusalem. The Company tried to control and "balance" the socio-economic and religious characteristics of the community by regulating the size and layout of apartments, and by choosing its own candidates for the purchase of apartments, but this was at best only partially successful. From the very beginning, the percentage of religious residents and the average number of children per household were higher than planned. Although the planners realized this, they did not adjust their plans, for example, by allocating more classrooms. It was left to the municipality to find locations for educational, health, and recreational facilities, usually in renovated apartments or in spaces originally intended for tourism and commerce. The residents' legal status was inferior; apartments were not registered in the land registry (*tabu*), and they were accorded the status of "secondary tenants" or lessees, for a period of 49 years, with the option of renewing their contract with the Company.

Residents noted in 1975:

> The Company...was founded in order to build, in a reasonable amount of time, a community that would establish a Jewish presence in this important historic, religious, national and political site—central to the State of Israel and to worldwide Jewry. We see ourselves as establishing that presence..., as partners in every forum..., The Company must listen to our opinions before making decisions.[161]

The founding of HaKotel and other *yeshivot* and student dormitories, renovation of synagogues and other institutions, research and cultural activities of semi-private bodies such as Yad Ben-Zvi Institute, did much to enrich visitors' experiences and to strengthen the new community of the quarter. A similar process of preservation and development took place at the same time in York, England. However in York, it led to a flourishing tourism-based economy, and in the Jewish Quarter it led to the flourishing of institutions. These not only settled the Jewish Quarter, they bequeathed their heritage to it. Almost every Jewish ethnic group and sect had once had a presence there. After 1967, new and old sought to establish a presence in the newly rebuilt quarter. Today there are five separate pre-school and elementary school systems and about twenty post-high school educational institutions, with more than 2,000 students, most of whom commute to the Jewish Quarter. English speakers predominate in many of these institutions (Kailani 2007, 96). Almost none of these existed before 1948. This is one of the most obvious changes in Jewish Quarter demography and institutional representation.

Many of the modern institutions were unsuccessful in launching large-scale cultural or tourism projects in the quarter. Institutions such as Bar Ilan University, the Pinchas Sapir Center for Jewish Heritage, and Writers' House all left the Jewish Quarter in the 1980s or shortly thereafter. The Rabbinic High Court did so as well. No major religious center (such as the seat of the Chief Rabbinate) is situated in the quarter, nor has any major national or municipal administrative or cultural institution located there, perhaps due to accessibility difficulties.

As in the Mandate Period, holy and historic sites attracted tourism, and this became the principle function of the historic Old City. Guided tours were initiated by semi-public bodies such as the Yad Ben-Zvi Institute, Writers' House, and the like. Non-Jewish tourism continued to be managed internally, in accordance with the needs and interest of each ethnic group and sect, as in the past. Development of tourism sites was also aided by private bodies. One example of this is the reconstruction of the Herodian Quarter (underneath the campus of HaKotel Yeshiva) as the Wohl Archaeological Museum. As one of the major donors to the HaKotel Yeshiva building fund, Maurice and Vivienne Wohl also contributed to the archaeological excavations beneath it.

In this framework, individuals and private groups succeeded in pushing through their own projects, some of which have proven immensely successful. These private initiatives are barely mentioned in official documentation, although they occurred concurrently with the centralized planning and development described above.

Current Trends and Instruments

Since the 1967 unification of Jerusalem more than fifty years ago, approaches to the revival of historic city centers in the western world have changed vastly: Renovation and development of the Jewish Quarter began in the 1960s and 1970s, against a backdrop of flourishing preservation activity in the western world. Preservation was conceived of as an end in itself, didactic in purpose and independent of economic or tourism profits. The first preservation activities in York, England and in Bruges, Belgium illustrate this trend. In the 1960s, the Safed Municipality tried to encourage residents and entrepreneurs to engage in conservation by offering them bonuses. This program was only partially successful, due to lack of financial resources. Renovation of the Old City of Jaffa, on the other hand, was one of the first Israeli projects fueled by the demographic and tourism potential for profit.

Until the end of the 20th century, public participation in the renovation of historic European city centers was quite rare. (Meethan 1996, 322–40) In York and in Bruges, the first demands for preservation came from the residents themselves. However, it was the government that decided and carried out the preservation activities. Likewise, the conservation and renovation of Old Jaffa was carried out by a government company for economic and tourism development, with no public involvement. In the Jewish Quarter, responsibility for planning and renovation was given neither to the municipality nor to the private sector, but rather to the Company for the Reconstruction and Development of the Jewish Quarter in the Old City of Jerusalem, authorized by and supposedly representing all relevant government bodies.

The latest international development in approaches to conservation is public-private partnership—involving the private sector in the planning, renovation, development, and conservation of heritage tourism. In York, Great Britain, this led to the creation of the York Tourism Bureau, the Tourism Strategy Forum, and the Jorvik Center. The private sector has also initiated cultural and tourism attractions in the United States. This approach developed in the 1980s, more than a decade after planning began for the restoration of the Jewish Quarter.

In Old Jaffa, the introduction of a bourgeois middle to upper-class population, including many artists who enjoyed significant benefits not granted to the local, lower-class population already residing in Jaffa, led to widening the gap between the two segments, segregating the renovated area from the wider urban environment. This same mistake was repeated in the Jewish Quarter, and has still to be corrected. Today, "islands" are no longer renovated without treating the surrounding areas and interaction between them. It is recognized that the policy of trying to create an "island" surrounded by poverty, crime, and political antagonism, will not draw tourists or appeal to residents seeking gentrified living. Particularly in Old Jerusalem, it may be advisable in the future to adopt a more holistic planning approach, one that will consider the character and interaction of all four Quarters together. In Jaffa today, the policy is to renew large tracts of land around the city center and to create a continuum of attractions and tourism sites all the way from Old Jaffa to Tel Aviv.

Gentrification through "evacuation and compensation" is no longer the only option. All over the world, neighborhoods are being renewed not only physically, but also socially, by helping local residents raise their standard of living and improve their living conditions with the aid of voluntary organizations. This conservation policy aims to inculcate heritage values in the residents as a means of motivating them to participate in efforts to preserve their historic neighborhoods (Fitch 1990). The Company for the Development of Old Acre is using this approach today to renovate Crusader and Ottoman Period architecture in the old city. A comparison of the approach taken in the renovation of Old Jaffa in the 1960s with the renovation of Old Acre in the 1990s and on illustrates the social gains that may be achieved from conservation, and the mutual influence of social and tourism gains.

Another topic worthy of further research is the involvement of UNESCO in Jerusalem. In 1981, UNESCO declared the Old City of Jerusalem and its walls a World Heritage site in response to Jordan's nomination of the city, although it had not been under Jordanian rule for more than a decade. In 1982, Jerusalem was proclaimed "a heritage site in danger." Jerusalem is the only city on the UNESCO World Heritage list that does not designate its nation, due to refusal of most members of the UN to recognize Israeli sovereignty. Although, according to UNESCO, Jerusalem is stateless, only the State of Israel has invested seriously in its conservation. There is universal consensus that the city has extraordinary cultural, religious, and historical significance, and that UNESCO has politicized its conservation, but no practical steps have been taken to ameliorate the situation. When Jordan nominated Jerusalem, the United States objected, arguing that it was improper for one country to nominate a site that would be preserved by another, and that this would lead to complications and to politicization of the World Heritage Committee.[162] To the best of our knowledge, no research has been published on the effect of this on the actual conservation of Jerusalem. The politicization of the United Nations Educational, Scientific, and Cultural Organization's World Heritage Council in regard to Israel and Jerusalem accelerated in 2016–2017, when it denounced Israeli activity in the Old City of Jerusalem, ignored the Jewish people's historic ties to Jerusalem, and referred to the Temple Mount compound solely as "a Muslim holy site of worship." (Lazaroff, *Jerusalem Post*, 6 July 2017).

In 1998, Israel began to participate in world heritage endeavors together with the EU (EUROMED); conservation work has been ongoing in this framework. In 1999, Israel signed the World Heritage Charter, promising to protect, preserve, present, and pass on its heritage to future generations. Following its signature, Tel Aviv and Acre were declared World Heritage sites. This declaration promises to promote conservation and rejuvenation, including socio-economic rejuvenation of the cities. It will be interesting to evaluate the effect of this involvement on the renovation of Israel's historic cities, particularly Acre. The declaration may lead to economic investment and professional involvement of the relevant bodies in the conservation process.

The Place of Heritage

The power of the historic city lies in its integration of time and place in the city fabric. As with Ezekiel"s prophecy (37:1–14), the existence of dry bones is a prerequisite to their resurrection. So too, the physical environment is the basis for heritage preservation and presentation.

Preservation of the city is crucial to creation of collective memory. By selecting the heritage to be preserved, its presentation in well-defined conditions and settings, and interpretation (visual/graphic or literary/textual/written), not only do we preserve heritage, we also to some extent create it (Barthel 1996, 345–64).

The fall of the Jewish Quarter and the division of Jerusalem in 1948 had a great impact on Israeli society. Jordan's subsequent desecration and prohibition of visits to Jewish holy sites under its control led to a deep longing for the Western Wall and the Old City. Following Israel's victory in 1967, a euphoric atmosphere pervaded the country. People seemed to hear the Messiah's footsteps approaching and expected universal peace to be just around the corner. However, this bubble soon burst, and in its place came a pledge that Jerusalem would never again be divided. Memories of the heavy price paid to unite it further strengthened the resolve for irreversible Israeli sovereignty.

Putting this resolve into practice by restoring the Jewish Quarter of Old Jerusalem was not easy. In order to overcome the tremendous physical obstacles and hardships, residents needed not only physical stamina and determination, socio-institutional support, and hopes for the future, but also a religious, national, and/or emotional tie to the area, whether it was an individual or a collective identification. Until the mid-1980s, the Jewish community was fairly heterogeneous; from the 1980s on, the percentage of secular Jewish residents plummeted and the percentage of orthodox English-speakers affiliated with educational institutions (or individuals with one or more of the above qualifications) in the quarter increased greatly.

This may be attributed to several factors: First, the rise in real-estate value of properties along with increasing physical inconvenience of isolation, lack of parking and adequate transportation, and the numerous excavation and building sites discussed above, motivated many to move out. Second, these demographic and socio-economic changes, as previously mentioned, were accompanied by an increase in the number of educational institutions. Many new residents are motivated by the plentitude of religious institutions and proximity to the Western Wall. In many of these institutions, English is the language of prayer, study, and conversation.

As noted above, dormitory institutions have definite advantages in populating the quarter: Adults and young people living and studying or working in the Jewish Quarter are less bothered by transportation inadequacy. The institution housing them provides physical and social support.

Educational institutions may be viewed as part of the "museumization" process, receiving Jewish students from all over Israel and the Diaspora... thus contributing to the Quarter's intensive Jewish life.... If all the Jewish Quarter's space were invested in dwellings for permanent residents, only a very limited number of Jews would be able to experience the holy meaning of living in the place (Kailani 2007, 94–95).

Additionally, an institution has an advantage over commercial or cultural services in that it is a permanent 24-hour-a-day presence. Thus the majority of those walking on the streets of the Jewish Quarter are transients—either students and teachers or tourists and visitors. This enhances the significance of the heritage presented but it also invites simplified presentation suitable to all. In addition, the residents are to some extent part of this grand exhibition.

The Jewish Quarter is unique—to the tourist, the resident, the business sector, and the institutions—in that all are living in history. Advantage or disadvantage—the past is both a tangible and an intangible fourth dimension in our streets and in our lives.

Bibliography

Archives and Collections

Company for the Reconstruction and Development of the Jewish Quarter Archive, Jerusalem.
HaKotel Yeshiva Archive, Jerusalem.
Hebrew University of Jerusalem Map Library, Mount Scopus, Jerusalem.
Israel State Archive, Jerusalem (ISA).
Jerusalem City Archive, Jerusalem (JCA).
Library of Congress, Washington, D.C., G. Eric and Edith Matson Photograph Collection.
Life Magazine online archive at Google.com
Livnot and Lehibanot Archive, Safed.
Mira Yehudai Archive, Kibbutz Ein Harod Meuchad.
Personal Collection, Bracha Slae.
Personal Collection, David Cassuto
Personal Collection, Dov Gavish
Personal Collection, Ruth Kark.
Personal Collection, Eliezer Shefer
Ruzhin Yeshiva Archive, Jerusalem.
World Karaite Jewry Archive

Websites

American Association for State and Local History http://www.aaslh.org
City Population, State of Israel http://www.citypopulation.de/Israel.html
Council for Conservation of Heritage Sites in Israel. http://eng.shimur.org//
Government Press Office National Photo Collection http://gpophoto.gov.il/haetonot/Eng_Default.aspx
ICCROM http://www.iccrom.org
ICOMOS http://www.icomos.org/en
ICOMOS (United States) www.usicomos.org/preservation
Israel Central Bureau of Statistics http://cbs.gov.il/reader/shnatonenew_site.htm
International Conservation Center Città di Roma https://www.studyabroad.com/institutions/the-international-conservation-center-citt-di-roma/saving-the-stones-286061
Israel Antiquities Authority http://www.antiquities.org.il
Israel Antiquities Authority, Scientific Archive of the Mandatory AntiquitiesDepartment, 1919–1948. http://www.iaa-archives.org.il/Search.aspx?loc_id=4189
Israel Knesset http://knesset.gov.il/laws/special/eng/HolyPlaces.htm
Jacobson, Michael, Backyard Blog on Old Jaffa https://michaelarch.wordpress.com/2009/04/16/
https://www.atlas.co.il/heb/market-house-tel-aviv
Old Acre Development Company http://www.akko.org.il/en/
Old Jaffa Development Company Ltd. https://www.oldjaffa.co.il/
UNESCO: https://en.unesco.org
UNESCO World Heritage Site, Acre http://whc.unesco.org/en/list/1042
Western Galil website http://english.wgalil.ac.il/category/English_Site

Newspapers and Periodicals

Australian Jewish News
Haaretz; Haaretz.com
HaModia
Hazofeh
Israel Digest
Jerusalem Post
The Times of Israel
Yediot Aharonot
Yisrael HaYom

Books, Articles, Dissertations and Official Publications

Aaronson, Shlomo, Peter Bogod, and Esther Niv-Krendel "A Proposal for Renovation and Reconstruction of HaYehudim Street Area" [in Hebrew]. In *Jerusalem Rebuilt* [in Hebrew]. Edited by David Kotler. Jerusalem: Ministry of Education and Culture, 1972.

Abbasi, Mustafa. *Safad during the Mandate Period.* Ph.D. diss., Haifa University, 1999.

Abramowitz, Leah. "Renovations in the Rova." *Jerusalem Post*, 25 Jan. 1980.

Ajami, Moshe, "Cultural Heritage Management: The Flea Market and Clock Tower Square Excavations, In *The History and Archaeology of Jaffa 1*. Edited by Martin Peilstocker and Aaron A. Burke. Los Angeles: Cotsen Institute of Archaeology Press, UCLA, 2010. 33–36.

Alfasi, Nurit and Roy Fabian. "Preserving Urban Heritage: From Old Jaffa to Modern Tel-Aviv." *Israel Studies* 14, no. 3 (2009): 137–56.

Amir, Ruth. "Review of Michael Dumper 'The Politics of Jerusalem since 1967,'" *Canadian Journal of Political Science* 32 (1999).

Araoz, Gustavo. "Historic Preservation in the United States." US ICOMOS http://www.usicomos.org/preservation (accessed June 2009).

al-'Āref, 'Āref. *Al-Mufaṣṣal fī Tārīkh al-Quds* [A detailed history of Jerusalem]. Jerusalem: Maktabat al-Andalus, 1961.

Ashworth, Gregory J. "Old cities, new pasts: Heritage planning in selected cities of Central Europe." *GeoJournal* 49, no. 1 (Sept 1999): 105–16.

———. *War and the City*. London: Routledge, 2002.

———. "Preservation, Conservation and Heritage: Approaches to the Past in the Present through the Built Environment." *Asian Anthropology* 10:1 (2011): 1–18.

——— and Tunbridge, J. E. *The Tourist Historic City*. London: Belhaven Press, 1990.

Assi, Eman. "Islamic Waqf and Management of Cultural Heritage in Palestine," *International Journal of Heritage Studies* 14, no. 4 (2008) 380–85.

Avnieli, Moshe. "The Jewish Quarter Renovated" [in Hebrew]. In *Jerusalem Rebuilt*. Edited by J. David Kotler. Jerusalem, 1976.

Avshalom-Gorni, Dina, Avner Hillman, and Carmiel Romano. "Historic Safed: Activities of the IAA in the City" [in Hebrew]. *Dvar Avar—Journal of the Israel Antiquities Authority* 18 (Jan. 2013).

———. Nirit Koren-Lawrence, Avner Hillman, and Shelly Ann-Peleg. "The Conservation Trustees Project in Safed" [in Hebrew]. *Dvar Avar—Journal of the Israel Antiquities Authority* 18 (Jan. 2013).

Bahaire, Tim and Martin Elliott-White. "Community Participation in Tourism Planning and Development in the Historic City of York, England." *Current Issues in Tourism* 2, nos. 2–3 (1999), 243–76.

Bahat, Dan. "Discovering the Past in the Old City and Environs" [in Hebrew]. In *Twenty Years in Jerusalem, 1967–1987*. Edited by Joshua Prawer and Ora Ahimei. Jerusalem: Jerusalem Institute for Israel Studies, 1988.

Baker, Alan. "The Self Destruction of UNESCO." *Jerusalem Post*, 19 Apr. 2016.

Barnes, John Robert. *An Introduction to Religious Foundations in the Ottoman Empire*. Leiden: Brill, 1987.

Bartal, Yisrael, Yossi Ben-Artzi, and Elchanan Reiner, eds. *Nof Moladto*. Jerusalem: Magnes Press, 2000.

Ben-Arieh, Yehoshua. *Jerusalem in the 19th Century. The Old City*. Jerusalem: Yad Izhak Ben-Zvi and St. Martin's Press, 1984.

———. "The New Jewish Jerusalem during the British Mandate." Council for Conservation of Heritage Sites in Israel. http://eng.shimur.org//viewArticle.aspx?articleID=166.

Ben Eliezer, Shimon. *Destruction and Renewal, The Synagogues of the Jewish Quarter*. Jerusalem: Rubin Mass, 1975.

Ben Solomon, Ariel. "A fight for the future of Acre's Old City." *Jerusalem Post*, 28 Mar. 2013.

Benziman, Uzi. *City Without a Wall* [in Hebrew]. Tel Aviv: Shocken, 1973.

Bianca, Stefano. "Morphology as the Study of City Form and Layering." In *Reconnecting the City: The Historic Urban Landscape Approach and the Future of Urban Heritage*. Edited by Francesco Bandarin and Ron Van Oers. Hoboken, N.J.: John Wiley and Sons, 2014.

Bier, Aharon. *For the Sake of Jerusalem: 3000 Years of Jewish Sites and History within the Walls*. Edited, translated, and expanded by Bracha Slae. Jerusalem: Mazo Publishers, 2006, 2010.

Bold, John and Robert Pickard. "Reconstructing Europe: The Need for Guidelines." *The Historic Environment* 4, no. 2 (Oct. 2013): 105–28.

Bollens, Scott. "Bounding Cities as a Means of Managing Conflict: Sarajevo, Beirut, and Jerusalem." *Peacebuilding* 1 (2) (2013): 186–206.

Burke, Aaron A. and Martin Peilstocker. "The Jaffa Cultural Heritage Project: Objectives, Organization, Strategies and Implementation." In *The History and Archaeology of Jaffa 1*. Edited by Martin Peilstocker and Aaron Burke. Los Angeles: Cotsen Institute of Archaeology Press, UCLA, 2010.

Calame, Jon. "Divided cities and ethnic conflict in the urban domain." In *Cultural Heritage in Postwar Recovery*. ICCROM Forum (2005): 40.

——— and Esther Charlesworth. *Divided Cities: Belfast, Beirut, Jerusalem, Mostar, and Nicosia*. Philadelphia: University of Pennsylvania Press, 2009.

Caner, Gizem and Fulin Bolen. "Urban planning approaches in divided cities." *ITU A|Z* (Istanbul Technical University School of Architecture) 13, no. 1 (Mar. 2016): 139–56.

Cassuto, David, ed. *The Hurva Rebuilt, Proposals and Criticisms Regarding Renovation of the Hurva Synagogue* [in Hebrew]. Third Annual Congress of Jewish Ritual Art, Jerusalem, 1970.

———. "Four Sephardi Synagogues in the Old City." In *Jerusalem Revealed, Archaeology in the Holy City 1968–1974*. Edited by Yigael Yadin. New Haven: Yale University Press and Israel Exploration Society, 1976.

———. "Symposium on Renovation of the Jewish Quarter," winter 1968, in David Kotler, ed., *Jerusalem Rebuilt* (Hebrew), Jerusalem, 1976, 71-74.

———. "Restoration of Old Synagogues in the Old City of Jerusalem." In *Planning and Conserving Jerusalem*. Edited by Eyal Meiron and Doron Bar. Jerusalem: Yad Yitzhak Ben-Zvi, 2009.

Cohen-Hattab, Kobi, "Historical Research and Tourism Analysis: The Case for the Tourist–Historic City of Jerusalem." *Tourism Geographies* 6, no. 3 (Aug. 2004): 279–302.

———. *Tour the Land, Tourism in Palestine during the British Mandate Period 1917–1948* [in Hebrew]. Jerusalem; Yad Yitzhak Ben-Zvi, 2006.

———. "Pilgrimage and Tourism—Organization and Infrastructure" [in Hebrew]. In *The History of Jerusalem—The Late Ottoman Period (1800–1917)*. Edited by Israel Bartal and Haim Goren. Jerusalem: Yad Yitzhak Ben-Zvi, 2010.

——— and Doron Bar. "Tradition and Innovation among Christian Pilgrims and Tourists in Late Ottoman Jerusalem" [in Hebrew]. In *A City Reflected through Its Research*. Edited by Kobi Cohen-Hattab, Assaf Selzer, and Doron Bar. Jerusalem: Hebrew University Magnes Press, 2011.

——— and Noam Shoval. *Tourism, Religion, and Pilgrimage in Jerusalem*. London: Routledge, 2014.

De la Torre, Marta and Randall Mason. "Introduction." In *Assessing the Values of Cultural Heritage Research Report*. Edited by Marta de la Torre. Los Angeles: Getty Conservation Institute, 2002.

Diefendorf, Jeffry M. "Planning Postwar Vienna." *Planning Perspectives* 8:1 (1993): 1–19.

Dumper, Michael. *The Politics of Jerusalem since 1967*. New York: Columbia University Press, 1997.

Efrat, Elisha, *Changes in the Town Planning Concepts of Jerusalem 1919–1969*. Jerusalem: Ministry of the Interior Planning Department, 1971.

———. "British town planning perspectives of Jerusalem in transition." *Planning Perspectives* 8:4 (1993): 377–93.

Efroni and Sheinberg, Architects Ltd. Report on the State of Planning and Construction of the Jewish Quarter in the Old City of Jerusalem, Dec. 1975.

Fitch, James Marston. *Historic Preservation: Curatorial Management of the Built World*. Charlottesville, Va.: University of Virginia Press, 1990.

Frankel, Eliezer, Ora Ya'ar, and Ya'akov Ya'ar. *Proposed Urban Design for the Jewish Quarter in the Old City of Jerusalem*. Jerusalem: Yad Yitzhak Ben-Zvi Library, 1968.

Fuhrmann-Naaman, Yael. *Conservation and the Construction of the National Space 1948–1967, A Case Study of Old Acre*. M.S. Thesis, Technion Institute for Urban and Regional Planning, Haifa, 2008.

Gardi, Shalom. "Restoration of the Jewish Quarter in the Old City of Jerusalem," *Jerusalem Papers 1 and 2, Proceedings from the International Workshop on Heritage and Conservation, Jerusalem as Laboratory*. Edited by Michael Turner. Jerusalem: Jerusalem Center for Planning in Historic Cities, 1986.

———. Outline Scheme for the Jewish Quarter of Old Jerusalem, Programme and Principles of Planning [in Hebrew]. Jerusalem: JQDC, 1972.

Gavish, Dov. "Aerial Perspectives of Past Landscapes," In *The Land That Become Israel: Studies in Historical Geography*. Edited by Ruth Kark. New Haven: Yale University Press and Hebrew University Magnes Press, 1989. 316–319.

Geva, Hillel. "The Renewal of the Jewish Quarter in the Old City of Jerusalem—40 years later." Lecture presented at the annual conference of the Association for Jewish Art, 6 May 2007.

Gilbert, Martin. *Jerusalem Illustrated History Atlas*. Jerusalem: Steimatsky's Agency and Cambridge: Burlington Press, 1977.

Glass, Joseph, and Rassem Khamaisi. "Report on the Socio-Economic Conditions in the Old City of Jerusalem." The Jerusalem Project, Munk Centre for International Studies, University of Toronto, 2007 https://www.researchgate.net/publication/265659724_Report_on_the_Socio-Economic_Conditions_in_the_Old_City_of_Jerusalem (accessed Dec. 2017).

Gliński, Micolaj. "How Warsaw Came Close to Never Being Rebuilt," 3 Feb. 2015, http://culture.pl/en/article/how-warsaw-came-close-to-never-being-rebuilt.

Gotkind, Naomi. "The Jewish Quarter: Lights and Shadows." Interview with the director of the Company. *Hatzofe*, 4 Aug. 1976.

Graham, Brian. J., G. J. Ashworth, and J. E. Tunbridge. *A Geography of Heritage: Power, Culture, and Economy*. London: Arnold, 2000.

Guinn, David E. *Protecting Jerusalem's Holy Sites: A Strategy for Negotiating a Sacred Peace*. New York: Cambridge University Press, 2006.

Hall, P. "Planning: millennial retrospect and prospect." *Progress in Planning* 57 (2002): 263–84

Har Noy, Shmuel, and Gali Gilady. "The Stories of Historic Hospitals in Safed: The Hospital of the London Association for Promotion of Christianity among Jews, Late the Yosef Bussel Convalescent Home, and the Historic Rothschild-Hadassah Hospital Building" [in Hebrew]. *Sites Magazine of the Council for Conservation of Heritage Sites in Israel* 6 (2016): 119–26.

Hashimshony, Aviya, Yosef Schweid, and Zion Hashimshony. *Jerusalem Master Plan 1968*. vol. 2. Jerusalem, 1973.

Havivi, Lavi. *Synagogues in the Old City of Jerusalem* [in Hebrew]. Jerusalem: Society for Protection of Nature, 1984.

Hopkins, Ian W. J. "Tourism in Jerusalem: A Report for the Ministry of Tourism, Israel." Durham, 1969.

Hyman, Benjamin. *British Planners in Palestine 1918–1936*. Ph.D. diss. London School of Economics and Political Science. London, 1994.

Israel Information Centre., *The Jewish Quarter, Ruins and Restoration*. Jerusalem: Israel Information Centre, 1973.

Izrael, Rami. *Quartertour*. Jerusalem: Youval Tal Ltd., 1983.

———. "From the Heart of Jewish Settlement to a Slum under Siege." *The Jewish Quarter in Jerusalem* [in Hebrew]. Edited by Mordechai Naor. Jerusalem: The Company for the Reconstruction and Development of the Jewish Quarter of the Old City, Ltd., 1987.

Jerusalem Municipality. *Master Plan 1968*. vol. 1. Jerusalem: Jerusalem Municipality, 1972.

Jerusalem Municipality. *Out of Jerusalem*. Jerusalem: Jerusalem Municipality, summer 1982.

Jokilehto, Jukka. ICCROM and Conservation of Cultural Heritage. Rome: ICCROM, 2011.

Kailani, Wasfi. *Identities in the Jewish Quarter of the Old City of Jerusalem: American Orthodox Jews between the Holy and the Mundane*. Ph.D diss., Hebrew University of Jerusalem, 2007.

Kark, Ruth. "Changing patterns of landownership in nineteenth-century Palestine: the European influence." *Journal of Historical Geography* 10, no. 4 (1984): 357–84.

———. *Jaffa, A City in Evolution, 1799–1917*. Jerusalem: Yad Yitzhak Ben-Zvi, 1990.

———. "Planning, Housing and Land Policy 1948–1952: The Formation of Concepts and Governmental Frameworks," In *Israel, The First Decade of Independence*. Edited by I. Troen and N. Lucas. New York: SUNY, 1995. 480–94.

———. "From Pilgrimage to Budding Tourism: The Role of Thomas Cook in Rediscovery of the Holy Land in the Nineteenth Century." In *Travellers in the Levant: Voyages and Visionaries*. Edited by Sarah Searight and Malcom Wagstaff. Durham: Astene, 2001.

———. "Ottoman Jaffa: From Ruin to Central City in Palestine." In *The History and Archaeology of Jaffa 1*. Edited by Martin Peilstocker and Aaron A. Burke. Los Angeles: Cotsen Institute of Archaeology Press, UCLA, 2010.

——— and Michal Oren-Nordheim. "Colonial Cities in Palestine—Jerusalem under the British Mandate." *Israel Affairs* (1996) 50-94.

———. *Jerusalem and Its Environs: Quarters, Neighborhoods, Villages, 1800–1948*. Jerusalem: Hebrew University Magnes Press, 2001.

Kendall, Henry. *Jerusalem, the City Plan: Preservation and Development during the British Mandate 1918–1948.* London, 1948.

Kesten, Alex. *Ancient Acre: Survey and Town Plan.* Acre: Old Acre Development Company, 1962.

———. *Ancient Acre: Reexamination and Comments.* Acre: Old Acre Development Company, 1993.

Khalaf, Samir. *Beirut Reclaimed—Reflections on Urban Design and the Restoration of Civility.* Beirut: Dar An-Nahar, 1993.

——— and Philip S. Khoury. *Recovering Beirut, Urban Design and Post-War Reconstruction.* Leiden: Brill, 1993.

Khamaisi, Rassem. "A Comprehensive Plan for the Revitalization of the Arab Parts of the Old City." In *Planning and Conserving Jerusalem: The Challenge of an Ancient City.* Edited by E. Meiron and D. Bar. Jerusalem: Yad Yitzhak Ben-Zvi, 2009. 66–69.

———. "The contribution of the Waqf and other Islamic institutions to the preservation of the Old City." In *Planning and Conserving Jerusalem: The Challenge of an Ancient City.* Edited by E. Meiron and D. Bar. Jerusalem: Yad Yitzhak Ben-Zvi, 2009. 280–89.

Kletter, Raz. *Just Past?: The Making of Israeli Archaeology.* London: Routledge, 2005.

Klinghoffer, Doron. An Investigation of the Commercial Network in the Jewish Quarter of the Old City of Jerusalem and Suggestions for Planning its Renovation and Development [Hebrew]. Tel Aviv: On behalf of the JQDC, 1970.

Kroyanker, David. *Developing Jerusalem 1967–1975.* Jerusalem: Jerusalem Foundation, 1975.

———. "Heart and Soul of Jerusalem." Eulogy for Mayor Teddy Kollek. Haaretz.com, 4 Jan. 2007.

Lazaroff, Bytovah. "Palestinians: UNESCO vote proves Israel's Jerusalem Narrative false." *Jerusalem Post,* 6 July 2017.

Lichfield, Nathanel and Yosef Schweid. *Preservation of Built Heritage in Israel* [in Hebrew]. Jerusalem: Jerusalem Institute for Research on Israel, 1986.

Lowenthal, David. *Heritage Crusade and the Spoils of History.* Cambridge: Cambridge University Press, UK, 1998.

———. *The Past Is a Foreign Country — Revisited.* Cambridge: Cambridge University Press, UK, 2015.

Luncz, Avraham Moshe. *The Ways of Zion and of Jerusalem.* [in Hebrew]. Jerusalem, 1876, reprint Jerusalem: Ariel Publishing House, 1979.

Margalit, A. "Future Generations Will Cry over [the renovation of] the Old City." *HaModia,* 28 June 1976.

McDowell, Sara. "Selling Conflict Heritage through Tourism in Peacetime Northern Ireland: Transforming Conflict or Exacerbating Difference?." *International Journal of Heritage Studies* 14, no. 5 (Sept. 2008): 405–21.

Meethan, Kevin. "Consuming in the Civilized City." *Annals of Tourism Research.* 23, no. 2 (1996): 322–40.

———. "York: Managing the Tourist City." *Cities* 14, no. 6 (1997): 333–42.

Meiron, Eyal and Doron Bar. *Planning and Conserving Jerusalem.* Jerusalem: Yad Yitzhak Ben Zvi, 2009.

Milstein, Faina. "The Old City of Jerusalem Tiferet Yisrael Synagogue, A Historical, Architectural and Engineering Survey." Jerusalem: Israel Antiquities Authority, 2010.

Ministry for Foreign Affairs. *Desecration.* Jerusalem: Ministry for Foreign Affairs, International Division, Nov. 1967.

Mualam, Nir. "New Trajectories in Historic Preservation: The Rise of Built-Heritage Protection in Israel." *Journal of Urban Affairs* 37, no. 5 (2016): 620–42.

N.a. "Yeshivat HaKotel Revitalizes Jewish Quarter," *Israel Digest* 13 (1969).

N.a. *Development of Ancient Acre.* [in Hebrew]. 1993.

N.a. "Allon's New Neighbor." *Australian Jewish News*, 8 Aug.1969.

Naor, Mordechai. *The Jewish Quarter in Jerusalem* [in Hebrew]. Jerusalem: Mossad Bialek, 1987.

Narkis, Uzi. *A Jerusalem Soldier* [in Hebrew]. Tel Aviv: Defense Ministry, 1991.

Nasr, Joe. "The Reconstructions of Beirut." In *The City in the Islamic World*. Edited by Salma K. Jayyusi, Renata Holod, Attilio Petruccioli, and André Raymond. Leiden: Brill, 2008. 1116–41.

Nasser, Noha. "Urban Design Principles of a Historic Part of Cairo." Ph.D. diss., School of Architecture, University of England, Birmingham, 2000.

———. "Cultural Continuity and Meaning of Place: Sustaining Historic Cities of the Islamicate World." *Journal of Architectural Conservation* 9:1 (2003): 74–89.

———. "A Historiography of Tourism in Cairo: A Spatial Perspective." in *Tourism in the Middle East: Continuity, Change and Transformation*. Edited by Rami Farouk Daher. Clevedon UK, 2007. 70–94.

Nour, Haysam Mohamed Hazem Mohamed Maamoun Hassan. *Awqaf and Heritage, Urban Conservation in Historic Muslim Cities. The Case of Waqf Institution in Historic Cairo*. Ph.D.diss. Politecnico di Milano Faculty of Architecture and Society, 2012.

Orbasli, Aylin. *Tourists in Historic Towns, Urban Conservation and Heritage Management*. London New York: E and FN Spon, 2000.

Pan, Shahar. "Tours and Vacations in the Land of Israel and the Middle East during the Mandate." Lecture presented at Yad Yitzhak Ben-Zvi, Jerusalem, 9 Dec. 2014.

Papastathis, K. and R. Kark. "The Politics of Church Land Administration: The Case of the Orthodox Patriarchate of Jerusalem in Late Ottoman and Mandatory Palestine, 1875–1948." *Byzantine and Modern Greek Studies* 40 (2) (2016): 264–82.

Paz, Yair. "*Preserving Architectural Heritage in Deserted Neighborhoods after Independence War* [in Hebrew]. *Cathedra* 88 (1998): 95–134.

Peilstocker, Martin and Aaron A. Burke, eds. *The History and Archaeology of Jaffa 1*. Los Angeles: Cotsen Institute of Archaeology Press, UCLA, 2010.

Perry, Noam and Ruth Kark. *Ethnographic Museums in Israel*. New York: Israel Academic Press, 2017.

Philips, Jon. *A Will to Survive*. New York: Dial Press, 1976.

Pierotti, Ermete. *Jerusalem Explored*. London, 1864. Gutenberg Project: http://www.gutenberg.org/files/44241/44241-h/44241-h.htm.

Price, Nicholas Stanley, ed. *Cultural Heritage in Postwar Recovery*. Papers from the ICCROM Forum held on 4–6 Oct. 2005. edited by *ICCROM Conservation Studies* 6. Introduction and Chapter 2. http://www.iccrom.org/.

Rabinovich, Abraham. "Modernizing in the Old City." *Jerusalem Post*, 18 July 1969.

Regev, Ofer. "The First 30 Years 1984–2014." Yehuda Dekel Library, Council for Conservation of Heritage Sites in Israel, http://eng.shimur.org//viewArticle.aspx?articleID=166.

Reiner, Elchanan. "The Hurva of Rabbi Yehuda Hechasid—Ideas Regarding Its Construction and Function in the Renewed Neighborhood" [in Hebrew]. Edited by Michael Levin. Jerusalem: Ministry of Education and Hebrew University Department of Jewish Art, 1978. 14.

———. "Traditions of Holy Places in Medieval Palestine. Oral versus Written." In *Offerings from Jerusalem. Portrayals of Holy Places by Jewish Artists: Exhibition Catalogue*. Jerusalem: Israel Museum, 2002. 9–19.

Reiter, Yitzhak, "The Muslim Waqf in Jerusalem under the British Mandate as Reflected in the Records of the Shari'a Court." Ph.D. diss. Hebrew University of Jerusalem, 1990.

———. *Islamic Awqaf in Jerusalem 1948–1990*. Jerusalem: Jerusalem Institute for Israel Studies, 1991.

———, ed. *Sovereignty of God and Man: Sanctity and Political Centrality on the Temple Mount*. Jerusalem: Jerusalem Institute for Israel Studies, 2001.

Ricca, Simone. *Reinventing Jerusalem: Israel's Reconstruction of the Jewish Quarter after 1967*. London: I. B. Tauris, 2007.

Safdie, Moshe. "A Description of Porat Yosef" [in Hebrew]. In *Jerusalem Rebuilt*. Edited by David Kotler. Jerusalem: Ministry of Education and Culture, 1972.

———. *If I Forget You O Jerusalem—Between Memory and Identity, Museum Architecture 1971–1998*. Tel Aviv: Tel Aviv University, 1998.

Sarkis, Hashim. "Territorial Claims: Architecture and Post-War Attitudes toward the Built Environment." In *Recovering Beirut, Urban Design and Post-War Reconstruction*. Edited by S. Khalaf and P. S. Khoury. Leiden: Brill, 1993. 101–27.

Schaffer, Yaakov. "Physical Restoration and Conservation of Buildings and Sites. In *Planning and Conserving Jerusalem* Edited by Eyal Meiron and Doron Bar. Jerusalem: Yad Yitzhak Ben-Zvi, 2009. 238–65.

Schweid [Shavid], Yosef. *Outline Plan Proposal for Jerusalem*. Jerusalem: Dept. of City Planning, Jerusalem Municipality, 1975.

———. "Symposium on Renovation of the Jewish Quarter, Winter 1968" [in Hebrew]. In *Jerusalem Rebuilt*. Edited by David Kotler. Jerusalem: Ministry of Education and Culture, 1972, 1976. 66–69.

Shalem, Diane. *Jerusalem*. Jerusalem: Jerusalem Municipality, 1968.

Shamir, Shimon. "The Beginning of Modern Times in the History of Palestine" [in Hebrew]. *Cathedra* 40 (1986): 138–58.

Sharon, Arieh. Radio lecture. 2 Aug. 1949. Mira Yehudai Archive, Kibbutz Ein Harod Meuchad.

———, Eliezer Brutzkus, and Eldar Sharon. *Planning Jerusalem: The Old City and its Environs*. Jerusalem: Ministry of the Interior and the Jerusalem Municipality, 1973.

Sheeran, George. Memorandum to the Select Committee on Office of the Deputy Prime Minister: Housing, Planning, Local Government and the Regions, Written Evidence, The United Kingdom Parliament. 2003. http://parliament.the.stationery-office.co.uk/pa/cm200304/cmselect/cmodpm/47/47we48.htm.

Shtern, Marik. "Polarized Labor Integration: East Jerusalem Palestinians in the City's Employment Market." Jerusalem: Jerusalem Institute for Policy Research, 2017.

Skaf, Isabelle "Introduction to the Economic Valorisation of Cultural Heritage." In *Conservation of Cultural Heritage in the Arab Region, Issues in the Conservation and Management of Heritage Sites*. ICCROM, 2013. 125–32. http://www.iccrom.org.

Stanley-Price, Nicholas, ed. "Cultural Heritage in Postwar Recovery." ICCROM, http://www.iccrom.org/downloads/ 2007.

Steinberg, Jessica. "Port city of Acre is making a comeback, one acre at a time." *Times of Israel*. http://www.timesofisrael.com/port-city-of-acre-is-making-a-comeback-one-acre-at-a-time (accessed Aug. 2016).

Strul, Lilach, "Conservation Projects, 41-52." In *The History and Archaeology of Jaffa 1*. Edited by Martin Peilstocker and Aaron A. Burke. Los Angeles: Cotsen Institute of Archaeology Press, UCLA, 2010.

Stubbs, John H. *Time Honored: A Global View of Architectural Conservation*. Hoboken, N.J.: John Wiley and Sons, 2009, Appendix B: Organizations and Resources Relating to International Architectural Conservation.

Sutton, Keith and Wael Fahmi. "The Rehabilitation of Old Cairo." *Habitat International* 26 (2002): 73–93.

Tanai [Tani], Dan. "From the Ramban to the Hurva—Synagogue Renovations" [in Hebrew]. In *Chapters in the History of the Jewish Community in Jerusalem*. Vol. 1. Edited by Yehuda Ben-Porat, Yehoshua Ben-Zion, and Aharon Keidar. Jerusalem: Yad Yitzhak Ben-Zvi, 1973, 1977.

———. "The Ben-Zakkai Synagogues—Reconstruction and Restoration." In *Jerusalem Revealed, Archaeology in the Holy City*. Edited by Yigael Yadin. New Haven: Yale University Press and Israel Exploration Society, 1976.

Tunbridge, J. E., and G. J. Ashworth. *Dissonant Heritage*. Hoboken, N.J.; John Wiley and Sons, 1996.

Tung, Anthony M. *Preserving the World's Great Cities—The Destruction and Renewal of the Historic Metropolis*. New York: Clarkson Potter, 2001.

Waterman, Stanley. *Some Aspects of the Urban Geography of Acre, Israel*. Unpubl. Ph.D. diss., Trinity College, Dublin, 1969.

———. "Early Post-State Planning in Israel—the 1949 Plan for Acre." *Horizons in Geography* 1 (Haifa University, 1975): 107–16.

Williams, Caroline. "Islamic Cairo: A Past Imperiled." *Massachusetts Review* 42, no. 4 (Egypt, 2001–2002): 591–608.

Wilson, John, *The Land of the Bible*. Vol. 2. Edinburgh, 1847.

Wise, Nicholas A. and Ivo Mulec. "Headlining Dubrovnik's Tourism Image: Transitioning Representations/ Narratives of War and Heritage Preservation, 1991–2010." *Tourism Recreation Research* 37 (2012): 57–69.

Witztum, Eliezer and Moshe Kalian. *Jerusalem of Holiness and Madness* [in Hebrew]. Tel Aviv: Aryeh Nir Publishers Ltd., 2013.

Yaffe, Amikam. *Annual Report of 1967–1968*. Jerusalem: Jerusalem Municipality, 1968.

Yahya, Maha. "Let the Dead be Dead: Memory, Urban Narratives and the Post–Civil War Reconstitution of Beirut." Lecture delivered at the symposium "Urban Traumas. The City and Disasters." Center of Contemporary Culture of Barcelona, 7–11 July 2004. http://publicspace.org/en/text-library/eng/a032-let-the-dead-be-dead-memory-urban-narratives-and-the-post-civil-war-reconstitution-of-beirut.

Interviews and Oral Communications

Elimelech Ben-Pazi, Chief Administrator of HaKotel *Yeshiva*, 1968–1998, by Bracha Slae, Jerusalem, 6 July 2005.

Shalom Gardi, Chief Architect of the Company, 1970–1980, by Bracha Slae, Mevaseret Zion, 23 Oct. 2007.

Yossi Glatt, First Executive Director of Hakotel *Yeshiva*, 1969–1978, by Bracha Slae, Jerusalem, 1 June 2008.

Rabbi Yeshayahu Hadari, Dean of Hakotel *Yeshiva*, by Bracha Slae, Jerusalem, 6 July 2005.

Rami Izrael, historian and guide, by Bracha Slae, Yitzhak Ben-Zvi Institute, Jerusalem, 24 Feb. 2008.

Ra'anan Kislev, conservation architect and head of the conservation authority of the Israel Antiquities Authority, by Bracha Slae, Jerusalem, 30 Nov. 2016.

Sa'adia Mandel, architect, by Bracha Slae, Rishpon, 3 June 2006.

Yisrael Markovitz, IDF Nachal soldier and Jewish Quarter resident, by Esther Sternberg, Jerusalem Jewish Quarter, 02 Feb. 1998.

Amiel Meitav, M.A., Tour guide, historian, and former Old City coordinator for Israel's domestic security agency, presently coordinator for development of infrastructure and tourism in the Old City of Jerusalem, by Bracha Slae, Jerusalem, 18 Dec. 2017.

Ehud Menczel [Netzer], Chief Architect of the Jewish Quarter, 1967–1970, by Bracha Slae, Jerusalem, 7 Dec. 2005.

Eliezer Shefer, Coordinator of the Nachal, 1968–1975, by Bracha Slae, Jerusalem Jewish Quarter, 30 May 2008.

David Zifroni, assistant executive director of the Company, 1967–1983, by Bracha Slae, Jerusalem Jewish Quarter, 31 May 2005.

Endnotes

1. ICOMOS http://www.usicomos.org/preservation (accessed Aug. 2017).

2. UNESCO (United Nations Educational, Scientific and Cultural Organization) attempts to build intercultural understanding through protection of heritage and support for cultural diversity. ICCROM (International Centre for the Study of the Preservation and Restoration of Cultural Property) is an intergovernmental organization with a worldwide mandate to promote the conservation of all types of cultural heritage through training, information, research, cooperation, and advocacy. ICOMOS is a non-governmental international organization dedicated to the conservation of the world's monuments and sites.

3. Araoz, "Historic Preservation in the United States," US ICOMOS website: http://www.usicomos.org/preservation (accessed Aug. 2017).

4. Mead, opening quotation of the voluntary national organization, American Association for State and Local History website, http://www.aaslh.org/ (accessed 2009).

5. "Smashing the Image: The Destruction of Archaeology by ISIS," Discussion held at the Van Leer Jerusalem Institute, 19 Sept. 2016; Report, international symposium on protection and destruction of cultural heritage, held at Ancient Olympia, 1–7 Sept. 2015, http://www.iccrom.org/olympia-resolution-the-importance-of-international-collaboration-for-the-protection-of-national-cultural-properties/#more-12016 (accessed Sept. 2016).

6. See map from November 1967 listing Jewish-owned property in the Jewish Quarter, ISA 130, 2981\HZ-24; Avraham Halperin, map of the Jewish Quarter on the eve of the War of Independence (ca. 1946), Hebrew University of Jerusalem Mount Scopus Map Library.

7. The UNESCO website on Jerusalem as a World Heritage Site (sponsored by Jordan), lists 220 historic monuments within the Old City and Environs. http://whc.unesco.org/en/list/148/, the most important being the Dome of the Rock and the Holy Sepulcher. See Map 2.

8. Ruhi al-Khatib, Jordanian Mayor of Jerusalem, "Development in Jerusalem from the 15th May 1948 to the 30th Sept. 1966," ISA 93, 4293\HZ-2.

9. 'Aref al-'Aref, *Taarich El-Kuds*, 491–504; quoted by Yaakov Yehoshua, historical overview of Muslim institutions in the Old City for the Foreign Ministry, 1968, ISA 93, 4293\HZ-2.

10. Information on the state of the Old City under Jordan, disseminated by the Foreign Ministry December 1967, ISA 93, 63\HZ-17.

11. Ibid.

12. Population Census of East Jerusalem, Central Bureau of Statistics, 22 Nov. 1967, ISA 109, 4948\G-19.

13. See portfolio of the Ministerial Committee on Jerusalem, ISA 43, 6306\G-3.

14. Municipality protocol, 8 June 1967 and 9 July 1967, JCA; Amikam Yaffe, Jerusalem City Engineer, Annual Report of 1967–1968, Jerusalem Municipality, 1968.

15. Dan Tanai, Director General of the Housing Ministry, Correspondence, 25 June 1967. ISA 74, 5688\G-20; 109, 4890\G-10.

16. Housing Ministry Report, 8 June 1967, ISA 109, 5314\G-7.

17. Text of the law: http://knesset.gov.il/laws/special/eng/HolyPlaces.htm (accessed June 2015).

18. "Urgent" letter, Chairman of the Jerusalem Regional Planning Committee to the Jerusalem Local Planning Committee, 4 July 1967, JCA,776; ISA 56, 12055\GL-11.

19. Protocol, Municipality meeting 34, 8 Aug. 1967, JCA, Municipality protocols, vol. 3.

20. Yael Uzai, Secretary of State, correspondence with the Prime Minister regarding Decision 731 of the government, 13 Aug. 1967, ISA 43, 6306\G-1.

21. ISA 43, 6304\ *2-4\6304.*

22 See JCA, 3302, 41/67; ISA 43, 6423\G-8.

23 Outline Plan of the Old City and Environs, Jerusalem Municipality, December 1971, JCA 9033.

24 Outline Plan for the Old City and Environs AM/9 Summary of Proceedings of the Secondary Committee, Urban Planning Unit of the Jerusalem Municipality, December 1971, JCA 9033; protocols of the committee, July 1967–June 1971, JCA 3302.

25 See building plans submitted to the Secondary Committee in its protocols, 1967–1968, ISA 56, 4010\G-18. The Municipality itself undertook building projects throughout the Old City such as renovation of Zedekiah's Cave with no building permit. These projects were granted de facto legitimacy by the Secondary Committee, often after construction had begun. They often related to a specific project and ignored the larger context. See Proceedings of the Secondary Committee, JCA 3922, and ISA 56, 4010\G-18; 3999\GL-6 and 3419\GL-2.

26 Yosef Schweid, Lecture on the Master Plan, 8 Aug. 1967, JCA 1921, III.

27 Jerusalem Municipality, Master Plan 1968, vol. 1, 1972.

28 Schweid, Master Plan; JCA 1921, III.

29 Correspondence, Shimshoni (JCA 1601) and Brutzkus (ISA, 56); preservation site index of the Jerusalem Master Plan Office, May 1968, 2-5, JCA, 9036.

30 See Master Plan Portfolio III, JCA, 1921; Menachem Barish, "Report on the Outline Plan," *Yediot Aharonot*, 3 Mar. 1970, 5. Today, there are some 40,000 inhabitants in the Old City, a number much greater than its carrying capacity: According to Israel's Central Bureau of Statistics, there are 30,000 or more in the Muslim Quarter, 4,000 in the Jewish Quarter and about 6,000 in the Christian and Armenian Quarters. The Muslim Quarter constitutes about 50% of the area of the Old City today. No "thinning out" has occurred; in fact, the population has more than doubled.

31 See, for example, architect Eliezer Brutzkus's comments on the Master Plan, ISA 56, 2742/GL-1.

32 See report, Ministers' Committee on Jerusalem, ISA 43, 7283\A-16; JCA, 1125 and 9099.

33 See Shlomo Aronson, Peter Bogod, and Esther Niv-Krandell, "The Cardo: Competition, Planning, and Development," Feb. 1977, JCA 9049.

34 Protocols and publications of the Jerusalem Committee, JCA, 1601. The Committee meets in Jerusalem every two years and serves as an international council concerned with the restoration and development of the city, and the preservation of Jerusalem's special character and unique pluralistic heritage.

35 Ruhi al-Khatib, Mayor of Jerusalem, Jordan, "Development in Jerusalem from the 15th May 1948 to the 30th September 1966," ISA, Records of Foreign Minister Shlomo Hillel, 1968, 4293\HZ-2.

36 See endnote 25.

37 Portfolio of the Ministerial Committee on Jerusalem, ISA, RG 43, 6306/G-3.

38 See portfolios of the CRDJQ, 1969–1975 in ISA, 59, 13342\ GL-1; 13342\GL-2; 9118\GL-3; 77, 7314\A-3.

39 Ehud Menczel-Netzer was then a young architect, later completing a doctorate in archaeology at the Hebrew University of Jerusalem. He is best known for his discovery in Jericho of the oldest known synagogue, and for the excavation of Herodium and identification of Herod's tomb in 2007. He was killed in a work accident on the site on 28 Oct. 2010.

40 Ya'ar, Mandel, and Frankel, Proposal for the Renovation of Old Jerusalem, 1970, JCA, 776

41 Government report of decisions, Aug.–Sept. 1967, ISA, 43, 6306\G-1; 153, 7920\A-8.

42 See Jewish Quarter map listing Jewish-owned property, completed November 1967, ISA, 130, 2981\HZ-24; Avraham Halperin, map of the Jewish Quarter on the eve of the War of Independence; IDF map of Jewish Holy Sites, 1967, both in Hebrew University Map Library, Mount Scopus.

43 Although Habad Street is the western border, Jewish property west of Habad Street is part of the Jewish Quarter, and non-Jewish property to its east is not.

44 The borders of the Jewish Quarter were set at Chains Street on the north, Habad Street on the west (but also including Jewish properties west of Habad Street), the road running parallel to the city walls from Zion to Dung Gate on the south, and the Western Wall Plaza on the east. Netzer himself advised extending the Jewish Quarter's borders to include Jewish property in the Hebron neighborhood north of Chains Street, but the government did not approve.

45 Moshe Ben Ze'ev to the directorate of the JQDC, 18 Sept. 1969, ISA, 109, 5574\GL-1; Protocol of the Ministerial Committee on Jerusalem, Aug.–Sept. 1967, ISA, 43, 6306\G-2; 56, 4948\G-19.

46 Protocol of the Ministerial Committee on Jerusalem, ISA, RG 43, 6306\G-2; 56, 4948\G-19.

47 Interior Ministry Planning Dept., ISA, 56, 4948\G-19 (date unknown).

48 Protocol of Housing Ministry, Sept. 1968, JCA, 776.

49 Portfolio of the Ministry of Religion, 1967–1970, ISA, 98, 2931\G-1; Portfolio of the Prime Minister's office, 43, 7284\A-16.

50 E. Brutzkus, "First Comments on Planning United Jerusalem," June 20, 1967, ISA, 142, 3075\GL-1.

51 Reports on the establishment of the Company, April 1969, ISA, RG 44, 7283\AA-16; RG 109, 4936\GL-30; RG 109, 4890\GL-10; RG 77.8, 7314/A-2.

52 Nachmanides (Ramban) is credited with re-establishing the Jewish community of Jerusalem in 1267 at the beginning of Egyptian Mameuk rule. This community existed uninterrupted until the fall of the Jewish Quarter on 28 May 1948.

53 Report of the Company (May 1972), JCA, 8032. Today there are no more than 100 shops and small businesses in the Jewish Quarter, including those directed primarily to residents. Only the Temple Institute has a museum shop. The Cardo Culinarium, now closed, was the only heritage-oriented commercial undertaking in the quarter. Customers were served "authentic Roman" food, eating with a spoon and knife while seated at low benches, wearing togas and laurel wreaths, in the spirit of the times.

54 According to Ynet, during 2013 Israel had 3.5 million foreign tourists of whom almost 70% visited the Wall and about 50% visited Christian sites in and around the Old City, http://www.ynet.co.il/articles/0,7340,L-4474551,00.html, (accessed 09/02/2015).

55 http://www.ynetnews.com/articles/0,7340,L-4475168,00.html (accessed Sept. 2016).

56 Transportation Master Plan Team and the Jerusalem Municipality, Survey of Visitors to the Old City, 22 July 2014. According to the survey, between 18,000 to 35,000 people entered through Jaffa Gate (the number varying from weekday to holiday); 7,000 to 17,000 through Dung Gate; 5,000 to 10,000 through Zion Gate; and 30,000 to 37,000 through gates leading to the Muslim and Christian Quarters.

57 See Avnieli's report on the summer course, Aug. 1971, ISA, 59, 13342\GL-1.

58 See protocols of the Company, 1970–1973, ISA, 61, 9118\GL-2.

59 For example, the renovated structures of the Batei Mahse neighborhood that had originally housed families were converted to classrooms. In the destroyed areas nearby, new apartment houses were constructed. The residents of these apartments suffer from their proximity to the educational complex and from cultural programs in the plaza. The plaza, intended to be an open area for cultural events, has become a playground on school days.

60 Pamphlet of the JQDC and Ministry of Tourism, Dec. 1971, JCA, 4943.

61 Protocols of municipality meetings, no. 47, 16 June 1968; compare old and new lanes and street names on maps of the Jewish Quarter in the Mandate period and the present; and see section on street names on the Jerusalem Municipality website: https://www.jerusalem.muni.il/City/Streetnames/Pages/default.aspx.

62 See protocols of the Company Treasury Committee's meetings, 1969–1974, ISA, State Comptroller files, 13342\GL-2.

63 On 25 Sept. 1967, the Housing Ministry allocated IL 300,000 compensation to minority groups, most of whom were evacuated from the Jewish Quarter; see also Mr. Sleifer, Housing Ministry to the Treasury Ministry, authorizing payments of up to IL 80,000 each, 17 June 1968, ISA, 109, 4936\GL-30.

64 See correspondence, State Legal Advisor Meir Shamgar and City Councilor Meiron Benvenisti, 27 Aug. 1970, ISA, 109, 5997\G-3.

65 Based on list of eligible voters for the first Resident's Committee, submitted by Ruth Steiner, an elected member of the committee, 1971; records of the CDJQ, ISA, RG 61, 9118\GL-1, 91118\GL-2, 9118\GL-3, 109, 4890\GL-10.

66 Residents' Committee to Prime Minister Rabin, to members of the Jerusalem Ministers' Committee, to the Company's Executive Director Ronny Gluskinas, and to Chairman Irwin Shimron and the directorate, 12 Jan. 1975, ISA, RG 43.4, 6722\G-4.

67 Informal report by Yehuda Tamir, 5 Jan. 1969, ISA, 98, 2932/GL-1.

68 Interviews with Glatt, Ben-Pazi, and Rabbi Hadari; *Kotlenu* newsletter of HaKotel Yeshiva, Feb. 1972. See correspondence between Ministry of Religion officials, Jerusalem Municipality, the National Bnei Akiva movement, and others, ISA, 140, 11653\GL-10.

69 List of eligible voters in the first Residents' Committee elections, May 1972, submitted by Ruth Steiner, Jewish Quarter resident and an elected member of the first Residents' Committee; list of household heads who signed contracts with the Company, JQDC protocols, ISA, 61, 9118\GL-1, 9118\GL-2, 9118\GL-3, 4890\GL-10, 3083\GL-14.

70 State Comptroller's report, ISA 59, 13342\GL-2.

71 The Jewish Quarter Residents Committee turned to the Justice Ministry with such a request due to the difficult living conditions and the Company's refusal to involve residents in the planning and decision making processes. They wanted "to return a strong Jewish presence to the quarter, whose national value is of top priority, and to make it a living city" (correspondence between the Company, the Municipality, and the residents, 1973–1975, ISA, 43.4, 6721\G-20).

72 See correspondence, Meir Aran: "[T]he government was aware of the political implications of renewal and settlement of the Jewish Quarter, and [therefore] awarded the Justice Minister the main part of the Company's stock. This was an exceptional case, and the Justice Minister has now decided to present to the government a proposal to normalize the structure of the Company," ISA, Rabin portfolio, 6722\G-4.

73 In recent years commercial, healthcare, and recreation areas in the Old City and environs have become less polarized. This may reflect developments throughout Jerusalem. See Marik Shtern, "Polarized Labor Integration: East Jerusalem Palestinians in the City's Employment Market," Jerusalem Institute for Policy Research, Jerusalem 2017.

74 See protocols, Company for the Development of East Jerusalem, 1971, ISA, 61, 9121\GL-2; correspondence of the JQDC with Teddy Kollek, 1971–1972, JCA, 2060; correspondence between Kollek and Zvi Ron, mayor's counselor on East Jerusalem and the Minister of Justice, the director of the JQDC, and others, 1971–1974, JCA, 2060.

75 Tushia Engineers, Tel Aviv, *Survey of Buildings in the Moslem Quarter of the Old City* [in Hebrew], Jerusalem Municipality, City Engineer Dept., May 1973.

76 Letter to Kollek urging speeding up renewal of the Jewish Quarter and improving the security situation, 15 May 1974. Kollek acknowledged that Soen was right, but blamed lack of financial resources and the government for the failure, 30 May 1974, JHA, 2060, 41/51. At that time, the population of the Muslim Quarter stood at more than 20,000. The population of the Muslim Quarter in 1967 was 13,500 according to Hebrew University Census for the National Urban Planning Council, June 1967, and CBS Census, Nov. 1967, ISA, 56, 4948\G-19. Today it is more than 30,000. (Jerusalem Municipality website, https://www.jerusalem.muni.il/City/Neighborhood/Statistics/Pages/hrova-hmoslemi.aspx (Accessed Aug. 2015).

77 See correspondence between Kollek, Benvenisti and others from 1967 and on, JCA, 2060, 41\51.

78 Synagogues on this route include the Habad, Ramban, Hurva (either reconstructed, built as a modern synagogue, or left in ruins), the Sephardi Complex, Karaite, and Tiferet Yisrael Synagogues. Also on the route are the Sidna Omar Mosque, Bet El, and Sephardic Yeshivot, a memorial square by the Hurva Synagogue, archaeological excavations, a Turkish Bazaar with coffee shop, a Crusader-era church complex, and new campuses of HaKotel and Porat Yosef Yeshivot. See Plan 5.

79 Jerusalem Master Plan Office, May 1968, pp. 2–5, JCA, 9036; Gardi 1986, 177.

80   Teddy Kollek to Simcha Dinitz, advisor to the Prime Minister, 12 Jan. 1971, JCA, 2060, 41\51.
81   Recent excavations beneath the ruins of Tiferet Yisrael Synagogue have produced similar impressive finds.
82   Ermete Pierotti was a colorful adventurer who served as Chief Engineer of Jerusalem from 1854–1864, and made many important archaeological discoveries in Jerusalem. His book, *Jerusalem Explored* is available online at the Gutenberg Project.
83   Tamir to Minister of Justice Hayyim Zadok, requesting his help in dealing with archaeologists' demands to delay planning until completion of excavations, 7 May 1974, JCA 2060, 41/51.
84   Property belonging to a Jewish charitable organization is *hekdesh*, and its legal status is similar to that of the Moslem *waqf*.
85   Notes on the meeting of the board of directors of the Company with the mayor and members of the Jerusalem city council, 5 July 1970, JCA, Protocols of city council meetings.
86   Habad Synagogue was renovated largely due to the efforts of Rabbi Moshe Zvi Segal. Rivka Weingarten, founder of the Old Yishuv Court Museum, almost singlehandedly renewed services in the Or HaHayyim Synagogue. These two-century-old synagogues and Torat Hayyim Yeshiva on HaGai Street in the Muslim Quarter resumed services and studies in the summer of 1967. Initial attempts to restore the partially destroyed two-story courtyard structure of Beit El Yeshiva for the study of Kabbala, founded in 1733, were unsuccessful. When Rabbi Meir Yehuda Getz, Rabbi of the Western Wall, became Dean of the yeshiva in 1974, the building was renovated. In August 1967, the administration of the Hayyei Olam Hassidic Yeshiva re-opened its Jewish Quarter branch, but closed by 1973. In 1972, descendants of the Gemilut Hasadim synagogue and Degel HaTorah yeshiva renovated the building and opened a new yeshiva. Etz Hayyim Yeshiva in the Hurva synagogue complex had also been damaged but not destroyed. The yeshiva administration immediately began to renew the structure and to reinstate study programs but a few years later closed its doors.
87   The identification is not definite. Reiner (2000, 277) places Nachmanides' synagogue on or near Mount Zion.
88   Minister Warhaftig's report on the Ministry of Religious Affairs activities, Protocol of the Seventh Knesset, 31 May 1971, ISA, Knesset Protocols, 189\5-C.
89   Avraham Ades, Report on the synagogues on behalf of the Ministry of Religious Affairs, 7 Aug. 1967, ISA, 98, 2931\GL-1.
90   From a brochure of the Sephardic Council, date and author unspecified, JCA 4945.
91   Shapiro to Kollek, 19 Mar. 1971, JHA, 2060, 41\51.
92   Correspondence and sketches Shem Or sent to the mayor, 14 Mar. 1968, and to President Shazar, 7 Apr. 1968, JCA, City Engineer files 1224/2/22/10; ISA, 98, 2931\GK-1.
93   Speeches of Rabbi She'ar Yashuv Cohen, Yehuda HaEzrachi, and Dan Alrod at the symposium, 1970.
94   Ehud Netzer, Dan Tanai, and Rabbi She'ar Yashuv Cohen, at the symposium, 1970.
95   Dr. Ze'ev Gothold, architect Ram Carmi, David Reznick, Dan Tanai, and others.
96   Correspondence between CEO Nissim Arzi, Meir Porush, and Gilad Baniel, 10 June 1997, Archives of JQDC; letter from CEO Nissim Arzi to the committee for Tiferet Yisrael, 7 May 2008, Archives of the JQDC; correspondence between the Company and the directorate of Ruzhin Yeshiva, Archives of Ruzhin Yeshiva.
97   Wikipedia, Armenian Orthodox Patriarchate website https://en.wikipedia.org/wiki/Armenian_Patriarchate_of_Jerusalem (accessed 10 Dec. 2015).
98   History of the Aish HaTorah Building, on Aish website: http://www.aish.com/ai/bn/ji/96862084.html (accessed 20 Nov. 2017).
99   Report of Tourism Ministry on Renovation of the Jewish Quarter, Dec. 1971, JCA 4945; University of Bar Ilan Rector Harel Fisch to Yehuda Tamir, 23 Sept. 1969, ISA, 98, 2931\GL-1; protocols of the Company's finance committee 1969–1974, ISA 59, 13342\GL-2.
100 Report of Tourism Ministry on Renovation of the Jewish Quarter, Dec. 1971, JCA 4945.
101 Rachel Yanait was Ben-Zvi's wife and a distinguished public figure in her own right. See Ben-Zvi Institute website: http://www.ybz.org.il/?CategoryID=210&ArticleID=147#.Vvfk2_nRi70 (accessed 27 Mar. 2016).

102 http://www.shimur.org/Kaplan-Yishuv-Court/ (accessed 27 Mar. 2016).

103 Report of Tourism Ministry on Renovation of the Jewish Quarter, Dec. 1971, JCA 4945; telegram from Eliashar to Prime Minister Yitzhak Rabin, 1 Oct. 1975, ISA, 43.4, 6721\G-20.

104 http://siebenberghouse.com/ (accessed 27 Mar. 2016).

105 All these sites and the Hurva Synagogue are under the authority of the JQDC. http://www.rova-yehudi.org.il/touristic-sites/?mypage=1 (accessed 27 Mar. 2016).

106 Temple Institute: https://www.templeinstitute.org/about.htm (accessed 16 Mar. 2016).

107 Protocol of the public competition to plan the Cardo in the Jewish Quarter, 01 Dec. 1971, JQDC, JCA 2060, 51\41; Peter Bogod, "The Cardo: Planning and Development," Feb. 1977, JCA 9049.

108 Correspondence between Municipality officials, the Jerusalem Fund, the National Parks Authority, and the Company, 1974–1975, JCA 2060, 41\51.

109 Gustavo Araoz, Historic Preservation in the United States, US ICOMOS Website, http://www.usicomos.org/preservation. (accessed June 2009).

110 See Antiquities Authority website, http://www.antiquities.org.il.

111 Council website: http://eng.shimur.org/viewStaticPage.aspx?pageID=258 (accessed Jan. 2017).

112 See Landmarks website: https://landmarks.gov.il/ (accessed Feb. 2017).

113 Michael Jacobson, Backyard Blog on Old Jaffa https://michaelarch.wordpress.com/2009/04/16/ (accessed Dece. 2017).

114 Documentation can be found in the files of the Old Jaffa Company, ISA, 43.4, 6305\G-25; see also articles on Old Jaffa on the Israel Antiquities Authority website: http://www.antiquities.org.il, (accessed Sept. 2014), and on the Company's website: http://www.oldjaffa.co.il/?CategoryID=212&ArticleID=353 (accessed Aug. 2016).

115 See the history of the Old Jaffa Development Company Ltd. on its website http://www.oldjaffa.co.il, (accessed Aug. 2016).

116 Michael Jacobson, Backyard Blog on Old Jaffa https://michaelarch.wordpress.com/2009/04/16/ (accessed Dec. 2017).

117 See JCHP website: http://www.antiquities.org.il/jaffa/ (accessed Aug. 2016).

118 See summary of the Old Jaffa Development Project of the 1960s and of today on the websites of the Antiquities Authority http://www.antiquities.org.il and of the Tel Aviv Municipality https://www.tel-aviv.gov.il/en/Pages/HomePage.aspx; and on the website of architect Michael Jacobson, "Old Jaffa—The Case of Urban Renewals of the 1960's," Backyard Blog [in Hebrew] https://michaelarch.wordpress.com/2009/04/16 (all accessed Sept. 2017).

119 International conservation center in Acre. Historic Assessment 2007, http://www.iaa-conservation.org.il/article_Item_eng.asp?subject_id=36&id=78 (accessed Jan. 2017).

120 G. F. Lowick, Memorandum on Acre: Conclusion http://www.iaa-archives.org.il/zoom/zoom.aspx?folder_id=6&type_id=&id=553 (accessed Feb. 2017).

121 C. T. Evans, district commissioner Galilee District, to the assistant District Commissioner in Acre, Jan. 1946, Acre folder in British Mandate archives in IAA website, http://www.iaa-archives.org.il/ShowFolder.aspx?id=35&loc_id=1&type_id (accessed Sept. 2017).

122 Memorandum on government policy towards Old Acre, 8 Sept. 1949, ISA, 5451\G-6.

123 UNESCO site, http://whc.unesco.org/en/ (accessed Dec. 2016).

124 Yael Fuhrmann-Naaman and Yael Alef, "Old Acre—A World Heritage City," Antiquities Authority website, Conservation Department, http://www.iaa-conservation.org.il/article_Item_heb.asp?subject_id=31&id=60 (accessed 27 June 2016); Tsilli Giladi, Old 'Akko—Conservation, Development and Inspection, IAA website: http://www.iaa-conservation.org.il/article_Item_eng.asp?id=198&subject_id=31 (accessed Aug. 2016); Central Bureau of Statistics, 2014, publication no. 1642.

125 http://www.iaa-conservation.org.il/article_Item_eng.asp?subject_id=36&id=176.

126 Ram Shoef and Yael Fuhrmann-Naaman, Rehabilitation of a Residential Quarter in Old Akko, Nov. 2008. IAA website, http://www.iaa-conservation.org.il/article_Item_eng.asp?subject_id=31&id=103, (accessed Aug. 2016).

127 http://www.wgalil.ac.il/category/English_Conservation_Studies (accessed June 2016).

128 Western Galilee College, http://www.wgalil.ac.il/category/about; International Conservation Center Città di Roma https://www.studyabroad.com/institutions/the-international-conservation-center-citt-di-roma/saving-the-stones-286061 (both accessed Aug. 2017).

129 See Old Acre Development Company website: http://www.akko.org.il/en/About-us (accessed Aug. 2016).

130 See Palestine census of 1922, https://archive.org/stream/PalestineCensus1922/Palestine%20Census%20%281922%29#page/n8/mode/1up. (accessed Dec. 2016).

131 CZA, KKL5/7002,S/25/7255, 24 Nov. 1934.

132 The scientific Archive 1919–1948, IAA archive of British Department of Antiquities, Safad Folder http://www.iaa-archives.org.il/Search.aspx?loc_id=4189 (accessed Feb. 2017).

133 Ibid.

134 Safed Town Plan 195-260, undated, scale 1:10,000, lists antiquities, monuments and Muslim, Christian, and Jewish public buildings such as church, tomb, mosque, Talmud Torah, etc. (Scientific Archive of the Mandatory Antiquities Department, 1919–1948. http://www.iaa-archives.org.il/Search.aspx?loc_id=4189 (accessed Aug. 2017).

135 http://www.zefat.muni.il/visitors/Pages/history.aspx#6 (accessed Dec. 2016).

136 Central Bureau of Statistics 2014, publication no. 1642. The total population of Jerusalem's Old City reached 36,830 in 2014.

137 http://www.zefat.net/2011-06-05-13-43-53/ (accessed Dec. 2016).

138 See Safed Academic College website: www.zefat.ac.il (accessed Aug. 2016), and the Faculty of Medicine in the Galilee website: http://medicine.biu.ac.il/en/node/3 (accessed Aug. 2016).

139 Israel Antiquities Authority website on the project: http://www.iaa-conservation.org.il/Projects_Item_eng.asp?site_id=4&subject_id=6 (accessed Aug. 2016).

140 Outline scheme 552, http://www.land.gov.il/IturTabot2/taba1.aspx (accessed Feb. 2017).

141 Israel Antiquities Authority, http://www.iaaconservation.org.il/article_Item_eng.asp?id=138&subject_id=45 (accessed June 2016).

142 Nadav Shragai, "Turkish Intervention on the Temple Mount" [in Hebrew], *Yisrael HaYom*, 21 June 2017; idem, "The Turks are Coming" [in Hebrew], *Yisrael HaYom*, 22 June 2017 and 24 June 2017; Taawon Welfare Association website on the Old City of Jerusalem Revitalization Programme: http://ocjrp.welfare-association.org/en/ (accessed Dec.r 2017).

143 Michael Jacobson, "Backyard Blog" [in Hebrew] https://michaelarch.wordpress.com/2009/04/16 (accessed Dec. 2017).

144 This synagogue, built in 882 C.E., housed the Cairo Geniza—an invaluable accumulation of almost 200,000 Jewish manuscripts dating from about 870 to as late as 1880; Cambridge Digital Library, http://cudl.lib.cam.ac.uk/collections/genizah, (accessed July 2016).

145 See the Egyptian Guide to Islamic Cairo, Egypt, http://www.touregypt.net/cairo/cairoislamic.htm (accessed Feb. 2017).

146 *Waqf khairi* is a revenue-bearing property (mostly land or a building) endowed for charitable purposes as defined by Islam, such as religious and cultural institutes (for example, mosques, schools, hospitals, and orphanages). There is also *waqf ahli*, namely family *waqf*, devoted to the general benefit of the children and other relatives. These kinds of *waqf* are safe from expropriation or confiscation, and cannot be sold, but only leased. The discussion in the text above refers to *waqf khairi*, not *waqf ahli*. Two kinds of *waqf* were recognized under Ottoman law, *waqf-i sahih* (true *waqf*) and *waqf-i gayr-i sahih* (untrue *waqf*), the main difference being the land endowed. True *waqf* is based on private property (*mulk*) while untrue *waqf* is based on *miri* land. With true *waqf* the full ownership (*raqaba*) on the land is transferred to the *waqf*, while in untrue *waqf* only the usufruct rights are given.

147 UNESCO, Operational Guidelines for the Implementation of the World Heritage Convention, http://whc.unesco.org/en/guidelines/ (accessed July 2016).

148 The Muslim Quarter was already overpopulated in 1967, with most of its 16,000 inhabitants in densely crowded slums. Today, that number has exceeded 27,000; see CBS 2014.

149 Archive of Warsaw Reconstruction Office, UNESCO website: http://www.unesco.org/new/en/communication-and-information/flagship-project-activities/memory-of-the-world/register/full-list-of-registered-heritage/registered-heritage-page-1/archive-of-warsaw-reconstruction-office/ (accessed Feb. 2017).

150 History of York website, http://www.historyofyork.org.uk (accessed Nov. 2013).

151 "Post-medieval York," *Secrets beneath Your Feet*. York Archaeological Trust website, 1998, www.yorkarchaeology.co.uk/ (accessed July 2009).

152 http://www.yorkairraids.wordpress.com/tag/world-war-2/;http://www.historyofyork.org.uk/timeline/20th-century (both accessed June 2014).

153 "Conservation Area 1" (PDF). City of York Council https://www.york.gov.uk/ (accessed June 2009). [dead link]

154 http://www.historyofyork.org.uk/themes/20th-century/a-new-vision-for-york, (accessed Mar. 2017).

155 One of the initiatives is Residents' Weekend when residents receive free admission to a range of York attractions; another involves training youngsters and pensioners as volunteer guides.

156 2002 census key statistics, e-mail, Simon Daubeney to Bracha Slae, 30 May 2003. 95% of York city's residents were born in the UK and 98% are white. 75% are Christian and 24% report no religion. Only 3% are unemployed.

157 http://www.rova-yehudi.org.il/areas-of-activity-2/the-planning-construction-and-development-department (accessed July 2017).

158 http://www.rova-yehudi.org.il/areas-of-activity-2/the-planning-construction-and-development-department/ (accessed July 2017).

159 Suggestion by Tamir at Company meeting, 26 Mar.1968, ISA 77, 7314\A-2.

160 Correspondence between Warhaftig and Prime Minister Eshkol, Oct. 1967, ISA, 43, 6304\G-4.

161 Residents' Committee (Ben-Zur, Bar-Giora, Wasserteil, Yuval, and Rosovsky) to Prime Minister Rabin, to the ministers who were members of the Jerusalem Ministers' Committee, to the Company's executive Director Gluskinas, and to Chairman Shimron and the directorate, 12 Jan. 1975, ISA, 43.4, 6722\G-4.

162 See UNESCO website for discussion on 1981 inscription of Jerusalem as a World Heritage Site, http://whc.unesco.org/en/sessions/01EXTCOM/documents/ and http://whc.unesco.org/archive/repext81.htm#148, and list of other Israeli sites declared World Heritage sites at http://whc.unesco.org/en/

Made in the USA
Columbia, SC
24 November 2022